MICHIGAN STATE UNIVERSITY
LIBRARIES

Y0-ASQ-618

MAR 10 2023

WITHDRAWN

RETURNING MATERIALS:
Place in book drop to
remove this checkout from
your record. FINES will
be charged if book is
returned after the date
stamped below.

JAN 0 5 1993

SEP 1 1 1994

SEP 2 3 1995

Myth, Man and Sovereign Saint

American University Studies

Series II
Romance Languages and Literature

Vol. 11

PETER LANG
New York · Berne · Frankfurt am Main

Maureen Slattery

Myth, Man and Sovereign Saint

King Louis IX in Jean de Joinville's Sources

PETER LANG
New York · Berne · Frankfurt am Main

Library of Congress Cataloging in Publication Data

Slattery, Maureen, 1940–
  Myth, Man, and Sovereign Saint.

  (American University Studies. Series II, Romance Languages and Literature; vol. 11)
    Bibliography: p.
    1. Louis IX, King of France, 1214–1270. 2. France – History – Louis IX, 1226–1270 – Historiography.
  3. Joinville, Jean sire de, 1224?–1317?   I. Title.
  II. Series.
  DC91.S57   1985   944'.023   84-47532
  ISBN 0-8204-0111-0
  ISSN 0740-9257

CIP-Kurztitelaufnahme der Deutschen Bibliothek

Slattery, Maureen:
Myth, Man and Sovereign Saint; King Louis IX in Jean de Joinville's Sources / Maureen Slattery. – New York; Berne; Frankfurt am Main: Lang, 1985.
  (American University Studies: Ser. 2, Romance
  Languages and Literature; Vol. 11)
  ISBN 0-8204-0111-0

NE: American University Studies / 02

© Peter Lang Publishing, Inc., New York 1985

All rights reserved.
Reprint or reproduction, even partially, in all forms such as microfilm, xerography, microfiche, microcard, offset prohibited.

Printed by Lang Druck Inc., Liebefeld/Berne (Switzerland)

To Carolyn and Tara,

my two lovely daughters who know of

King Louis IX

TABLE OF CONTENTS

PREFACE ... v

ABBREVIATIONS ... x

CHAPTER ONE: INTRODUCTION
- The Critical Tradition on Joinville ... 1
- Classical Works on Kings and Saints ... 3
- The Author ... 5
- The Work ... 8
- History of the Text ... 9
- The Origins of Joinville's Work ... 12
- The Purpose and Composition of Joinville's Book ... 16
- Methodology ... 20
- Notes ... 21

CHAPTER TWO: THE KING IN JOINVILLE'S ORAL SOURCES
- Introduction ... 33
- The Hermeneutics of Kingship ... 39
- The Good King Externalizes Evil ... 42
- Conquest and Conversion ... 44
- Objects of Power and Abundance ... 45
- A Divine King of Conquest ... 47
- Gesta Dei Per Regem ... 48
- Success and Oral History ... 50
- The King, Failure and Oral Custom ... 51
- The Shaping Force of Oral Custom ... 52
- The Suffering Servant ... 54
- A New Messiah ... 58
- Conclusion ... 60
- Notes ... 67

CHAPTER THREE: THE KING IN JOINVILLE'S VISUAL SOURCE

    Introduction   79

    The Medieval Eye-Witness   80

    The Places, the People, the Words and the Deeds   83

    Joinville as a Medieval Eye-Witness   85

    Perceptual Development in Contemporary Art of the Period   88

    The Perfect Prud'Homme of the Court   90

        King of Justice   91

        King of Holiness   93

        King of Chivalry   95

        Conclusion   98

    The Stylized Crusading King   99

        Military Might and Aristocratic Abundance   99

        Solo and Corporate Spaces   101

        An Intimate Space   103

        Conclusion   104

    One in One Thousand   105

    Royal Alliance   108

        The Payment of Ransom   109

        A Tap on the Toe   110

        A Bond of Conscience   111

    A Human Prud'Homme of the Holy Land   115

        Perfect King of Holiness?   115

        Perfect King of Chivalry?   120

        Perfect King of Justice?   123

    Conclusion   126

    Notes   127

CHAPTER FOUR: THE KING IN JOINVILLE'S WRITTEN SOURCES

Introduction	135
Latin Works of the Twelfth Century	135
Translations by the Monks	136
The Work of Guillaume de Nangis	137
Guillaume de Nangis and the <u>Grandes Chroniques</u>	137
How He Wrote His Life of the King	139
What Writings Joinville Borrowed	140
Nangis as a Supplement to Joinville	142
The Complementary Perspective of Nangis	143
The Official Saint	146
King of the Poor and the Suffering	148
King of Religious Orders	149
A King Immune to Clerical Influence	150
A King who Punished Blasphemy	150
A King with the Grace of Final Perserverance	151
The Official King	152
The King's Legal Correction of <u>Baillis</u>, <u>Prevôts</u> and <u>Maieurs</u>	153
The King's Judicial Centralization	155
The King Corrects the Corruption of the Paris <u>Prevôt</u>	156
The Official Father	157
Conclusion	160
Notes	162

CHAPTER FIVE: CONCLUSION
              Introduction   171
              Portrait Summaries
                  The Portrait of the Oral Sources   173
                  The Portrait in the Visual Source   174
                  The Portrait in the Written Sources   175
              The Secondary Source-Material
                  General Character and Comparative Content   177
                      Historical Epistemology   177
                      Social Anthropology   179
                      Political Beliefs   182
                  Joinville's Privileged Oral Witness   184
                  Common Themes   186
              The Primary Source-Material   188

BIBLIOGRAPHY   193

PREFACE

My aim is to critically examine in the light of its sources, the "Mémoires" of the illustrious seneschal Jean de Joinville, born in (c.) 1225, died a nonagenarian in (c.) 1317. The true title of this text, so often reproduced since the celebrated edition of Natalis de Wailly in 1874, is worth noting: Le Livre des saintes paroles et des bons faiz de notre roy saint Looys.

    A significant title, because in the times I have studied this portrait of Louis IX by his aimiable biographer and been struck by the conversational tone of the dictated work, there have appeared Henri Marrou's Sur la connaissance historique, Faire de l'histoire as well as the interdisciplinary perspectives of The New History - the 1980's and Beyond.

    Under the impact of psychology, sociology and anthropology, historians are investigating their manner of reading ancient texts.

    The startling insight which emerges from the scientific research of Freud and is incorporated into such pioneering works as Erikson's Young Man Luther is that historical change is a fusion of conscious and unconscious factors. In the aftermath of Freud, with the object-relations research of Otto Kernberg, the ego-psychology studies of Peter Blos, the growing understanding of the pre-oedipal and life-cycle developmental processes, psychological findings continue to broaden our historical horizons.

    In the light of psychology, an historical document can reveal conscious and unconscious processes within the mentality of its author, milieu and period. Not only the words used, but their familial and cultural contexts, their associations, their images; not only the events described but the manner in which an author emotionally related to and signified the event; not only the accomplished structures but the conflicts from within which the accomplished was created, become the motivating dynamics of historical problems. In this regard, John Benton's Introduction to the memoirs of Guibert of Nogent has made a useful contribution to our psychological understanding of a medieval text and its author. [2]

With the findings of modern sociology, it becomes essential to distinguish the class or caste-consciousness attached to an historical text. Its social strata reveals the specific limitations of a document and its relation to the society as a whole. Durkheim, Tonnies, Wirth and Weber have all attached importance to social values, norms, ideals and communication systems of human groups. Weber's study of converging Protestant religious mentalities with social structures of the mercantile class, his analysis of patriarchal, bureaucratic and charismatic authority, Pareto's treatment of the élite, Durkheim's attention to <u>anomie</u> have introduced historians to the varying conditions of social consciousness within historical texts and their authors. Sociology has made the historian aware that one cannot thoughtlessly blanket an age with the mentality of one caste, interest-group or sex, especially that of an élite. However, by the same token, this does not exclude the study of an élite's creation of meaning and its influence upon a society. Andrew Lewis' treatment of the lineage and kinship factors in Capetian dynastic succession has successfully brought the French medieval monarchy closer to its societal matrix.[3]

Concerned with historical problems of cultural development, ethnologists and social anthropologists have illustrated that human life is a complex result of interconnected fields of development. Since the demise of the world colonial system and the corresponding collapse of the related unilinear notion of history, the work of anthropologists has exercised considerable influence on historians. Spender and Tylor in discussing the underlying processes of human culture, have joined with R.H. Lowie, A.L. Kroeber and P. Bourdieu in emphasizing the multilinear lines of human evolution in society. Rural forms of oral medieval European society survived the urban humanism of the Renaissance, the literate rationalism of the Enlightenment and the middle-class scientism of the Industrial Revolution. Documentation of these societies has been undertaken by ethnologists and folklorists such as Barbeau and Miner in French-Canada, C.M. Arensberg in Ireland. Fruitful study of the rural Albigensians in southern France has been accomplished with anthropological questions by the medieval historian, Emmanuel Le Roy Ladurie.[4]

Ethnologists and anthropologists have focussed attention on the value of oral sources as the appropriate index to the cultural and religious mentalities of traditional societies. Mircea Eliade has shown that almost all oral sources in a traditional society belong one way or another to sacred literature.[5] In showing how historical time and events are often assimilated through eternal archetypes in traditional societies, Eliade clears a path for historical study of the workings of events in these societies. Moreover, when history is transformed into exemplary myth by a society's people, these myths become a source for the historian who is anthropologically informed. Through anthropology, the historian sees that events of the past cannot be understood without sensitivity to the mental structures surrounding and creating these events and their significance. When we realize the relativity of our own mental structures, anthropology becomes an invaluable tool towards historical comprehension. In societies like the medieval where the vast majority were illiteratus, a word almost synonymous with 'lay', oral sources can introduce us to mental structures of an oral traditional society.

Psychology, sociology and anthropology have all drawn the historian to attend to new problems and questions, new methods and frame-works. Interestingly, all three sister disciplines have gained expertise in methods relying on oral testimony of individuals, families or groups. These methods can be useful to historians interested in studying orally dictated documents or oral sources in medieval historiography. It may be that historians can be of some help to psychologists, sociologists, anthropologists, some of whom confess that their respective discipline has not dealt very satisfactorily with problems of cultural change.[6]

Faced with these new avenues of historical knowledge, I became convinced that it was possible to widen our understanding of Joinville's medieval text by studying his triple sources of what was seen, what was listened to and what was read in order to better understand the cultural and religious mentalities surrounding the king-saint, Louis IX of France.

It was Voltaire who dreamed of writing a history of the human spirit and it was his generation which began to believe that the mental attitudes of men have not been the same throughout the ages. Since the eighteenth century, historical research has acquired tools from the developing sister disciplines to update the agenda of Voltaire's dream. We are now reading classical texts with new attention to their cultural mentality and to their source-material. As Duby aptly says in "Histoire des Mentalités":

> Divertissant ou exemplaire, diplomatique ou
> moralisant, le récit historique - celui de
> Plutarque ou de Joinville comme celui de
> Commynes - fait ainsi sa place à l'analyse
> plus ou moins subtile des états d'âme.[7]

PREFACE

NOTES

[1] Henri Marrou, *Sur la connaissance historique* (Paris, 1954); J. Le Goff and P. Nora, eds., *Faire de l'histoire* (Paris, 1974), 3 vols.; T. K. Rabb and R. I. Rotberg, eds., *The New History - The 1980's and Beyond - Studies in Interdisciplinary History* (Princeton, New Jersey, 1982).

[2] John Benton, ed., *Self and Society in Medieval France: The Memoirs of Abbot Guibert of Nogent* (New York, 1970), Introduction.

[3] Andrew W. Lewis, *Royal Succession in Capetian France: Studies on Familial Order and the State* (Cambridge, Mass., 1981).

[4] Emmanuel Le Roy Ladurie, *Montaillou - The Promised Land of Error*, tr. Barbara Bray (New York, 1979).

[5] Mircea Eliade, "Littérature orale", *Histoire des littératures* (Paris, 1955), 1:4.

[6] William J. Bouwsma, "From History of Ideas to History of Meaning", *The New History...*, p. 289.

[7] Georges Duby, "Histoire des mentalités", *L'Histoire et ses méthodes* (Paris, 1961), pp. 937-938.

ABBREVIATIONS

Jean de Joinville's Edited Work

HSL — *Histoire de Saint Louis, Credo et Lettre à Louis IX,* ed. Natalis de Wailly (Paris, 1874).

LSL — *The Life of St. Louis,* tr. René Hague (London, 1955).

CHAPTER ONE
INTRODUCTION

THE CRITICAL TRADITION ON JOINVILLE
Few would care to contest Bacon's observation that the invention of printing, gunpowder and the compass changed the form of civilization. But many of our medieval sources have been studied as if they had been written after the invention of the printing press. The majority of studies on Joinville's "Mémoires", as most historians persist in calling them, have succumbed to the magic of printing.[1] Depending on an historical method of a Langlois and Seignobos or even a Bernheim, these studies have taken the written document as the first if not the only criterion for our historical knowledge.

   Before the accomplishemnt of the scientific edition of Natalis de Wailly, one read and reread Joinville's text as if it had been composed in the sixteenth century with Rieux's edition or the seventeenth century with Claude Menard's edition, or even the nineteenth century with Daunou and Naudet's edition of 1840. Rarely was it mentioned that Joinville could have composed his work from not only written sources but from what he had heard and seen. For Auguste Molinier, this master of Les Sources de l'Histoire de France, the work of Joinville was "un écrit un peu incohèrent au début et à la fin, et non exempt de redites, la partie centrale, la première rédigée, restant la meilleure."[2]

   Other commentators have not ceased to call our attention to the 'special' language of Joinville, his familiar tone. Natalis de Wailly acknowledged the monotonous repetitions, the triviality of some details but saw Joinville's greater qualities. Gaston Paris referred to the opening section as a "laborieuse compilation de faits mal reliés entre eux." René Hague, Joinville's English translator, mentioned that his subject "had little aptitude to the writing of history."[3]

   Critics have been puzzled that the opening and closing sections of Joinville's work present King Louis IX in short symbolic scenes with hagiographic style, while the central and longest sections describe him in running narrative form. Discussion has centred on dating the written composition of the dictated work. One eminent group of commentators,

Gaston Paris, Molinier, Jeanroy and Bossuat, believe that the work was composed in two stages.[4] Paris maintains that the Crusade section (110-663) was an account of Joinville's adventures in the seventh Crusade with King Louis IX of France designed to entertain his family and friends of Champagne. Paris estimates that the tale was put to pen shortly after October, 1272, two years following the king's death. Thirty years later in 1304-5, Joinville was asked to write a life of Saint Louis for the royal court. At this time, he officially dictated his original Crusade story, adding appendages at the beginning and the end.

A smaller scholarly school, led by Bédier and supported by Alfred Foulet and Noel Corbett, believe that the book is a complex but single composition of 1305-6.[5] Alfred Foulet developed this hypothesis further in 1941, suggesting that the single composition of 1305-6 did develop in prior stages. He reasoned that Joinville's deposition during the canonization inquiry of 1282 together with the revision of Joinville's first written work, the Credo, in 1287, were initial steps in the composition of the finished product. Foulet even goes so far as to say that before 1282, Joinville "had doubtless narrated his memories of the king but it must have been in piecemeal fashion, without plan or perspective."[6]

Both schools have more in common than they have realized. Both groups of scholars stress the literary problem of dating the book's final rendering. Both teams date the work's final written form by internal textual date references. Apart from the fact that internal date references are not a conclusive method for dating the written composition of an orally dictated story, these critics have ignored the false anthropology of their literary priorities.

In our view, Paris and Foulet agree on the major character of the creation, but underestimate the fundamentally different consequences which such a character entails. Both scholars acknowledge that the work likely emerged from stages of both oral and written development. This common foundation merits our further attention and its takes us beyond our literary mind-sets.

It is simply in remembering that Joinville was first and foremost someone who saw bons faits and heard bonnes paroles long before the printing press that we can ask the question which is the subject of our

study: is it possible to read Joinville's 'book' in the light of his
visual and oral sources? Can we relegate to third rank his written
sources without denying their place in his final text? The portrait
which Joinville gives us of Louis IX is one of a witness who saw and
who heard about the king, then dictated his memories. His borrowed
written sources are auxiliary to this fundamental character of his work.

CLASSICAL WORKS ON KINGS AND SAINTS

Kings and saints have occupied the interest of many medieval studies.
Both figures were prototypes of Christian symbolism in an age which gave
them intriguing reverence. Louis IX of France, as king and saint, is a
touchstone of two central medieval traditions.

As charming as Joinville is, it is his subject which occupies our
curiousity because he reflects something so representative of the
thirteenth century. Canonized seventeen years after his death, King
Louis fulfilled his title: "most Christian of the Christian kings" and
a Capetian quest for legitimacy through holiness.

Historical studies on the medieval monarchy have made excellent use
of official documents surrounding the royal court. They have treated the
administrative, liturgical, legal, political and financial aspects of its
growth from theocratic to feudal to sovereign stages. During the reign
of Louis IX, the French monarchy grew from feudal to more sovereign
authority through the increasing territorial and legislative expansion
of the crown. By the time of Louis' death in 1270, no part of the kingdom was without some tie to the royal government. Royal lawyers formed
in the Roman law of Bologna and Montpellier began to affirm the imperium
of the king.

Delisle, Wallon, Berger, Lavisse, Petit-Dutaillis, Kern, Luchaire,
Lot, Langlois, Buisson, Glotz, Pfister, Funck-Brentano, Fawtier, David
and Kantorowicz have contributed inestimably to our understanding of the
French crown and Louis' reign. In a recent work, Jordan has illustrated
the major role of the Crusade in Louis IX's self-understanding as a king
and in his assumption of control after his mother's death in 1252. His
meticulous and thorough application of his suzerainty upon his return
from Crusade, coupled with his painfully won autonomy from his mother
made him a forceful ruler of his kingdom. Increasingly, his provincial

administration was controlled through his investigations of his <u>baillis</u> and seneschals and he strictly outlined their official duties in his ordinances of 1254 and 1256. Specialization of function began to develop his traditional feudal court into two bodies: a <u>parlement</u> who discussed judicial matters and a <u>curia in compotis</u> who dealt with financial affairs.

Louis continued the policy of his Capetian forbears by acquiring more land for the royal domain: Clermont-en-Beauvaisis, Mortain, Domfront and Maçon. By the treaty of Paris in 1258, Louis recognized Henry III of England as Duke of Aquitaine but won back France's claim to Normandy, Maine, Anjou, Touraine and Poitou. He maintained neutrality in the struggle between Emperor Frederick II and the papacy, kept firm control over episcopal appointments in his territory and permitted complaints against papal taxes. These instititutional aspects of Louis IX's reign have been extensively treated.

An important exception to this institutional emphasis on the French monarchy has been the study of Marc Bloch, <u>Les rois thaumaturges</u> which has unearthed the religious mentality and beliefs surrounding the medieval kings. His introduction explains the imbalance which his book attempts to right. Bloch says that it is not sufficient to understand the monarchy's administrative organization, judicial, financial or territorial changes. It is not sufficient to study the concepts of theoreticians which supported the divine right of kings or absolutism in the modern period:

> Il faut encore pénétrer les croyances et les fables qui fleurirent autour des maisons princières. Sur bien des points tout ce folklore nous en dit plus long que n'importe quel traité doctrinal. [7]

Marc Bloch's interest in the sacral beliefs surrounding medieval kings has been the inspiration for this study.

This work also takes its cue from a pioneer in medieval hagiography: Hippolyte Delehaye. Like kings, saints have also been studied in their legal, iconographic, homiletic, liturgical and pious aspects. Like kings, saints have been thoroughly documented as medieval events without much attention to the religious mentality surrounding them in their milieu. Rare is the study which treats the anthropology of sanctity in the medieval period.

The great contribution of Delehaye is that he presented the early medieval saint as an oral phenomena in a world of collective memory, symbolic representations and cultural rituals mirroring the divine. He illustrated how the oral memory retained simple, limited, similar incidents, describing saints who matched a type rather than an individual. Qualities and deeds which belonged to other local heros and heroines were often united under one head in the person of a saint. It was not uncommon to find exactly the same anecdote attributed to more than one saint. Delehaye explained how the oral memory relied on external signs to aid it: a monument, castle, feast-day or name-place preserved the tales attached to great people.[8] In analyzing the popular origins of medieval saints, Delehaye, like Bloch in his specific field, has enhanced our insight on the mentality of early medieval people, the way they thought about saints. Other scholars such as R. Aigrain, have built upon Delehaye's foundations. Aigrain has written on the methods and sources of hagiography in the esteemed Bollandist tradition.[9]

The cultivated perceptions and pioneering research of Bloch and Delehaye on medieval kings and saints form a basis from which to build. They show us the beginning of a methodology for studying the religious mentality surrounding the king-saint, Louis IX.

THE AUTHOR
Jean de Joinville's portrait of Louis is the best contemporary account of the king. When he dictated the closing words of his "livre des saintes paroles et bon faiz nostre roy saint Looys", it was the month of October, 1309.[10] The courtly seneschal was eighty four years old. The extraordinary monarch with whom he had fought in the seventh Crusade (1248-1254) had been dead almost forty years, and a canonized saint for almost twelve years. Joinville had known him privately and loved him well.

Others had eulogized the king: the Dominicans, Geoffroi de Beaulieu and Guillaume de Chartres;[11] the monk of St. Denis, Guillaume de Nangis[12]— all had composed hagiographies of the monarch before his canonization. Guillaume de St. Pathus,[13] Franciscan confessor to the king's daughter, Blanche, had put the finishing touches on his hagiography in 1303.

Joinville's product is a lay postscript to a clerical line. It is of particular value because it is the only lay biography on the lay king. Moreoever, it is composed by a reliable first-hand participant witness of the events described. This also made it unique as the other works on the king compile their presentation of him through written sources.

Joinville was a member of the lesser nobility of Champagne, the north-west county of the French kingdom. Born in 1225, eleven years after his royal subject, Louis, Joinville was the ninth lord of Joinville and likely served as a squire at the court of his overlord Thibaut IV, count of Champagne. Champagne had a proud and separate heritage from that of the direct royal domain of the French king. Joinville was very aware and proud of this distinct heritage.

His first known ancestor, Etienne de Vaux had founded the house of Joinville before 1027.[14] Since then, the house of Joinville had prospered by alliances with the families of Brienne and Broyes. John of Brienne twelfth king of Jerusalem was one of Joinville's family heroes. Joinville had a Crusading history to live up to in his family. Four generations of forbears had fought on Crusade before him: Geoffrey IV and V had won noble reputations on other Crusades and Joinville's own father, Simon, the son of Geoffrey V, had fought to take Damietta in 1219. Joinville inherited this Crusading tradition and eventually the title of seneschal of Champagne. This hereditary title made him an officer in the household of the count of Champagne, Thibaut.

Jean de Joinville received the courtly education of his time, learning to read and write with perhaps a bit of Latin. He was married at the age of fifteen and a year later accompanied his lord Thibaut to a great royal feast at Saumur, given by King Louis IX for his brother, the count of Poitiers. This was likely his first meeting with the king.

Joinville took the cross for the seventh Crusade at the same time as Louis IX in 1244. He set out in the summer of 1248 on the Crusading expedition for Egypt, from where the Crusaders planned to attack Syria from the south. He was captured and ransomed with Louis in Egypt. During the king's subsequent stay in the Holy Land, he became the king's closest confidante from 1250-1254. By an act of April, 1253, Joinville became a permanent vassal of the king with an annual income of 200 <u>livres tournois</u>.

While at Acre, Joinville composed a Scriptural elaboration of the Christian Creed known as the _Credo_ and intended as an oral reading to solace the dying.[15] The _Credo_ and his life of King Louis are the only two literary works we can positively attribute to him. Both reflect his serious moral character.

Upon his return to France in 1254, he divided his time between his fief, the Champagne court and the court of the king. He refused to go with Louis IX on his last Crusade, calling it folly. He never saw his royal friend again. Louis IX died of fever outside the walls of Tunis in 1270.

Early accounts of his Crusade experience were likely spoken to his peers upon his return to Champagne and possibly written during the 1270's. The final form of the work was composed at the request of his overlord, Jeanne of Navarre, heiress of Navarre and Champagne and wife of Philip IV of France. As she died in 1305, Joinville eventually dedicated the finished copy to her son, the future Louis X in 1309.

Joinville's officially recorded memories of Louis IX were politically pertinent. They gave prestige to the Capetian lineage and the dynasty which had produced a saint. Philippe IV and his wife Jeanne would not have been unaware of their political value.

Moreover, Joinville would have understood the possible moral value of his experience for future French kings. Philippe IV had ruthlessly departed from the ways of his grandfather Louis IX. Joinville's native province of Champagne had been acquired by Philippe III through the betrothal of Jeanne of Navarre to the future Philippe IV. Local administration in Champagne suffered under Philippe IV, whose political and ecclesiastical quarrels occupied his time.

As the seneschal closed his work on Saint Louis the Crusader, Philippe IV was proceeding against the Crusading Order of the Templars. He had ordered the arrest of every Templar in France, extracted an odious list of confessions and was bringing the Templars to trial to perjure themselves. Pope Clement V, at court in Avignon since 1308, was an impotent partner in the monarch's suppression.

Philippe le Bel's policies did not win him favour with the noble vassals of France. Joinville referred to him with distaste in his work:

>Si y preinge garde li roys qui ore est, car il est
>eschapez de aussi grant peril ou de plus que nous ne
>feimes: si s'amende de ses mesfais en tel maniere que
>Dieu ne fiere en li ne en ses choses cruelment.[16]

THE WORK

As a biography of a lay royal saint composed by a contemporary lay knight, Joinville's work is unique. The knight from Champagne was proud that his subject was a lay-man: "on pourra venir tout cher que onques hom lays de nostre temps ne vesqui si saintement de tout son temps..."[17]

Like the almost contemporary roman in verse, le roman du Comte d'Anjou, Joinville personified feudal personnages in himself and the king with secular biographical elements. However, his composition did not fall into any literary genre of exact definition. Sharing characteristics with the chronicles of Robert de Clari and his Champenois predecessor, Geoffroi de Villehardouin, Joinville nonetheless distinguished himself as both narrator and participant.[18]

The work consists of three basic sections:
1. Introductory section
   a) dedicatory letter to Louis Hutin (1-18);
   b) words and teachings of St. Louis (19-67);
2. Central section
   a) early life and reign of the king (68-105);
   b) deeds of the Crusade (106-664);
3. Closing section
   a) later years of the king (665-767);
   b) postscript to the book (767-769);

Both the opening and closing sections possess hagiographical elements. The opening section is based on Joinville's oral and visual sources, while the closing section is largely borrowed from the official hagiography of the king by Guillaume de Nangis, a Benedictine monk and official biographer of Louis IX for the dynasty. The central section is a narrative of the monarch and his trusty knight on Crusade. It is a blend of biography and autobiography.[19] Based on visual and oral witness, the central part is more chronological and eventful than the other two parts of the work which are divided into short symbolic scenes.

Joinville clearly designates when he uses augmenting oral report, borrows official written records and relies on his own first-hand witness throughout his work. For this reason, he makes an excellent choice for studying oral, visual and written reports on King Louis IX.

His primary source-material is his own inestimable witness of the monarch. His eye-witness account is part of a world in which visual witness was the beginning of a good oral tale. His evidence rings with the truth of his growing knowledge of the king and the unassuming details of human exchange inscribed in concrete examples.

His secondary evidence flows from the oral witnesses surrounding the king. The stories which Joinville heard about Louis illustrate the mentality of the milieu in which his own experience took shape and against which he measured his growing intimacy with the king. His oral sources are colourful anecdotes revealing the attitudes of the French noble Crusaders and their vassals towards the French king.

His tertiary sources are written material. He borrowed fairly long passages on law and short anecdotes on piety from Guillaume de Nangis' <u>Chroniques de Saint-Denys</u> and referred to at least one letter to refresh his memory. Joinville's major written source speaks for hagiographic and dynastic interests of a clerical milieu and its literary traditions quite distinct from Joinville's sociological grouping. Moreover, his written source relies on literary exemplars of sanctity and kingship which makes it an interesting point of comparison with Joinville's oral source-material.

Joinville's three sources are interwoven in refined discursive style with a careful choice of vocabulary.[20] We propose to separately examine the modes of perceiving the king in each source through a qualitative content-analysis.

HISTORY OF THE TEXT

Scholars rely on three manuscripts. The earliest, which dates from the fourteenth century, perhaps as early as 1320, is the Brussels MS., recovered by the Maréchal of Saxony in the eighteenth century. It is known as the Bibl. Nat. f. fr. Ms. 13568. The second is the Lucques MS. found by Saint-Palaye in the eighteenth century and known as Bibl. Nat.

f. fr. MS. 10148. The third is the Rheims manuscript, discovered by M. Brissart-Binet in the nineteenth century known as Bibl. Nat. f. fr. 6273. The last two manuscripts date from the sixteenth century and have been 'modernized'. It is believed they have a common source, independent of the Brussels manuscript and intermediate between them and the original. They are valuable in that they serve to correct each other and to qualify the Brussels manuscript, which is the most authentic of the three manuscripts.

In 1547, Pierre-Antoine de Rieux published the first known edition of Joinville's life of Saint Louis, based on a document he had found among the belongings of King René of Sicily.

Rieux published it only after he had polished its style, orthography and illuminations to sparkle with sixteenth century tastes. The MS which he used was subsequently lost. His edition not only distorted the manuscript but changed what seems to have been a defective manuscript.[21] Rieux's edition depicted Joinville handing his book to a king of France called Louis, whose mother, the widow of Saint Louis, had requested the work. This same historical error appeared in the next edition which relied on a similar, apparently defective copy of the original. Claude Menard published this second edition in 1617 and dedicated it to Louis XIII. The MS which he utilized was also lost. [22]

It was a literary event when the Maréchal Maurice of Saxony found an early manuscript in Brussels in the eighteenth century. Its language, orthography and illuminations bore the unmistakable characteristics of the fourteenth century. This Brussels text, now acknowledged as the most authentic manuscript, was published in 1761 by Melot, Allier and Capperonnier. It brought the oldest, most authoritative version of Joinville's work to the public. Capperonnier also had at his disposal the sixteenth century Lucques manuscript, a freshly discovered document. He published its variations as foot-notes to his edition. The Brussels MS. 13568 was hailed as the original text. Several editions followed its first publication: Daunou and Naudet's in 1840, more fully foot-noted than Capperonnier's; Francisque Michel's in 1850 and Michaud and Poujoulat's in 1851.

These nineteenth century editions had recourse to both the Lucques and Brussels documents but gave preference to the most ancient one of the two.

In the last half of the nineteenth century, Natalis de Wailly found a third manuscript supplied through M. Brissart-Binet of Rheims. The Rheims document seemed to be a more complete version of the sixteenth century Lucques manuscript and to originate from a similar or identical source. Natalis de Wailly's published edition is the final and fullest publication. It has been accepted as the standard edition of Joinville's work.

Using all three manuscripts and comparing them to the language of Joinville's scribe in various original charters, de Wailly came to the conclusion that the Brussels manuscript was not the original text. He thought it to be a later fourteenth century copy of the original with minor grammatical alterations. He took it upon himself to edit a new and 'more original' text in a pseudo-champenois dialect. Despite the fact that his changes are minor, his edition is an altered version of the closest document we possess to Joinville's original manuscript. It should be studied in this cautionary light.

H. Moranvillé has made a good case for dating the Brussels MS. 13568 between 1320-1330, almost contemporary with Joinville's death in 1313.[23] He disagrees with de Wailly and maintains that it is an unaltered sister to the original text offered by Joinville to the future Louis X. Moranvillé reaches this conclusion for four reasons: 1) it alone of all three manuscripts contains this closing: "Ce fu escript en l'an de grace mil CCC et IX au mois d'octovre"; 2) it alone contains a biting reference to Philippe le Bel quoted above; 3) it has several copying errors, many of which are carefully corrected by a contemporary hand; 4) the writing, illuminations etc., when carefully studied, date slightly later than the original manuscript of the <u>Vie de St. Louis</u> by Guillaume de St. Pathus which dates from approximately 1320. If this is indeed the case, the Brussels MS. 13568 may have been a Joinville family copy of the original text.[24]

THE ORIGINS OF JOINVILLE'S WORK

Joinville dedicated his work to the son of Philip IV of France, his future king. However, this king was to be the direct royal suzerain of Champagne, Joinville's native domain.

> A son bon signour Looys, fil dou roy de France,
> par la grace de Dieu roy de Navarre, de Champaigne
> et de Brie conte palazin, Jehans, sires de Joinville,
> ses seneschaus de Champaigne, salut et amour et
> honnour, et son servise appareillié. [25]

Joinville's work fulfilled a promise to his direct feudal suzerain, Jeanne de Navarre and de Champagne. Jeanne was the last independent feudal suzerain of Champagne. By Jeanne's marriage to Philip IV of France, Champagne came into the direct royal domain of the French monarchy:

> Chiers sire, je vous faiz à savoir que madame la
> royne vostre mere, qui mout m'amoit (à cui Dieu
> bone merci face!), me pria si à certes comme elle
> pot, que je li feisse faire un livre des saintes
> paroles et des bons faiz nostre roy saint Looys;
> je le li oi en couvenant, et à l'aide de Dieu li
> livres est assouvis en dous parties. [26]

This formal dedication at the opening of the seneschal's book was more than an external form such as we find employed in dedications of the fourteenth and fifteenth centuries. In the late thirteenth century, this dedication still represented the traditions of a feudal reality, tied to the heritage of Joinville's feudal service to the counts of Champagne and the honour of the royal service to Louis IX.

With his Crusading experience, Joinville represented a splendid Champenois history. The thirteenth century was the grand era of Champagne. The nobles of Champagne had married, fought and written well during this time. One can understand the influence such a glorious past might have on the imagination of the Champenois and the inspiration it might have given to Joinville's Crusading memories. One of Joinville's noble predecessors from Champagne had also written down his account of his Crusade experience. Like Joinville, this chronicler Villehardouin belonged to the noble ranks of Champagne society. Like the house of Joinville, the house of Villehardouin was well-connected by marriage or conquest in Europe:

> Les Chatillon devenaient comtes de Touraine,
> de Chartres et de Blois; les Dampierre
> héritaient du comté de Flandres. Les sires
> de Brenne allaient les uns conquérir le
> Sicile, les autres monter sur le trône de
> Jérusalem et sur celui de Constantinople:
> les Villehardouin se partageaient les débris
> de l'empire grec: Thibaut de Champagne
> ceignait la couronne de Navarre. On comprend
> l'influence que dut exercer sur l'imagination
> du peuple la splendeur de toutes les fortunes
> guerrières. L'honneur éveilla les muses, et
> la Champagne eut ses jours de gloire poétique
> et militaire. [27]

Joinville's work on King Louis was also feudal in the sense that it represented the antipathies and affections of an old and more independent Champagne before it came directly under the French crown. This heritage of territory and noble lineage, brought the customs, devotion, faith, independence and crusading spirit, to the service of the new seigneur of Champagne, the French monarch. The work of Joinville perpetuated the memory of Champagne's last independent seneschal, and the king who had been kindly to him.

The origins of Joinville's book lie not only in his Champenois traditions but in his family history. Joinville's kin-structure was one of distinction. Jean de Joinville was linked by the marriage of his great grandfather to the famed house of Brienne. In his work, he extolled at least two of the Brienne members as heroes: John of Brienne twelfth king of Jerusalem, whose glory ended in disaster on the banks of the Nile in 1219, and the "great count Walter" who was murdered in a Cairo prison after the Gaza defeat of 1244 and whom Joinville called a "martyr" as he likewise called Louis IX.[28]

Joinville was related to the Empress of Constantinople through the Brienne house. Mary, wife of Baldwin II was the daughter of John of Brienne. The Crusading seneschal devotes a telling passage of his work to her and recounts how the Empress of Constantinople chose Joinville and Erard as her kinsmen. Nor did Joinville fail to mention that the chief emir of the Saracens queried him about his royal connections when he was captured:

> Et il me demanda se je tenoie riens de lignaige
> à l'empereour Ferri d'Allemaigne, qui lors
> vivoit; et je li respondi que je entendoie que
> madame ma mere estoit sa cousine germainne; et
> il me dist que de tant m'en amoit-il miex. [29]

Joinville's maternal great-aunt Beatrice had married Frederick Barbarossa, Frederick II's grandfather. This was a prestigious series of family connections for the seneschal from Champagne.

It seems that Joinville's work, particularly his central Crusade account, was at the service of this familial and feudal heritage. In this regard, it cannot be ignored that there were two heroes to Joinville's tale. For there was Joinville, his lineage and all the traditions of Champagne's noble chivalry to be defended, as well as the king to be honoured.[30] As we shall see in Joinville's eye-witness story, Louis IX was sometimes compared and contrasted to Joinville's feudal chivalry.

The dual allegiance and origin of Joinville's work emerges from the opening of his Crusade account. On the one hand, Joinville is proud to have served under the great and holy monarch, Louis IX. On the other hand, he does not fail to remind his audience of his own chivalry, and that of his family and Champenois nobles. For example, Joinville praises his father's defense of the Champenois city of Troyes against the forces of the Brittany allies:

> Li bourgois de Troies, quant il virent que il
> avoient perdu le secours de lour signour, il
> manderent à Symon Signour de Joinville, le
> pere au Signour de Joinville qui ore est,
> qu'i les venist se courre. [31]

Joinville recounts how Simon de Joinville saved Troyes, the capital of Champagne, from the destruction of its baronial enemies. Once the major defense of the city was accomplished, the King of France arrived to complete Simon's work:

> Li roys de France, qui sot que il estoient
> là, il s'adreça tout droit là pour combattre
> à aus...[32]

With this anecdote, Joinville accomplishes two things. While praising his father's noble bravery, he also illustrates the fruitful alliance which operated between his family and the French crown. This theme persists throughout Joinville's Crusade tale. The themes of the seneschal's Crusading memories were tied to the traditions of two lineages: that of the family and territory of Champagne and that of the Capetians to which Champagne was later joined.

Moreover, it is possible that Joinville recalled his memories through the oral traditions of his family and province.[33] Jeanne de Navarre and Champagne asked her seneschal to collect and write down the anecdotes she may have heard Joinville relate to his peers so that they could be offered as a book to the royal court. As we have seen, scholars agree that Joinville had orally recounted his Crusading experiences to his Champenois peers long before his book's composition.

As a noble of Thibaut de Champagne's homeland, as an official of his Champagne court, as a proud member of a Crusading family, Joinville was raised in an environment where epic legends, songs of troubadours, verses of poets and tales of returning Crusaders formed a familiar part of noble gatherings. His work emerges from this oral atmosphere and took its first origins within this Champenois culture. It was to this Champenois audience that Joinville first orally addressed his Crusading memories. Like the songs, <u>romans</u> and <u>mises en prose</u> of thirteenth century Champagne, Joinville's Crusading tales were addressed to a noble audience who wanted entertainment, adventure and glory. It is perhaps even possible that the general characteristics of the historical epic which we find in Ambroise, Ernould, Robert de Clari, Philipe de Novare, Villehardouin and Joinville originated from within noble oral traditions.

In his work on King Louis and the Crusade, Joinville indicates that his personal memories of the Crusade would have an informal oral destiny. This was quite apart from and prior to any thought of composing an official book for the royal court. The seneschal assumes that his experiences would find their way into noble oral traditions. For example, in his description of the battle of Mansurah, when he and the count of Soisson were holding a bridge against a Saracen onslaught against the king, the count reminds him that one day, they would speak of their adventures in noble halls:

> Li bons cuens de Soissons, en ce point là où nous estiens, se moquoit à moy et me disoit: "Seneschaus, lessons hiver ceste chiennaille; que par la quoife dieu: (ainsi comme il juroit) encore en parlerons - nous, entre vous et moi, de ceste journée es chambres des dames." [34]

Within this context of the familial, feudal and oral origins of the work, it is well to recall that Joinville's final book resulted from the oral mentality of his medieval culture. His book was an important honour and official achievement. But his final work was the literary adornment on the oral and visual experience and on the earlier story-telling of the proud and loyal seigneur of Joinville, seneschal of Champagne, a chivalrous but independent vassal of the great King Louis IX of France.

THE PURPOSE AND COMPOSITION OF JOINVILLE'S BOOK

In Joinville's <u>Credo</u>, the miniatures have been recognized as "an integral part of the whole economy, not mere adornment." Emile Mâle, in <u>L'art religieux du XIIIe siècle en France</u> called attention to the literal interrelation of its text and its illuminations. [35] The text was to be listened to and the miniatures were to be looked at. Since the <u>Credo</u> was designed for the religious exhortation of the dying, this work sought to bring the matters of faith to the victim through the two principal senses: the eyes and the ears. [36]

Although Joinville's memories of Louis on Crusade were designed for the living, there is a parallel to be drawn between this work and the <u>Credo</u>. While his book was to be read, it was to be read to others in a comparable fashion as the <u>Credo</u>. Joinville's portrait of Saint Louis was designed both for reading as well as for listening.

In his dedication of the royal portrait, Joinville tells the young and future king of twenty-one that he dictated King Louis' good deeds and words with the hope of influencing future kings and noble lords:

> pour ce que vous et vostre frere et li autre qui l'orront, y puissent penre bon exemple, et les exemples mettre à oevre, par quoy Diex lour en sache grei.[37]

The Champagne knight expected that his work on the king would be listened to both literally and figuratively. He thought that his book would be read aloud to members of the royal court. He hoped that it would offer good examples which would influence the future leaders of France.

In effect, Joinville was speaking through a book.[38] He was addressing an audience who would have the book read to them. In his work on King Louis, Joinville recalls that the monarch used to read stories of kings to his own children before bed-time:

> Avant que il se couchast en son lit, il fesoit venir ses enfans devant li, et tous recordoit les faiz des bons roys et des bons empereours, et tous disoit que à tiex gens devoient-il penre exemple.[39]

Along with the good kings, Louis recounted the deeds of the bad so that his children would learn that if they were not good, God would be angry and they could lose their kingdom for their misdeeds:

> "Et ces choses, fesoit-il, vous ramentoif-je pour ce que vous vous en gardez, par quoy Diex ne se courousse à vous."[40]

Was not this the function which Joinville envisioned for his own book: "pour edefier ceuz qui les orront"?

In a similar vein, Joinville records the tale of a sermon given to the king by the Grey Friar, Brother Hugh. It was delivered to Louis at Hyères when he first returned to France from his disastrous campaign in Egypt. The homily had a profound effect on Louis. It reminded the king that in all important books, no kingdom was ever lost to a lord or a king without some misdeed from its ruler:

> en la fin de son sermon dist ainsi, que il
> avoit leue la Bible et les livres qui vont
> encoste la Bible, ne onques n'avoit veu, ne
> ou livre des créans, ne ou livre des mescréans,
> que nus royaumes ne nulle signourie fust onques
> perdue, ne changie de signourie en autre, ne de
> roy en autre, fors que par defaut de droit:
> "Or se gart, fist-il, li roys, puis que il en
> va en France, que il face te droiture à son
> peuple que en retiengne l'amour de Dieu, en
> tel maniere que Diex ne li toille le royaume
> de France à sa vie."[41]

While Joinville's <u>Credo</u> was composed to exhort the dying, Joinville dictated his book on Saint Louis to exhort the living. Like Brother Hugh's sermon which referred to authoritative books, Joinville's royal portrait had a homiletic purpose. This purpose was tied to the medieval custom of reading books aloud to appropriate audiences. Joinville's official audience for the final book was the royal court and its members.

In his book's final form, Joinville wished to primarily record what he had seen and heard during his six years in Palestine and Egypt with the king. To this central experience, he added other occasions on which he had seen the king at court. As such, he limited himself mainly to the roles of ear and eye-witness. At the very end of his composition, he included one major literary source. It consisted of several chapters from Guillaume de Nangis' life of the king. It is likely that Joinville added this official source on the Capetian monarchy to enhance the authoritative nature of his official book destined for the royal court. We shall evaluate this question further in the chapter on Joinville's written sources.

Finally, it must be acknowledged that the formal composition of Joinville's book was accomplished orally. He dictated it to a scribe: "Je... faiz escrire la vie notre saint roy Looys..."[42] He refers to his work as it "devise",[43] "parle",[44] "conte".[45]

Throughout Joinville's account, he uses expressions like:
"or disons donc que..."[46]
"je vous dirai..."[47]
"je vous ai dit devant..."[48]
" je vous avoie oublié à dire que..."[49]
"après ces choses desus dites..."[50]
"revenons à nostre matiere..."[51]
"vous faiz-je à savoir..."[52]
"je vous conteroie bien..."[53]
"or di-je à vous..."[54]

Joinville is speaking in his book, in a way similar to that in which he spoke to his Champenois peers upon his return from Crusade. The audience was slightly different: this was royalty he was addressing in his book. The purpose was somewhat more serious, long-lasting and moral: this book could influence the destiny of the French kingdom. But the basic aim of the message was similar: this addressed a live audience of listeners. Its oral purpose was a constant characteristic of Joinville's tale, from its first to last telling.

In his composition, Joinville addresses his audience as if he expects them to hear his words:

or ces choses vous ramentoif-je pour vous
faire entendant aucunes choses qui affierent
à ma matière...[55]

Joinville was utilizing a written vehicle for an oral tale to an audience of listeners.

METHODOLOGY

The method which we propose to adopt for this study is the separate analysis of Joinville's oral, visual and written sources on the king. We will examine each source-type's content and character with attention to the distinguishing traits and cultural values it attaches to the monarch. It is our hope that this methodological treatment of Joinville's designated source-material will lead to a fuller historical appreciation of the various mentalities surrounding the figure of the king in thirteenth century France.

First, we will analyze the royal portrait presented in Joinville's popular oral sources, then that presented in Joinville's eye-witness account and finally the portrait which appears in his written material.

CHAPTER ONE
NOTES

[1] See R. Marichal, "Manuscrit", Dictionnaire des lettres français, Le moyen âge, ed. R. Bossuat, L. Pichard, G. de Lage (Paris, 1964).

[2] Auguste Molinier, Les sources de l'histoire de France (Paris, 1903), 5: 28.

[3] HSL, de Wailly, introduction; Gaston Paris, "La composition du livre de Joinville", Romania 23 (1894), p. 516; LSL, Hague, introduction.

[4] Gaston Paris, "La Composition du livre de Joinville sur Saint Louis", Romania 23 (1894), p. 509; Molinier, Les sources, 3: 104-113; Robert Bossuat, "Jean de Joinville", Dictionnaire des lettres françaises, Le moyen âge (Paris, 1964), p. 418.

[5] Joséph Bédier, "Jean de Joinville", Histoire de la littérature française illustrée (Paris, 1923), 1:83; Alfred Foulet, "Notes sur La Vie de Saint Louis de Joinville", Romania 58 (1932), pp. 551-565; Noel Lynn Corbett, Joinville's Vie de Saint Louis, A Study of the Vocabulary, Syntax and Style (Ottawa National Library, Public Archives Microfilms, no. 12937, 1968), p. 1.

[6] Alfred Foulet, "When did Joinville write his Vie de Saint Louis?", Romanic Review 32 (1941), pp. 233-243; "Notes sur le texte de Joinville", Mél. Ronques 1(1951), pp. 59-62.

[7] Marc Bloch, Les rois thaumaturges (Paris, 1924), p. 19. Recent scholarship which departs from the traditional conception of the Capetian monarchy to place it in touch with its socio-cultural matrix includes the excellent work of Andrew W. Lewis, Royal Succession in Capetian France: Studies in Familial Order and the State (Cambridge, Mass., 1981). In studying the Capetian dynasty in relation to its context of the royal family, Lewis treats royal holiness as an attribute of birth "de saint liu", pp. 122-133.

[8] Hippolyte Delehaye, Les passions des martyrs et les genres littéraires (Brussels, 1921), p. 438.

[9] Robert Aigrain, L'hagiographie, ses sources, ses méthodes, son histoire (Paris, 1953). Recent scholarship which treats the popular

perceptions of saints includes: Weinstein, Donald and Bell,Rudolph M., Saints and Society: The Two Worlds of Western Christendom, 1000-1700 (Chicago, 1982); Delooz, Pierre, Sociologie et Canonisations (Liège, 1969); Goodich, Michael, Vita Perfecta: The Ideal of Sainthood in the Thirteenth Century (Stuttgart, 1982); Vauchez, André, La Sainteté en Occident aux derniers siècles du moyen âge: d'après les procès de canonisation et les documents hagiographiques (Rome, 1981).

[10] Joinville closed with the words: "Ce fu escrit en l'an de grace mil CCC et IX, ou moys d'octovre." Jean de Joinville, Histoire de Saint Louis, Credo et Lettre à Louis IX, ed. M. Natalis de Wailly (Paris, 1874), p. 412. (hereafter cited as HSL). A good readable version in the English language is by M.R.B. Shaw, as Life of Saint Louis, in Chronicles of the Crusades (London, 1963).

[11] Geoffrey de Beaulieu, Vita et sancta conversatio piae memoriae Ludovici regis, HGF (Paris, 1840), pp. 3-27; Guillaume de Chartres, De Vita et Actibus Regis Francorum Lucovici, HGF (Paris, 1840), pp. 27-41. For background see: R.B. Brooke, The Coming of the Friars(London/ N.Y., 1975); R.W. Emery, The Friars in Medieval France (London/N.Y., 1962).

[12] Guillaume de Nangis, Vita Sancti Ludovici, HGF (Paris, 1840), pp. 58- 121. See N. de Wailly, "Examen de quelques questions relatives à l'origine des chroniques de Saint Denys", Mém. Acad. Inscr. 17 (1874), 403-407; L. Delisle, "Mémoire sur les ouvrages de Guillaume de Nangis", Mém. Acad. Inscr. 27.2 (1873), 342; H.-F. Delaborde, "Notes sur Guillaume de Nangis", BEC 44 (1883), 195-196; H. Moranvillé, "Le texte latin de la Chronique abrégée de Guillaume de Nangis", BEC 51 (1890), 652-659; A. Molinier, "Les Grandes Chroniques de France au XIIIe siècle", Etudes d'histoire du moyen âge dédiées à Gabriel Monod (Paris, 1896), pp. 311-313.

[13] Guillaume de St. Pathus, Vie de Saint Louis, HGF(Paris, 1840), pp. 58-121. For background see: J. Moorman, A History of the Franciscan Order from its origins to the year 1517 (Oxford, 1968); L.K. Little, "Saint Louis' Involvement with the Friars", Church History 33 (1964), 125-148; Elizabeth M. Hallam, "Aspects of the Monastic Patronage of the English and French Houses, c. 1130-1270" (unpublished

doctoral dissertation, University of London, 1976), pp. 220-283.

[14] Henri Delaborde, Jean de Joinville et les Seigneurs de Joinville, suivi d'un catalogue de leurs actes (Paris, 1894), p. 619; pp. 4-24 for Joinville's first known ancestors. On the period see: G. Sivéry, Saint Louis et son siècle (Paris, 1983); Elizabeth M. Hallam, Capetian France, 987-1328 (London, 1980), ch. 5.

[15] Charles Langlois, "Le Credo de Joinville", La vie au moyen âge (Paris, 1928), 4: 1-22; also see D. O'Connell, The Teachings of Saint Louis: A Critical Text (Chapel Hill, 1972).

[16] HSL 7.42, p. 24. On Philip IV see: J. Favier, Philippe le Bel (Paris, 1978); M. Barber, The Trial of the Templars (London, 1978).

[17] HSL 1.1, p. 4.

[18] Albert Pauphilet,"Introduction to Joinville's Histoire de Saint Louis", Historiens et chroniqueurs du moyen âge (Paris, 1952), p. 197.

[19] Pauphilet emphasizes "deux portraits ou lieu d'un", in Historiens et chroniqueurs, p. 199. However, Georg Misch does not include Joinville in his autobiographers: Geschichte der Autobiographie im Mittelalter (Frankfurt, 1962).

[20] Corbett, Joinville's Vie, p. 13.

[21] HSL, p. 14, introduction.

[22] John of Joinville, The Life of St. Louis, tr. René Hague (London, 1955), p. 16.

[23] Henri Moranvillé, "Note sur le ms. français 13568 de la Bibl. Nat.: Histoire de saint Louis par le sire de Joinville" BEC 70 (1909), 303-312.

[24] For the sense of heritage attached to the Joinville family see: Sachy de Fourdrinoy and P. Schouver, "Famille de Joinville", Heraldique et Généalogie 7 (1975), 108-109. For an interesting comparison to the sense of Capetian heritage see: B. Guenée, "Les généalogies entre l'histoire et la politique: la fierté d'être Capétien, en France au moyen âge", Annales: Economies, Sociétés, Civilisations 33 (1978), 461 and passim.

[25] HSL 1.1, p. 2. On the prodigious uniformity of dedications in the Middle Ages and the presentation of a book as its formal time of publication see: K.J. Holzknecht, Literary Patronage in the Middle Ages (New York, 1966), ch. 8 and 9. MS. 13568 of Joinville's work contains an illumination which shows Joinville offering his book to Louis le Hutin, the future King of France.

[26] HSL 1.2, p. 2. Joinville responded to the request of Countess Jeanne of Champagne, Queen of Navarre, a grand-niece of Saint Louis and wife of his grandson, Philip IV. Eager to spread the cult of the saint she addressed herself to her seneschal, Jean de Joinville, to solidify his memories. She died on April 2, 1305, before her command had been carried out. Another princess of the Royal House had made a similar request, Blanche de la Cerda, a daughter of Louis IX, had commissioned her confessor, Guillaume de Saint-Pathus, to write an account of her father, the king. Saint-Pathus had completed his task during the year 1303. Joinville dedicated his work to the Queen of Navarre's son, Louis le Hutin, sometime after her death in 1305 and before Louis' accession to the throne of France on Nov. 29, 1314. The date of October 1309 in par. 769 of Joinville's work: "Ce fu escrit en l'an de grace mil CCC et IX, ou moys d'octovre", is found in only one of the three manuscripts and presumably refers to the presentation copy to Louis. Louis was born on October 4, 1289 and entered his twenty-first year in October, 1309. It is possible that this birthday prompted Joinville's presentation of his work. Par. 767 again refers to Louis le Hutin of Navarre in the hopes that he will send some of King Louis IX's relics to Joinville's chapel of Saint Laurent.

[27] P. Tarbe, Les chansonniers de Champagne aux XIIe et XIIIe siècles (Reims, 1850), p. VI. There was a common bond of identity and loyalty among the knights of Champagne which Joinville reflected. As Alfred Foulet remarks: "Joinville a un orgueil de caste très net..." Foulet, "La Vie...", Romania 58 (1932), p. 560. Joinville's knightly solidarity extended in particular to the men of Champagne, who had a reputation of their own. Canon Ricardo in his chronicle of the Crusade of King Richard says: "Est quedam pars franciae quae campania dicitur, et cum regio tota studiis armorum floreat, haec quodam militae privilegio

singularius excellit et praecellit." Ricardo, Canonico Sanctae Trinitatis Londoniensis, *Itinerarium Peregrinorum et Gesta Regis Ricardi*, ed. W. Stubbs (London: 1864), v. 1, liber 1, XXIX, p. 67. Thibaut de Champagne reflects this almost patriotic feeling at the end of a poem, when he cries: "salue nostre gent de Champaigne!" Thibaut was Joinville's literary count: Thibaut de Champagne, *Les Chansons de Thibaut de Champagne,* ed. A. Wallenskold (Paris, 1925), chanson V, p. 15, v. 44.

[28] Joinville also mentions his kinsmen when he describes his landing at Damietta: "A nostre main senestre, ariva li cuens de Japhe, qui estoit cousins germains le conte de Monbeliart, et dou lignaige de Joinville...": HSL 34. 158, p. 86. Joinville's concern for his family heritage is also evident in his solicitude to have epitaphs composed for his ancestors, e.g. the epitaph of Clairvaux to Geoffrey III reads: "Pour les grands faits qu'il fist decâ mer et au delà." Consult: H. F. Delaborde, *Jean de Joinville et les Seigneurs de Joinville suivi d'un catalogue de leurs actes* (Paris, 1894). See also: A. Firmin-Didot, *Etudes sur la vie et les travaux de Jean Sire de Joinville* (Paris, 1870), v. 1, p. 106 on epitaphs. Joinville was proud of his family's Crusading heritage: five of his ancestors had preceded him to the Holy Land. Bédier asks of Joinville: "Pour quoi s'est il croisé, quand son suzerain de Champagne ne se croisait pas? Nulle raison temporelle ne l'y forçait. Il s'est croisé pour se conformer à une belle tradition de famille: cinq de ses aieux l'avaient précédé en terre sainte, dont il tenait à honneur de fouler les traces..." J. Bedier, "Jean de Joinville", *Histoire de la littérature française illustrée* (Paris, 1923), v. 1, p. 84.

[29] HSL 65. 326, p. 178.

[30] For the epic traditions of this theme see: W.T.H. Jackson, *The Hero and the King: an Epic Theme* (New York, 1982), pp. 1- 109. He examines "the conflict between hero and king" as a common epic theme. According to Jackson, the basic heroic conditions are sadness, loyalty, exile and desire for fame, none of which are absent from Joinville's self-account while runs parallel to his account of the king. For an innovative work on the creative nexus of medieval art, epics and chronicles see Stephen G. Nichols, Jr., *Romanesque Signs* (New Haven, Conn.,

1983).

[31] Apart from this anecdote on his father (HSL 19.84, p. 48), Joinville includes other tales from Champagne in his early life of the king. After a few initial stories on the early troubles of Louis' reign, Joinville recounts the war of Thibaut of Champagne against the barons of France. Learned through oral tradition, Joinville's account is not entirely accurate: e.g. he gives the rupture of Thibaut's marriage to Ioland of Brittany as a reason for the war, although this rupture occurred two years after the fact. He also digresses into the history of Count Henry I of Champagne and an anecdote concerning Henry and Artaud de Nogent (ch. 18 and 20). On one other occasion, Joinville refers to an earlier Crusade and seige of Damietta at which Simon de Joinville, Jean's father had assisted, Behind his remarks, undoubtedly lay the memory of familiar stories from his father about this long seige. (HSL 25. 165, p. 90)

[32] HSL 19. 85, p. 48.

[33] e.g. Joinville's departure from his native land for the glory of the Crusade is recounted with similar ardour and attachment to the land, similar sadness and sense of fidelity to a cause that we find in the thirteenth century poets of Champagne. Joinville recalls with sadness: "Et endementieres que je aloie à blehecourt et à saint-Urbain, je ne voz onques retourner mes yex vers Joinville, pour ce que li cuers ne me attendrisist dou biau chastel que je lessoie et de mes dous enfans." HSL 27. 122, p. 68. In Girard de Vienne, the work of the talented troubadour of Champagne, Bertrand de Bas-sur-Aube, the four sons of Garin leave their paternal château in a quest for glory in much the same fashion. See Le roman de Girard de Viane, de Bertran de Bar-sur-Aube, pub. P. Tarbe (Reims, 1850). Jean Misrahi, in "Girard de Vienne et la Geste de Guillaume", Medium aevum IV, 1 (1935), p. 14, comments on Girard: "Le héros n'est jamais un homme isolé; il fait toujours parti de son 'lignage'." When the abbot of Cluny receives Girard and Renier, the first thing he asks them is : "... dont estes vos enfant? De quel lingnaje?..." This observation is almost as apt for Joinville, the sixth of his lineage to go the Holy Land, a form of not only holy war but holy exile. Also consult: G. Doutrepont, Les Mises en prose des épopées

des romans chevaleresques (Bruxelles, 1939) as the classic on the subject of the mises en prose. For a useful introduction to the differences between the auditory and visual memory and on the cultural transition from auditory to visual memory which started during Joinville's period, consult: H. J. Chaytor, From Script to Print (Cambridge, 1945), ch. II: "Reading and Writing", and ch. V, "Prose and Translation". Also refer to G. Chadwick, The Growth of Literature (Cambridge, 1936), for the transitions from script to print.

[34] HSL 49. 242, p. 134. Gaston Paris' belief expounded in Romania 23 (1894), pp. 508-524, is that the central and longest section on the Crusade was composed of Joinville's personal Crusade memories, spoken "es chambres des dames" upon his return, and heard by the queen of Navarre and Champagne, his suzerain. Paris contends that the main purpose of Joinville's Crusade memories was not to glorify the king but to entertain the family and friends of the seneschal of Champagne. This is the part of Paris' hypothesis which seems most plausible. H. F. Delaborde, in his Jean de Joinville, p. 146 makes an interesting observation on the oral origins of Joinville's work. He notes Joinville mentions (3.25, pp. 12-14) that he advised Philippe le Hardi against spending so much money on his embroideried tunics. Joinville reminds the son of his father's simpler dress and greater charity. Delaborde comments: "Si Philippe le Hardi lui donnait déjà l'occasion d'opposer à sa conduite celle de son glorieux prédécesseur, combine de fois, sous le règne suivant, si différent de celui de Louis IX, à la cour de France comme dans la chambre de sa suzeraine, la comtesse de Champagne, reine de France, à Paris comme dans son château de Joinville, aux jeunes princes qui n'avaient pas connu leur grant aieul comme à ses propres enfants, combien de fois le sénéchal dut-il parler de la piété du saint roi, de sa fermeté dans ces dangers qu'il avait partagés, de son équité dans ces jugements dont il avait été le témoin."

[35] Emile Male, L'art religieux de XIIIe siècle en France (Paris, 1948), p. 177, n. 1. Perdrizet has also considered the Credo with its close relation of text and illumination as a source for the study of medieval religious iconography consult: Speculum humanae salvationis, texte critique, traduction inédite de Jean Mielot;

J. Lutz et P. Perdrizet (Mulhouse, 1907), v. 1, p. 332.

[36] Jean de Joinville, <u>Credo</u>, ed. L. Friedman (Cambridge, Mass., 1958), p. 1. While the verbal text has been preserved in only one version, three versions of the iconographic text are extant. This has led to a number of scholarly discussions on the fashion in which the text was to be illuminated and on the relation of the miniatures to the text. MS. 4509 is incomplete in its illuminations although it is the only known complete text of the <u>Credo</u>. The second group of illustrations is a series of outline drawings, inspired by the <u>Credo</u> and found on folios $231r^0$ - $232r^0$ of MS. Latin 11907 of the Bibliothèque nationale. At least one folio is missing. The third set of illustrations is complete and even includes the scene of the captive French crusaders which establishes their origin in Joinville's work. This group was discovered by W. Bakhtine in a thirteenth century Breviary for the service of Saint-Niçaise of Rheims, and was executed before the canonization of Saint Louis. Friedman reproduces the later findings of Bakhtine on plates v-xxii, and discusses the problem comprehensibly, highlighting the tradition of scriptural testimony which appears in the <u>Credo</u>. According to Joinville's mentality, faith was a form of belief in oral tradition, <u>fides ex auditus:</u> of things not manifest, concerning which we have certainty through oral report. Scripture was considered the <u>divina auctoritas</u> of oral report. Joinville offered his scriptural references as final proof of his arguments. Friedman's analysis points to an informal relation of the text and illuminations based on Joinville's purpose which calls for the text to be read to a dying victim and the illustrations shown to him: "Et devent lou malade façons lire le romant.. si que par les eux et les oreilles mete l'on lou cuer dou malade si plain de la verraie cognoissance que li anemis... ne puisse riens metre ou malade dou sien..." (P. 51). See also L.J. Friedman, "On the structure of Joinville's <u>Credo</u>", <u>MP</u>, v. L1,(1953), pp. 1-8; G. Lozinski, "Recherches sur les sources du <u>Credo</u> de Joinville", <u>Neuphilologische Mitteilungen</u> 31 (1930), p. 200; Ch.-V. Langlois, "Observations sur un missel de Saint-Nicaise de Reims, conservé à la Bibliothèque de Leningrad", <u>Comptes-rendus de l'Académie des Inscriptions et Belles-Lettres</u> Bulletin de octobre-décembre (1928), pp. 362-368; H.F. Delaborde and

Ph. Lauer, "Un projet de décoration murale inspiré du Credo de Joinville", Monuments et mémoires publiés par l'Académie des inscriptions et Belles-Lettres (Paris, 1909), t. XVI, pp. 61-84.

[37] HSL 2.18, p. 10. Joinville's official purpose to influence the French crown to follow in the illustrious foot-steps of its great Saint Louis is found in this introductory section of his work, a second purpose which accrued to his earlier oral purpose to glorify the deeds of the Champagne knights and the family of Joinville. Natalis de Wailly, in his 1868 edition of Joinville's work on Louis made a guess that Joinville dictated his memories of the king to "un des clercs de sa chancellerie, c'est-à-dire à un homme qui avait sa confiance, qui était toujours à sa disposition, et qui, sans doute, avait eu plus d'une fois l'occasion d'écrire, sous la dictée de son maître, des lettres-missive ou des chartes..." See Joinville, Histoire de Saint Louis suivie du Credo et de la lettre à Louis X, ed. N. de Wailly, (Paris, 1868), p. xxi. De Wailly believed that the work was composed as a whole for the final dictation and his estimate therefore refers to the last rendering of Joinville's book for Jeanne de Navarre. On the other hand, Gaston Paris believed that Joinville dictated his Crusade memories in 1272 from his head without referring either to notes or to the version of the Credo he had composed in 1250 at Acre. Paris maintained that in 1305, the Crusade section was merely recopied by a scribe, while the remainder of Joinville's memories were dictated by Joinville at that time and the concluding chapters of his work were copied from the "romant" to which he referred at the end of the book. See G. Paris, "La Composition du Livre de Joinville sur Saint Louis", Romania 23 (1894), pp. 508-524. In his re-evaluation of the MS. 13568, H. Moranvillé defended the work's early orthography against de Wailly's and Paris' later dating of this MS. 13568. Moranvillé says: "rien ne pouvait que ce secrétaire eût fait partie de la chancellerie de Joinville..." He points out that secretaries travelled from house to house, château to château, and concludes that Joinville's scribe could have easily come from another part of France, hence with different grammar and orthography from a native Champenois of Joinville's region. See H. Moranvillé, "Note sur le MS français 13568...", BEC 70 (1909), p. 305.

[38] Ch.-V. Langlois, La Vie en France au moyen âge (Paris, 1928) t. IV, p. 3, describes it this way: "Dans le Credo, comme dans les Mémoires, on entend pour ainsi dire, parler cet homme délicieux."
[39] HSL 134. 689, p. 380.
[40] HSL 134. 689, p. 380.
[41] HSL 132. 659, p. 362.
[42] HSL 3. 19, p. 10.
[43] HSL 1.1, p. 2.
[44] HSL 1.1, p. 4.
[45] HSL 3.19, p. 10.
[46] HSL 103.407, p. 222.
[47] HSL 127.390, p. 212.
[48] HSL 91. 194, p. 106.
[49] HSL 34.160, p. 88.
[50] HSL 24. 106, p. 60.
[51] HSL 21. 93, p. 54.
[52] HSL 20, 89, p. 50.
[53] HSL 20. 89, p. 52.
[54] HSL 2, 18, p. 10.
[55] HSL 90. 189, p. 102. Joinville's oral style has been commented upon by H. Hatzfeld, "A Sketch of Joinville's prose style", Medieval Studies in honor of J.D.M. Ford (Cambridge, Mass., 1948), pp. 69-80. He describes Joinville's style as"'add as you write' language, more suitable for conversation than for literature", p. 75. This is one of the few articles which shows understanding of the oral nature of Joinville's style originating in his oral delivery. Another facet of Joinville's oral style is the manner in which his repetitions occur in his work: with the same themes and motifs but with an improvised variety of details. Gaston Paris noted this: "Le fait est particulièrement notable pour le récit, répété en tête du livre, des quatre occasions où saint Louis aventura sa vie pour son peuple: ici la répétition était légitime, et il semble que le sénéchal n'avait qu'à reprendre ce qu'il avait dit dans le corps du livre: mais il ne l'a pas fait, et tout en donnant au récit une forme beaucoup plus abrégée, il y a ajouté çà et là des détails qu'il avait omis dans la version

plus ample (c'est ainsi que le nombre des 'notonier' que le roi consulta n'est indiqué que dans le résumé); ainsi sa mémoire lui fournissait les mêmes récits avec une admirable exactitude, mais, ce qui est bien naturel, avec quelques variantes de détail." G. Paris, "La Composition...", p. 522.

CHAPTER TWO
THE KING IN JOINVILLE'S ORAL SOURCES

INTRODUCTION
Joinville was an assiduous collector of other people's tales about the king. He was a reliable witness who was careful to distinguish orally received information from both his eye-witness account and borrowed written material. He qualified the nature of his oral information, referring to his informants as 'people', men returning from campaign, the papal legate or the king himself. His craftsman's care with his source-material makes it feasible for the historian to analyze his oral sources.

Scattered throughout his Crusade section, present in both his introductory and concluding sections, his oral stories give a cohesive picture of Louis. The motifs of the monarch which emerge in Joinville's oral sources differ from those which appear in his visual and written sources respectively.

The seneschal's oral anecdotes about Louis introduce us to precious layers of popular beliefs and attitudes which circulated within the Crusading milieu. Oral source-material is infrequently studied in medieval historical literature as a separate data-base. These kinds of sources offer us valuable insights into an oral society beneath the superficial crust of its written literature.

In an oral society, where the vast majority of the population were functionally illiterate, most of our historical evidence comes from the élite sectors of the culture who left written documentation. Four out of five medieval annalists were clerics. Isolated reliance on this literature can give an ecclesiastical tone to our historiographical understanding of medieval culture and its mentalities.

By way of contrast, Joinville was one of the first lay nobles to dictate his memories of a Capetian monarch who was well-known to the chronicler. His work introduces us to the lay aristocratic mentality of his period. Moreover, the seneschal's well-cited oral sources reveal to us something of the popular perceptions of the king in his aristocratic milieu at court and on Crusade. Joinville's oral tales tell us of the common-sense collective notions of the king which circulated among the Crusading aristocracy and their vassals. These are distinct from Joinville's eye-witness which develops into a more individualized perception of Louis.

The king was the hero of the oral sources in Joinville's work. As Gaston Bouthoul shows in his work, <u>Les Mentalités</u>, all cultures whether they are religious, military, artistic or intellectual, are mirrored in their heroes.[1] Be they prophets, monarchs, saints, soldiers or poets, the heroes of a cultural tradition personify the culture's ideals, value-judgments and the intensity of its beliefs. The social, psychological and cultural character of a sub-group or élite's mentality within a civilization are partly revealed through the attributes it gives its heroes. As the popular hero of Joinville's oral sources, Louis and his attributes are an index of the nobles' caste mentality in the thirteenth century medieval west.

As these oral sources originate mainly from Crusading circles, they are associated with a time of war. Sociologists are careful to distinguish between mentalities of war and peace. Attitudes expressed during war-time can be a radical breach with the norms of the same people during peace-time. Generally, social psychologists consider the mentalities present during war to represent more primitive layers of belief latent within a society which emerge in a crisis.[2] Further research would be required in order to ascertain the degree of homogeneity or heterogeneity of these Crusading myths with the peace-time attitudes of a military caste.

Joinville's oral sources reveal the popular mentality of Crusading nobles towards their king and Crusader leader. As such, they are a useful guide to understanding the collective consciousness of these men. Jean-Luis Flandrin expresses the interest of historians of mentalities when he says that the human course of conduct can only be understood through the consciousness its participants had of it.[3]

Sociologists concede that the importance of social hierarchies is not only political and economic. The same kind of social hierarchies can accompany very different kinds of mentalities, values and attitudes. Bouthoul compares the social hierarchies of classical Antiquity with those of the Hindu castes, illustrating the different mentalities associated with the slaves of Greek Antiquity and that of the parias, their Hindu counterpart.[4] The ideologies which surround social hierarchies, and their castes, explains the manner in which a civilization conceives of differences between individuals according to sex, age, origin, function, personal aptitudes and culture.[5] These ideologies express a quality of consciousness which distinguishes one civilization from another, one caste or class from another's cultural counterpart. Delineating the common consciousness of his Crusading caste, Joinville's oral sources are a valuable cultural testament.

Recently, historians have begun to recognize the specific use of oral sources recounted in the written literature of oral societies such as the medieval. As Benoît Lacroix observes in L'Historien au moyen âge, the medieval period cannot be validly studied without attention to the predominance of oral sources, oral traditions and oral transmission particularly in its historiography, from Gregory of Tours to Villehardouin, Joinville to Monstrelet.[6] Fulcher of Chartres, Orderic Vitalis, Guibert of Nogent and William of Malmesbury, all for the most part, wrote their histories of the Crusaders without being Crusaders. These recorders relied on informed hearsay from returning Crusaders to fill their annals.

While the eye-witness was considered more authoritative, the oral conteur or key informer was the more common source of information.[7] The assertion of historical truth was based on the authoritative position of the informer, even if this was, to our modern eyes, extraneous to the factual narrative of verifiable events. As Jeannette Beer illustrates in Narrative Conventions of Truth in the Middle Ages, there was a necessary climate of dependence on the oral persuasiveness of an informer.[8] Poor communication, the uncertainty and length of travel between towns, monasteries and country villages, the scarcity of writings, popular preaching, reliance on the accounts of travellers, frequent wars and the prodigious memory of the illiterate elders among the lower castes favoured medieval reliance on oral news and oral history.[9]

Like the bricoleur who made new arrangements of old elements traditionally comprehensible to the senses, the noble oral reporter shaped contemporary events in narrative forms familiar to the oral traditions of caste and lineage. Joinville was an active participant in a richly coloured mosaic whose elements were constantly re-arranging themselves in traditional patterns. This commonly accepted mode of how the king was spoken about in noble circles is perhaps too simple a point to labour. But is also a subtle point which is easily overlooked. Individualistic habits of oral reporting were culturally almost impossible in the Middle Ages. Believability was rooted in collective tradition and authoritative attitudes.

Within this cultural context, Joinville's oral sources tell us not only how contemporary historical events were interpreted but how they were shaped. Historians are joining ethnologists, folklorists and anthropologists in comprehending the power of oral transmission through an elder or a social superior. In a world which was still close to magical thinking, where defeat was considered God's will and success was considered God's grace, authoritatively communicated oral news could be not only credible but normative. It served as a guide for the future. This is one of the explanations for the tenacity of customary ways of thinking in an oral society.[10]

Perhaps a few examples will suffice to illustrate the manner in which oral reports of authoritative witnesses could not only credibly interpret old events but influence the modelling of new ones. The modes of thought present in Joinville's oral sources were those of participation, analogy and symbol, associated with mental functions in primitive societies.[11]

We find one telling instance in Joinville's narrative of a "fiere merveille" which occurred to him and his Champenois knights while on their sea-voyage to Cyprus in order to join the king and his forces. The Crusaders sighted a mountain at the hour of Vespers off the Saracen coast of Barbary. The next day, they again found themselves before the same mountain. Unable to find their course, Joinville and his cousin, who had each nine knights with them, found themselves circling the mount two or three times. As the enemy coast was near, their alarm grew. Joinville recalls that the oral account of a priest,

called the dean of Maurupt, saved them. He told the men that when any
trial, drought or tempest hit his parish, one action had always
proved successful: "que aussi tost comme il avoit fait trois
processions par trois samedis, que Diex et sa Mere ne le delivrassent".[12]

It was a Saturday, so the sailors made their first procession
around the mast of the ship without delay. Joinville remembers that
he had to be carried, he was so sea-sick. He proudly records that
after their procession, they never saw the stubborn mountain again.
The Crusaders from Champagne arrived at Limassol, Cyprus on the third
Saturday, a few days after the king. Louis had landed on September
18th, 1248. Joinville believed that it was the procession which had
permitted their safe arrival.

At another dubious moment during the ensuing Crusade, the
grateful seneschal passed this custom on to the papal legate. After
a season's wait in Cyprus, the royal squadron sailed for Egypt, the
richest and most vulnerable province of the Ayubite Empire. In early
June of 1249, the Crusaders easily captured the port of Damietta. The
Crusaders delayed their march up the Nile over the summer months until
the river waters receded. When the Nile waters went down in October,
the Crusading troops impatiently waited for the crucial arrival of the
king's brother, the Count of Poitou with men and supplies. Time was
short for the march up the seasonally flooded Nile. The Crusaders grew
anxious. At this point, Joinville recalled the dean's testimony to the
processions and his own positive experience with the results of this
practice.

Upon Joinville's authoritative account to the papal legate, two
Saturday processions were held. Joinville participated with the king
and the rich men of the host in the procession from the papal legate's
lodging to the Saracen mosque.[13] By the third Saturday, October 24th,
the Count of Poitou had arrived safely.

Credible oral news carried word that these processions could
re-discover the sacred dimension of life in the present. It was
commonly accepted that this was history. Joinville's report responded to
a traditional and collective outlook which believed that history could
be made through participation in truth which was beyond human reach:

objective divine truth. As March Bloch says in Feudal Society:
> In the eyes of all who were capable of reflection,
> the material world was scarcely more than a sort
> of mask behind which took place all the really
> important things. It seemed to them also a
> language intended to express by signs a more
> profound reality.[14]

Analogy, amplification, anachronism, digression, cosmic events and the supernatural clung to the tales of the oral reporter as so many chips of colour to a mosaic pattern. Time and space were as implicit as the seasons, as cyclical as feast-days, as relative as King David and Charlemagne, as concrete as a church-bell and as symbolic as a procession from a papal legate's ledging to a Saracen mosque.

In La Civilisation de l'Occident au moyen âge, Jacques le Goff uses one of Joinville's oral sources to illustrate the long historical submission of the peasants to their king. He finds this submission rooted in the royal myth that the king would deliver the peasants from the tyranny of their seigneurial lord. This myth survived up until the final explosions of 1642-1649 in England and 1792-1793 in France.[15]

Le Goff quotes Joinville on Louis IX's memorable anecdote of his peasant support during his fragile minority rule as a young man. In 1227, when important French magnates, including Peter Mauclerc and supporters of Henry III of England, captured the king at Montlhéry, the militias of Paris and the Ile de France rescued the monarch and returned him to Paris. Louis recalled to his confidante that the road back to Paris had been filled with peasants who fêted him and prayed to God that he would live a long and good life, well-protected from his enemies.

These examples from Joinville's oral source-material indicate a level of mythic consciousness in both his aristocratic milieu and among peasants which was self-perpetuating. This contributes to our understanding of historical continuity. When common myths are modified, we can speak of a change in mentalities, an historical change.[16]

THE HERMENEUTICS OF KINGSHIP

The colourful anecdotes which Joinville heard about King Louis were part of a cluster of tales about rulers which entertained the Crusaders. Sultans, emirs and kings were a central topic of storytelling for the knights judging by the number of yarns which Joinville included about mysterious, powerful, rich and often evil foreign rulers.[17] Semi-divine and ritualized, these foreign rulers depicted by Joinville's informers were also curiously vulnerable to the worst of evil from their enemies with whom they were always at war.

Within this <u>genre</u>, there emerge the adventures of the King of France, the good king. In the most remote oral tales, Louis is simply 'the king', as if he could be any good king. He is a type. Tales accumulate around his function. He is the accumulation of the kings who have gone before him. The sound of his name is the echo of the centuries: Louis VIII, Charlemagne, David. In a moment of camaraderie, danger or relief, the aspirations and ideals of other royal stories are attributed to him. He is the powerful collective oral symbol of a people's belief. The sacred king of the eleventh and twelfth centuries described by Georges Duby and Marc Bloch is still a living force in the Crusaders' mental universe.[18]

Clustered around the name of the King of France were various stories which invoked the royal name in the human sphere as a substitute for the presence of God. The king's name had a hermeneutic and didactic nature.

A monk at the abbey of Clairvaux told Joinville a tale to illustrate the holiness of the Abbot of Cheminon. The sketch of the Abbot begins with the name of the king: "le jour d'une feste Nostre-Dame, que li sainz roy i estoit..."[19] The monarch's presence at the scene of the abbey assured listeners of its veracity and import.

In a similar manner, the king's appearance in an event made it meaningful news. The most important event which Joinville selects to record of his Paris visit before the first Crusade when the king was receiving the vows of the great barons to join the Crusade, was a rather innocuous anecdote about three men in a cart. Their claim to fame is their journey to the king.

Entering Paris, Joinville and his squire meet three dead men in a cart who are being brought before the king. Joinville's curiousity is aroused. He sends along his squire to find out the story surrounding their fate. He later learns the following circumstances:

> Et conta mes escuiers, que je y envoiai, que
> li roys, quant il issi de sa chapelle, ala au
> perron pour veoir les mors, et demanda au
> prevot de Paris comment ce avoit estei. [20]

The circumstances of the slaughter are recounted to Louis. The dead men are the provost's sergeants from the Châtelet. They had spent their time robbing people on deserted streets. Their last victim was a cleric who turned around and chased them with crossbow and cutlass. He struck one robber in the heart with his crossbow, cut off the leg of another with his cutlass and split the head of the third down to his teeth.

The king renders judgment by taking account of the canon law against clergy shedding others' blood. The cleric loses his canonical status but is enlisted as a Crusader.

> Sire clers, fist li roys, vous avez perdu à estre
> prestre par vostre proesce; et pour vostre preesce
> je vous retieing à mes gaiges, et en venrez avec
> moy outre mer. Et ceste chose vous faiz-je encore
> à savoir, pour ce que je vueil bien que ma gent
> voient que je ne les soustenrai en nulles de lour
> mauvestiés. [21]

In this anecdote, the king is the theatre for the meaning of events. This story illustrates the kind of chivalrous prowess needed of a Crusader. The tale enhanced the image of the Crusader, distinguished it from the clerical caste, and must have appealed to Joinville's circles. Since it was authoritatively judged by the king, the yarn's significance is sealed with the royal stamp of approval. This theme of the king as judge is strong in Joinville's oral sources. He is the judge of caste distinctions and status. Violence in self-defense is praised as an opening theme for the Crusade through this account.

The seneschal invokes a tale of the king's justice another time to bolster familial pride. The knight from Champagne says he had heard the king refused to oblige the Church in his justice. The French prelates had asked Louis IX to force their excommunicates to obtain absolution. Louis refused. He cited in defense the case of the Count of Brittany, excommunicated mistakenly for seven years, and finally released by the Court of Rome itself.

Joinville tells this incident twice.[22] The second time he recounts it, he follows it with an explanation of his own excommunication upon returning from Crusade. Preceding his experience, with an oral source on the king's judgment on erroneous Church excommunications, lends an aura of righteousness to his cause. Located in Joinville's feudal domain, the St. Urban monastery was searching for a new abbot. The seneschal of Champagne supported a monk who was not the local bishop's favoured candidate. The bishop excommunicated Joinville for keeping the monastery in his own hands until the matter was settled by Rome. Joinville uses an oral source on the king's inviolability and justice with regard to ecclesiastic politics to bolster his familial reputation. Once again, it is the king's figure which settles the truth of a matter both in judgment and in association.

On another occasion, Joinville quotes an oral source on Louis to bolster his chivalrous pride. He recalls that while on the island of Cyprus, the Empress of Constantinople arrived with only her cloak and surcoat after the shipwreck of her ship. Devoted relative that he was, Joinville sent the damsel in distress some good cloth for a new gown. Allied by the marriage of his great-grandfather to the house of Brienne, Joinville does not let his audience forget that the Empress was the daughter of John of Brienne, twelfth king of Jerusalem.

Another noble, Lord Philip of Nanteuil became jealous of Joinville's chivalry and connections. Joinville cites an oral source which says that this Philip went to complain about Joinville to the king. Once more, it is the king who sets his seal of approval on the importance of an event:

> Il ala au roy et li dist que grant honte avoie fait
> à li et aus autres barons, de ces robes que je li

avoie envoié, quant il ne s'ent estoient avisié
avant.[23]

We hear no judgment on the issue from the king. Apparently, the fact that a knight could be so jealous of Joinville's chivalrous generosity that he would report his dissatisfaction to the king is sufficient. The king had heard about Joinville's chivalry. This makes it important.

In this group of oral tales, the royal name attached to a story certified its veracity or importance. The king possessed a numinous quality of justice, truth and morality. He was the central environment for meaning in the lay aristocratic milieu. In short, the king structures the knights' experience with ultimate assurance and meaning.

These oral sources suggest that the kingship was considered an historical interpretation in and by itself for the lay aristocratic caste. The king did not even have to utter a word in a story for it to qualify as worthwhile news. Among Joinville's peers, the king was the accepted interpretation of an event. Moreover, the king was the interpreter of events. There is a divine finality about the king as a judge of the closed caste hierarchy, the separation of the spiritual from the temporal sword, the sacred meaning of Crusading violence.

THE GOOD KING EXTERNALIZES EVIL

In Joinville's oral sources, the king provides the figure who ties history to a cult which represents the theogonic drama.[24] In being idealized as the good king, his goodness is absolutized. Those who are excluded from his acceptance are therefore evil. One of the seneschal's oral sources re-creates this drama of the confrontation between good and evil through two rulers who stand between God and man. The tale recounts the meeting between King Louis and messengers from an evil ruler in the Levant. By means of the two rulers' symbolic exchanges, a cultural ritual is re-enacted and a certain vision of human existence is worked out. The dualism of the tale is marked.

After his disastrous Egyptian campaign to Mansurah and Crusading captivity, King Louis, Joinville and the Crusaders go to Acre. While there, Joinville hears of Louis' confrontations with representatives of the powerful Shi'ite sect known as the Assassins. Louis was to stay in Palestine for four years, fortifying the major Christian strongholds of Acre, Caesarea and 'Allit. The major port of the Palestinian coast was Acre. The Kingdom of Jerusalem had been reduced to the area of the northern coastal plain when the Egyptians occupied the entire south of Judea in 1244. Louis' aim was to try to find some compromise between rival parties in the Kingdom. The Assassins were one of these rival parties.

The largest component of the indigenous Moslem population consisted of Sunni Moslems but there were Shi'ite Moslems in the north at Nablus, Tiberias, Galilee and Tyre in the mountainous regions of Upper Galilee, Mount Hermon and South Lebanon. These were small communities of Isma'ilites, Nusairis (Assassins) and Druzes.[25] In 1126, the town of Bonias-Bêlinas was given to the Assassins by the ruler of Damascus. It was at the foot of Mount Hermon on the most important trading road for Acre - that to Damascus - and the Assassins held considerable commercial power over Acre.

Joinville records the tale he hears of Louis' confrontation with the messengers of the Shaik al-Jabal, known as the Old Man of the Mountain, head of the Assassins and known as the ruler 'who carries the death of kings between his hands'.[26]

The story opens in a typical fashion: the king is returning from Holy Mass in a chapel. He is confronted with sinister threats from the Shaik's men. He is told that he must pay tribute to the Old Man and release him from tribute to the Templars and Hospitallers, the two wealthy Crusading orders in the Kingdom of Jerusalem, or face the penalty of death. The first messenger presents the threat, the second presents three knives which fit into each other, and the third presents a large cloth which buries kings who have been assassinated with the knives.

In response, Louis requests the messengers to return to him three times. Three times, the messengers must face an increasingly powerful opposition. The first time they return, they find the king flanked by the Master of the Hospitallers on one side and the Master of the Templars on the other side:

> Lors li dist li roys que il li redeist ce que il
> avoit dit au matin; et il dist que il n'avoit pas
> consoil dou redire, mais que devant ceus qui

estoient au matin avec le roy. Lors li distrent
li dui maistre: "Nous vous commandons que vous
le dites."[27]

The messengers are forced to repeat their treats in the presence of the Masters concerned. Then, they are instructed to return again.

The next scene depicts the messengers alone with the two Masters. The king is absent. His power increases through the words of the Masters. The Masters tell the head emir that it was bold of their Shaik to send threatening messages to King Louis. They make it clear to the emir that it is only out of respect for their leader that they will not drown his messengers in the filthy waters of Acre harbour. The Shaik's men are sent back to their leader with orders to return to the king with a tribute of letters and jewels.

The final encounter demonstrates the king's victory. Shaik al-Jabal sends the monarch a shirt because it lies closer to the body than any other garment. He also sends him a ring with his name engraved on it in order to marry the king. The story ends when King Louis sends a missionary to the Old Man of the Mountain.

This is a tale which idealizes a ritual confrontation between a representative of good and representatives of evil. The theme is dualistic. Louis' enemy is almost a counterpart to his prototypical function as the good king.

The story blends ritual with fact, religious conversion with political victory and truth with power. Perhaps it is a tale which exaggerates Louis' victory in order to compensate for the grave disaster of the Egyptian campaign. It is an account which suggests some of the Crusaders' emotions about their Crusading mission. Their monarch is seen as the religious sword of the world.

CONQUEST AND CONVERSION

Another of Joinville's oral sources about a foreign ruler repeats this theme of conquest and religious conversion. Joinville had heard it from one of the king's envoys to the Tartar, people of the Mongol Empire.

The Mongols were the Assassins' fiercest enemy.[28] In 1253, a rumour reached Acre that one of the Mongol princes, Sartaq, had been converted to Christianity. Louis sent two Dominicans to his court in the hopes of winning his alliance and aid for Christians in Syria.

As the story goes, Louis sends the Tartar king a magnificent scarlet tent embroideried with many scenes of Christian belief. However, the tactful Tartar uses the tent to gain power. Displaying the artful tent as a symbol of his prestige with the king from France, the Tartar subdues several other Mongol princes to his suzerainty. Erecting the religious testament before his Mongol audience, he says:

> "Signour, li roys de France est venus en nostre merci
> et sugestion, et vez-ci le trēu que il nous envoie;
> et se vous ne venez en nostre merci, nous l'envoierons
> querre pour vous confondre..." [29]

The Mongol prince impresses those leaders he hopes to subdue with the sheer richness of an exotic gift from a famous ally. According to this report, the sight of the unusual tent was enough to win these peoples to the Tartar's side for they had heard of the French king's reputation: "Assez en y ot de ceus qui, pour la poour dou roy de France, se mistrent en la merci de celi roy." [30]

This story magnifies King Louis' power and fascinating wealth. It shows that the reputation of the Christian king had spread far and wide. His gifts alone were enough to subdue unknown tribes to the suzerainty of foreign rulers. Indirectly, even crudely but nonetheless effectively, Louis' religious symbolism caused foreign peoples to bow in political submission. Although the story does not explicitly speak of its secondary message, there is an implicit undertone to the story that the name of the king while powerful could also be misused. It is not the religious symbolism of the tent which wins the Tartar to ally with the Christians as Louis had hoped. It is the richness of the gift from an ally which leads the Tartar to subdue other Mongol princes. While Louis' name was exalted through the story, it was also somewhat misused in the story.

OBJECTS OF POWER AND ABUNDANCE

Objects of power and abundance evoked the king's name in Joinville's oral sources. When Joinville journeyed down the Rhône river to Lyon on his way to the port of Marseilles for the Crusade, he spotted a razed castle stark against the sky. Inquiring about its origin, Joinville hears the account that the king had caused this destruction. Louis had pursued the lord of this castle for his cruel crimes against the innocent pilgrims and merchants who passed by his land:

> A Lyon, entrames ou Rone pour aler à Alles le
> Blanc; et dedans le Rone trouvames un chastel
> que l'on appelle Roche de Glin, que li roys
> avoit fait abatre pour ce que Rogiers, li sires
> dou chastel, estoit criez de desrober les
> pelerins et les marchans.[31]

The tale conveys an image of a king of military might, a king who could wield a sword to punish in the name of his justice.

A similar story depicts an image of abundance associated with the king. As Joinville's Crusading ship later approaches Cyprus to join the king's forces after his sea-voyage, the land-lonely men see great barrels of wine piled high in the fields like wooden barns by the sea. This is a welcome sight. The wood-piles are surrounded by hills of green grass sprouting from heaps of wheat and barley.[32] Joinville hears a report that these sights are the royal provisions. The king has arrived. This nurturing sight is the first thing which Joinville records about his arrival in Cyprus.

Joinville's journey from his home to go on Crusade is marked by signs of the king he follows. The king leaves his signature on Joinville's horizon through securing signs of power and abundance. Travelling through a strange new world, Joinville finds that the king is a popular oral phenomenom which centres his experience with some connection to his needs for communication, provisions and military protection.

These two oral sources connect the king with fundamental human needs in a simple way. Both scenes aggrandize his function and attribute impressive visual sights to his power. Through these oral sources, we are introduced to the fear and wonder which Joinville and his men might have experienced at the time, emotions which may have increased their king's dimensions.

A DIVINE KING OF CONQUEST

The foregoing tales create the general atmosphere of the Crusaders' world. The king is its hermeneutic, its interpretation and interpreter. His numinous qualities speak of a sacred world beyond yet in him, a world he represents to this Crusading caste of nobles. As a prototype of good, he externalizes all evil in his opponents. As a missionary, he aims to be a conqueror of the Holy Land. His function is power, wealth and ultimate meaning for the knights who follow his dangerous mission. His divine representation is a strong theme.

These general Crusade tales set the emotional climate of the aristocratic milieu in which Joinville lived for six years in the Levant. This climate finds its apotheosis in a story about God as a King of Conquest. Joinville heard this yarn from Louis IX's envoy to the Tartars. The story projects onto God the very qualities of Louis' Crusading kingship praised in these oral sources described above.

A Tartar prince is said to have met God while travelling on a very high mountain. There he finds Him, arrayed on a throne of gold, better dressed and more beautiful than all the multitude who surround Him. Six jewelled kings and a throng of shining angels join the throng in worship and praise. When the Divine King spots the visiting prince from the earth, he bestows on the Tartar peoples the power to conquer the peoples of the earth.

The Tartar prince is uncertain that his king will believe this divine commission when he returns from the mountain. The prince asks the King of the world: "'... comment me croira-il?'" God gives the prince a sign to convince his king. He promises he will grant the Tartars victory over the Emperor of Persia: "'Tu li diras que il te croie, à tiex enseignes que... je te donrai victoire de desconfire l'empereour de Perse...'" [33] Royal conquest will be the sign of God's favour on the Tartars.

This anecdote cloaks God with desires for conquest of his earth through the actions of his favoured kings. God is imagined as the superlative of every aristocratic quality: personally radiant, seated on a golden throne, more elegantly attired than any nobleman. He is the Supreme King of the World. He is worshipped by kings, angels, men.

He grants to kings the right to the military conquest of foreign rulers and their peoples. God proves his favourable presence on the battlefield of the conqueror.

The Great Khan of the Tartars had indeed been victorious. His empire stretched across the girth of Asia during King Louis' reign. As a hopeful ally of King Louis, the Tartars were included in the Crusaders' vision of good rulers. Perhaps they hoped that their leader, a good Christian king and God-fearing man, would share in the Tartars' divine dispensation described in the tale. One can see what popularity this story might have had among these Crusaders who suffered an unfortunate military catastrophe in Egypt before coming to the Holy Land.

GESTA DEI PER REGEM

During the account of the Crusade itself, we perceive the king in two different but merging images in Joinville's oral sources: the arm of a God who lives in oral custom and military conquest,[34] and the Suffering Servant of Christ who achieves moral victory despite defeat. In the early part of the Crusade, victory is the consistent preoccupation of Joinville's oral sources. The king is seen as the arm of a Divine Conqueror.

It is interesting and perhaps significant that Joinville's first mention of the Crusade comes from an oral source. It reveals the underlying cause of the Crusade as God's will. In so doing, the story indicates that the religious mentality surrounding Crusades as a Divine Mission was still very much alive in Joinville's lay aristocratic milieu.

In the account, King Louis is prepared from on high to become God's chosen leader of a Crusade by falling deathly ill:

> Ainsi comme Diex vout, que une grans maladie prist le roy à Paris, dont il fu à tel meschief, si comme on le disoit, que l'une des dames qui le gardoit, li vouloit traire le drap sus le visaige, et disoit que il estoit mors.[35]

Royal sickness was a traditional event in medieval chronicles which could give a sign of God's disposition to His people. It seems that in this tale, this tradition was still part of the nobles' beliefs.

The oral source recounts that the two attending ladies to the sick king believed that he was dead. They covered his face with a sheet:

> Et comme il oyt le descort de ces dous dames
> Nostre-Sires ouvra en li et li envoia santei
> tantost; car il estoit esmuyz et ne pouoit
> parler. Et si tost qu'il fu en estat pour
> parler, il requist que on li donnast la croiz
> et si fist-on.[36]

It is God who saves the king from death. Upon recovery, the king's first words are to request the cross of the Crusade. The Crusade is depicted as a Divine Recompense. Whatever deformation, simplification or *amplificatio* are present in this oral source, it reflects the mentality of Joinville's environment.[37] The Crusade is seen as a divine war willed by God through his chosen instrument, the King of France.

On the tail of this oral account comes a list of the knights who followed the king and took the Cross: "Après ce que il fu croisiez, se croisierent Robers li cuens d'Artois, Auphons cuens de Poitiers, Charles cuens d'Anjou..."[38] At the bottom of this feudal hierarchy emanating from the king, comes the name of the author: Jean de Joinville. In the sequence, it is as if the Divine design enters the world through his king and descends the social hierarchy of his people's ranks through the noble aristocracy. In this interpretation of the Crusade's origin, we see how the king-figure of the nobles' oral tales was an inner source of aristocratic cohesion and loyalty to the Crusading cause.

Throughout the Crusade narrative, Joinville's oral sources fill the specific role of tracing the progress of the Crusade events through the figure of the king as a religious motif of meaning. The Crusade is interpreted through the king's relationship with God. In these oral sources, the king is a ritual centre through whom the transcendent truth emerges and the Crusade progress is gauged.

SUCCESS AND ORAL HISTORY

The best estimate of the number of troops who fought under Louis' command is 15,000 men. For the period, this was a sizable army. It is estimated that there were 2,500-2,800 knights, 1,000 lower ranking troops of crossbowmen and mounted sergeants, the rest composed of well-armed infantry, numbering approximately 10,000 fighting men.[39]

There was also a very high number of Champenois knights on this Crusade, approximately 1,000 troops in all. Joinville was fighting within a collective experience and tradition of a large number of his country-men. Many of these knights carried with them on Crusade the memory of their fathers' and grandfathers' tales of other Crusades. Such accounts were passed down from one generation to another.

The Crusaders' first success surpasses the oral history of the Crusades. Damietta falls to the troops without a seige. Victory is swift and unprecedented. Oral report sees God's grace in this royal triumph:

> Or disons donc que grant grace nous fist Diex li
> touz puissans, quant il nous deffendi de mort et
> de peril à l'arriver, là où nous arivames à pié,
> et courumes sus à nos ennemis, qui estoient à
> cheval.[40]

The grace is all the greater because the victory overcomes the oral precedent of the Crusaders' forefather. In 1219, the Crusaders had had to battle an eighteen month seige before taking this port-city of Egypt. Jean de Joinville's father, Simon, had been there:

> Grant grace nous fist Nostre Sires, de Damiete que
> il nous delivra, laquel nous ne deussiens pas avoir
> prise sanz affamer; et ce poons-nous ou tens de nos
> pères.[41]

The success is referred to previous oral history.

THE KING, FAILURE AND ORAL CUSTOM

In Joinville's oral reports, the king is the key to both success and failure. The Lord of Courtenay and John of Saillenay told Joinville that the king saved the day at the battle of Mansurah. After an arduous trek up the Nile river to Mansurah from Damietta, the king and his men engaged the Mameluks on the banks of the Nile ford, Bahr as-Saghir. Robert of Artois, the king's brother, had rashly attacked the Mameluks before he was joined by the king's forces. He had charged the Egyptians as they fled into Mansurah and eventually been killed, his men decimated. When King Louis crossed the ford, he heard of this disaster.

Louis at once drew up his front line to meet the attack of the Mameluks who greeted his men upon his arrival across the ford. His corps of crossbowmen had not yet crossed the ford to give him back-up. The king held his men to the charging arrows of the Mameluks. When their ammunition ran low, he ordered a counter-attack. He and his calvalry swept the Saracen forces back, but another savage charge was made against him by the Mameluk forces. Another counter-charge finally saved him. Almost surrounded by six Saracens, King Louis gave great blows to them with his sword:

> Et quant sa gent virent que li roys metoit
> deffense en li, il pristrent cuer, et
> lessierent le passaige dou flum plusours
> d'aus, et se trestrent vers le roy pour li
> aidier.[42]

As the king's name brought meaning to oral reports, his presence brought decisive meaning to battle. "Et dist l'on que nous estiens trestuit perdu dès celle journée, se li cors le roy ne fust." [43]

When failure hit the Crusaders, it was the king whom oral report faulted. King Louis waited for eight weeks at the camp before Mansurah, fending off the Mameluks and hoping for a court revolution in Cairo after the Sultan's death. Instead, Turanshah, the late Sultan's son, arrived at the Egyptian camp. A squadron of light boats were transported by camel to the lower reaches of the Nile. These Egyptian boats began to intercept the Crusaders' precious supplies from Damietta. The Crusaders fell ill with famine, dysentery and typhoid.

How to interpret so miserable an ending to so promising a start? Joinville refers to his oral sources. Word had it that the king was the cause. He had broken with "les bones coustumes anciennes".[44] When he had entered Damietta, he had violated a sacred custom. As in the Old Testament, such actions are punishable by God:

> Autant puet dire Nostre Sires de nous comme
> il dist des fiz Israel, là où il dist: <u>Et pro</u>
> <u>nichilo habuerunt terram desiderabilem.</u> Et
> que dist-il après? Il dist que il oublierent
> Dieu, qui sauvez les avoit.[45]

The custom was that an occupying king could take only one third of the town's booty for himself and his men. The rest should be left for the pilgrims. Louis had taken more than his share of the booty.

Other kings had respected this oral custom:

> Et ceste coustume tint bien li roys Jehan
> quant il prist Damiete; et ainsi comme li
> ancien dient, li roy de Jerusalem qui furent
> devant le roy Jehan, tindrent bien ceste
> coustume...[46]

The elder Crusaders remembered that this oral custom had been revered in the days of their forefathers. The king had not listened to the lone voice of John of Walery who had reminded him of the tradition. Instead, he had followed the majority counsel of his barons and taken the wheat, barley, rice and other food, leaving just six thousand pounds worth of goods to the pilgrims. In the galling light of defeat, oral report identifies God's will with this oral custom, and his punishment with the aftermath of Mansurah. The moral sense of oral custom which was attached to the king-figure was strong.

THE SHAPING FORCE OF ORAL CUSTOM

We see the shaping force of oral custom on the king in another oral account. After release from the captivity of 1250 by the Saracens, the king goes to the coast of the Holy Land. This tale finds him at Jaffa. He is informed that the Sultan of Damascus will permit him to visit Jerusalem under safe-conduct. This time, Louis listens to the voice of oral custom.

The royal Council recalls that King Richard had refused to visit Jerusalem unless he could deliver it from the hands of the enemies. Joinville heard that the king's Council pressed Louis to follow King Richard's example. They request him to heed this custom not only for the sake of the past precedent but for the sake of the future:

> Ceste exemple moustra l'on au roy, pour ce
> que se il, qui estoit li plus grans roys des
> Crestiens, fesoit son pelerinaige sanz
> delivrer la citei des ennemis Dieu, tuit li
> autre roy et li autre pelerin qui après li
> venroient, se tenroient tuit apaié de faire
> lour pelerinaige aussi comme li roys de France,
> averoit fait, ne ne feroient force de la
> delivrance de Jerusalem.[47]

According to this oral source, "li plus grans roys des Crestiens" fulfills past oral custom and sets its future.[48]

This oral source reflects an old Germanic and feudal attitude to kingship. As Kern and Carlyle describe it, custom, the first element in the conception of feudal law, was not made by the king or even by the community but was a part of its life.[49] The king relives the past heritage of his kingship in being below this customary law. Oral custom carries forth God's kingship to future kings. Joinville's oral sources seem to reflect this early medieval attitude towards unwritten custom and law.

In this group of oral tales, King Louis is an exemplar of a sacred monarchy which reaches from the oral past into the future. In his words and actions can be found the plenitude of Providence. <u>Gesta Dei per regem.</u>

THE SUFFERING SERVANT

It is telling that when the prize of conquest slips from their hands, the Crusaders' oral reports diminish. For the remainder of the doomed Egyptian campaign, Joinville's oral sources begin to rely on the privileged words from the king himself. The earlier theme of a divinely appointed king of conquest and covenant shifts. Joinville's oral hermeneutic of the king is transformed. A second theme emerges. In this section of the Crusade captivity and ransom, the king appears as a Suffering Servant, a figure of Christ. Here we observe a redemptive vision of defeat.

Since the thirteenth century was a time when the Passion and humanity of Christ gained wide popularity, since Louis IX eventually became a martyr-hero in his native land of France despite his misfortune, this second theme was not foreign to Joinville's culture. We hear its refrain beyond Louis' oral account in supporting oral sources from Joinville and his peers.

Cut off from their vital supplies, struck down with famine and fever, the weary Crusaders are forced to retreat back to Damietta. The camp is struck on the 5th of April, 1250. Joinville recalls the solemn exodus, the misery of the men. Louis is suffering from camp fever and severe dysentery but he gallantly insists on staying close to his men. Joinville records what he heard of the king's words: "... se Dieu plaisoit, il ne lairoit jà son peuple." [50] In his deep distress, the king appears as head of a Mystical Body of men. United in their sacred mission, they are also united in their suffering.

An oral rumour deals the final blow. Just as Geoffrey of Sargines had negotiated with the king his quiet exit from the royal bodyguard to a village cottage, a treacherous rumour spreads like wild-fire through the troops. A sergeant named Marcel, bribed perhaps by the Egyptians, rides through the ranks instructing the commanders in the King's name to surrender without condition. The rumour has it that if the Crusaders do not surrender, the king will be killed.[51] The men lay down their arms, and are led into captivity. This rumour was spread just as Philip of Montfort had persuaded the Egyptian generals to allow the Crusaders the free departure of their army for the return of

Damietta. We witness the immense power of oral rumour in this sad saga.

Later, Louis IX describes his painful retreat from Mansurah to Joinville: "et me conta li roys que il estoit montez sur un petit roncin, une houce de soye vestue."[52] The monarch recalls his gratitude to Geoffrey of Sargines who protects his master from the Saracen swords as a good servant protects his master's cup from flies:

> Car toutes les foiz que le Sarrazin l'approchoient,
> il prenoit son espié, que il avoit mis entre le et
> l'arçon de sa selle, et le metoit desous s'essele,
> et lour recouroit sus, et les chassoit en sus dou
> roy.[53]

In this group of oral sources, the king reveals himself as more human, more corporate and more dependent upon his men than the themes of conquest allowed in the first group of oral sources.

Like Christ before the Sanhedrin, the king surrenders himself to torture for the sake of God and his people. It is unlikely that it was anyone but the king himself who told Joinville about this threat and torture. The advisors of the sultan ask Louis to promise to deliver the Castles of the Templars and Hospitallers in the Holy Land in return for the Crusaders' release. If the king refuses, he will get the torture known as the bernicles.

Joinville explains to his audience that the bernicles are two pliable lengths of wood, armed at one end with teeth. The victim's legs are placed between the teeth and not six inches of bone are left unbroken. After three days, when the victim's legs are still swollen, they are freshly broken.

To this threat, the king resists. He replies: "que il estoit lour prisonniers, et que il pouoient faire de li lour volentei."[54] The monarch's willingness to suffer for a principle dismays and defeats the Saracens:

> Quant il virent que il ne pourroient vaincre le
> bon roy par menaces, si revindrent à le et li
> demanderent combien il vourroit donner au soudanc
> d' argent, et avec ce lour rendist Damiete.[55]

Louis goes on to say that the lands in Syria do not belong to him but to the Emperor's son and only the Emperor himself can give them away. Astounded at Louis' courage, the Moslems drop their threat.

The new Saracen terms of money payments are slowly met by the king. According to the oral account to Joinville, Louis negotiates with his enemies in a slow, repetitive and amplified fashion. The king says he will ask the queen in Damietta if she can meet the payments, he says he knows she will oblige because she is his wife but he wants the Saracen oath of promise that they will deliver the Crusaders if the queen pays the five hundred thousand French pounds <u>tournois</u>. Finally, it is agreed that over this vast sum, equivalent to one million besants, the Sultan will free the monarch and his men.

Oral report from the Saracen side confirms that the French monarch has won a spiritual victory in the midst of material loss. It is said that the Sultan acknowledged the greatness of this king:

> Quant li soudans oy ce, il dist: "Par my foi!
> larges est le Frans quant il n'a pas barguignié
> sur si grant somme de deniers. Or li alés dire,
> fist li soudans, que je li doing cent mile livres
> pour la reançon paier." [56]

According to the wishful thinking of this account, the Sultan is so impressed with the Christian king's generosity, that he thinks of reducing the French debt.

When the Saracen emirs ask the king for certain oaths to assure his sincerity in the agreement, King Louis agrees to all oaths but one. The last oath they ask of the king is this: if he breaks the settlement he will be like the Christians who denounce God and stamp on His Cross. Louis refuses to blaspheme with this oath.

When the emirs and Master Nicholas warn the king that if he does not take this oath, the Saracens will behead him and his troops, the monarch responds that he prefers death to blasphemy. Again, he is willing to suffer for the sake of Christian principles:

> Li roys respondi que il ne pooient faire lour
> volentei; car il amoit miex mourir bons crestiens,
> que ce que il vesquit ou courrous Dieu et sa Mere.[57]

The oral account continues that the king even stands up to the threatened torture of the eighty year-old Patriarch of Jerusalem. The Saracens tie the old gentleman so tightly to a tent-pole that his hands swell to the size of his head and blood spurts from his nails. The Patriarch cries out to the king for mercy. The elder says he will take the king's oath upon his soul. Joinville admits: "je ne sai pas comment li sairemens fu atiriez; mais li amiral se tindrent bien apaie.." The sentiments in the account resemble those engaged in a morality play. The oral report leaves the scene unfinished. The authority of the king and the Patriarch is left intact. [58]

The Saracens are reported to have come to the king's tent to ask him to be their new Sultan. According to this dubious report, Louis asks Joinville if he should accept the zenith of tributes:

> Et il me demanda se je cuidoie que il eust pris
> le royaume de Babiloine, se il li eussent presentei.
> Et je li dis que il eust mout fait que fous, à ce
> que il avoient lour signour occis; et il me dist
> que vraiement il ne l'eust mie refusei. [59]

Saracen talk says that Louis is the firmest Christian that could be found. They speak with awe of how they saw this monarch lie in the form of a cross on the ground.

Through the Saracen tributes, King Louis appears not only as Suffering Servant of all Christians but king of all rulers. It is his principled perseverance as Suffering Servant of Christ which wins him this moral victory. Louis becomes another kind of hero through the Crusade catastrophe. Martyrs to the faith can be heroes to Christians. Their God died on a cross. But to Saracens? This oral source serves as the final proof that Louis had converted the Saracens to the ethical power of his vision as Christian.

However, Joinville's personal reflection on this tribute sounds an ambivalent note to this compliment. If the Saracens murdered their own Sultan, what would they do to a Christian monarch as their leader? Joinville does not wholeheartedly endorse this kind of success.

In this second theme of Joinville's oral sources about the Crusade expedition, the king's religious suffering in defeat is still viewed

in terms of its measure of victory over the Saracens. The Suffering
Servant theme is somewhat subordinated to this triumphant aim through
the two oral reports which praise the king from the Saracen side.
Suffering is seen as a kind of self-made mastery because the king does
it nobly, courageously and with resistance to temptation. This is
a religious victory. It is also a political success because it is
recognized as extraordinary by the Saracen enemy. In this indirect
fashion, religious victory is linked with conversion of the Moslems
and moral conquest.

In this cluster of oral reports, Louis IX's personal interpretation
of his kingship as a salvific mystery is expressed. The theme of Louis
as a figure of Christ, the Suffering Servant is heard. Through the
addition of Saracen sources, a latent schema of dualism and conquest
emerges. Through Saracen recognition of the heroism in this principled
Christlike suffering, a theme of moral conquest and conversion emerges.
The king's oral stories of his capture place no explicit value on
suffering for the sake of conquest. However, the underlying motif of
dualism between good and evil, Christian and Moslem is present in his
accounts. In this way, both Louis' oral report and the Saracen
commentaries are coloured with a dualism which seems to lie at the heart
of these Crusading oral excerpts.

A NEW MESSIAH

The theme of the king as a Suffering Servant reveals a mystical
dimension to the meaning of the kingship. This aura to the kingship
is also expressed in three short oral reports which Joinville includes
at the beginning and end of his work. In each case, he embellishes
these traditional royal events with liturgical mysticism.

Joinville followed the medieval chronicler's custom of relating
the king's birth, coronation and death as central events in his reign.
He describes Louis IX's birth, coronation and death as prophetic rites of
passage. He sees them as times when the customs of the Christian kingship
are fulfilled in the person of the king.

The seneschal's brief information on these three events is from oral
report. He embellishes on this summary information to heighten the
prophetic quality of the kingship. This monarch is envisioned as a new

Christ. The religious practices of his day of birth, the liturgical words for his coronation Mass and the Biblical hour of his death are utilized to amplify this spiritual meaning.

It was King Louis who had informed Joinville about the day he was born: "aussi comme je li oy dire, il fu nez le jour saint Marc euvangeliste après Pasques." [60] Joinville recalls that the religious custom of this feast is to carry black crosses in procession. He believes that this was a sign of prophecy concerning the many Crusaders who would die on Louis' two Crusades. Contained in his birth were the funerals of his followers. Joinville reflects that these crosses would be cause for great joy in heaven but severe sorrow on earth. Joinville contrasts the earthly desires for conquest with the heavenly meaning of defeat and even death. This tale, based on oral information, reflects specifically on Joinville's commentary and introduces a theme of Crucifixion and Resurrection to the king. In Joinville's remarks are contained both sides of his oral sources' themes: earthly conquest and heavenly victory in principled defeat.

Joinville had also heard about the royal coronation. He reports on its liturgical significance in the same prophetic vein. He injects the specific Christian nature of the kingship through a special God-man relationship. Louis was crowned on the first Sunday of Advent and his reign was to mirror the words of the liturgical rite:

> Li commencemens de celi dymanche de la messe si est,
>
> <u>Ad te levavi animam meam</u>, et ce qui s'en suit après;
>
> et dit ainsi: "Biaus Sire Diex, je leveray m'amme
>
> à toy, je me fi en toy." [61]

Joinville's passage illustrates that Louis' faith made the sacred rites of his coronation live throughout his life.

It was the Count of Alençon, Louis IX's son, who told Joinville of his father's death. Louis died before the walls of Tunis on a bed of ashes at the opening of his second and last Crusade disaster. Fever quenched his life and those of many of his men. The source notes that the king died at the same hour that Christ had died on the cross to save the world. In his death as in his life, this king had, like the Suffering Servant, Christ, given himself to God for the salvation of his people. The salvific nature of the Christian kingship is the concluding note of this oral source:

> Après, se fist li sains roys couchier en un lit couvert de cendre, et mist ses mains sus sa poitrine, et en regardant vers le ciel rendi à nostre Creatour son esperit, en celle hore meisme que li Fiz Dieu morut pour le salut dou monde en la croiz.[62]

According to these brief, almost ornamental oral sources, Louis IX's birth, coronation and death stand as messianic announcements of the kingship and the personal faith of this king. In these religious rites of passage, the king is at once God's anointed and the Suffering Servant of Christ.

CONCLUSION

In these oral sources, the kingship holds a primordial function within the mentality of the Crusading milieu. Joinville's general oral accounts represent a collective mythology about the king which was popular in the knights' circles during Crusade. In these reports, Louis appears as the embodiment of his kingship more than as an individual king. By way of contrast, Louis IX's oral testimony gives us a vivid portrayal of his more personal interpretation of his kingship and Crusade leadership. In these more privileged oral sources, the mystical aspect of the king as Suffering Servant and Head of a Mystical Body of Christ is illustrated. It is not possible to speculate on the wider meaning these themes possessed for the king himself during his reign in France. These sources are limited to a terrible time of trial for the king. However, it is possible to draw some tentative conclusions about the manner in which Joinville utilized the king's oral reports within the context of his Crusading account. Our conclusion is limited to this question.

As a ritual centre of meaning, as the interpretation of events, the king is tinted with the values and ideals of the lay aristocratic caste while on Crusade. The Crusading king is presented as the idealization of caste hopes for the justification of their mission to fight the Saracens and win back the Holy Land for the Christians. The king-figure creates peer cohesion and diffuses peer revenge and rivalry. However, the king is more than a sociological rite for these knights. He responds to primordial needs of these fighting men. He is spoken of at moments of their deepest moments of mystery. He is close to their most profound emotions of terror, wonder, awe and the unknown. Most profoundly, the king appears as a religious myth.

As Paul Ricoeur shows,[63] religious myth combines and transcends the inner contradictions of human experience. In this sense, the king reconciles the contradictions of the Crusaders' experience. These are experiences of birth and death, crucifixion and resurrection, defeat and victory. Their aspirations surround him with good deeds and wise words of epic proportion. Tales and anecdotes multiply around him. Louis appears as a kind of Hebraic David dubbed King of the Franks, the new Chosen People. Few occasions are missed to aggrandize the monarch traditionally loved or the sultan traditionally feared.

Joinville recounts the religious and barbaric heredity of his hero as well as the military values in which his milieu flourished. Louis IX appears close to the rituals of collective symbols and aspirations. Through these rituals, the king appears present to his Crusaders' paternal needs, and contained in ambivalent and even contradictory archetypal functions of theocratic or feudal heritage. Louis emerges as a sacred myth unifying the Crusaders: on the one hand, a Warrior-God's lone leader in a Crusading battle for the world against the agents of the Devil and on the other hand, a caste Christ-figure who can redeem his men even in defeat. We hear of the king in the midst of a very difficult Crusade and captivity which went against the basic pride of the Crusaders' purpose far from home in a foreign land.

In the general early tales which we analyzed, kingship externalizes a Divinely-appointed monarch of power, wealth and conquest. The God he serves structures the events of human history through the actions of his chosen kings. This Divine King grants conquest of the earth to those He favours in the struggle against the evil dichotomies of the earth. This basic dualism remains close to the heart of almost all of Joinville's Crusading oral sources. It indicates that this interpretation of the world divided into the good who conquer and the bad who go down to defeat seems to have been a fundamental part of the noble mentality on Crusade.

In the light of these general oral tales, conquest appears as a semi-religious rite of Christian kingship. Running right through almost all of the Crusade oral sources, it continues to play a role in the Saracen interpretations of the Egyptian disaster itself. Through these Saracen accounts, the Christians win a kind of spiritual triumph through the amazing fortitude of their king.

In the early yarn of the Old Man of the Mountain, we see some indication of the importance of the just use of power. Louis conquers the Assassin ruler's threats by a series of ritualized threats, visual impressions and insinuations of revenge. These are all directed towards the defense of the Christians in the Holy Land and towards the moral end of the Assassin's conversion. Conversion as a form of Crusading conquest appears as one of the tale's morals.

This pattern is repeated in the Saracen commentaries on Louis' captivity. Louis receives the tribute of a Saracen request to become their leader as a sign of their possible conversion to his faith which triumphs over defeat. Again, in the Tartar tale of God on the mountain, conquest itself becomes a form of conversion. The Tartars' subsequent success against the Persian forces is described as proof that their prince did see God on a mountain foretelling their win. Their triumph over Persians is a way of converting the Tartar troops that God is indeed with them.

In this fashion, conquest is seen as a form of conversion to God. As a religious ritual, military battle is accomplished in consort with the Divine. Conversion as a conquest and military conquest as conversion are themes which indicate how closely martial glories were tied to religious experience in the noble order while on Crusade. This motif is continued in aristocratic oral sources of Joinville's early Crusade account. This simplistic world-view is a fairly constant companion in the seneschal's oral reports. The world is divided into two camps. The noble fighters try to keep themselves on the side of God through their king. Their mission is to conquer and convert the evil forces to their religious mission.

Joinville's oral sources give meaning and purpose to the terrors of battle, the desires for eternal reward and the mysteries of their life and death. The king supplies the human touchstone. For the nobles who shared these tales, kingship was both the bridge from the order of values and from the disorder of their experience to God. In the process of tale-telling, the function of kingship is sometimes divinized. On the other hand, the person of God is sometimes anthropomorphized as in the tale of God on the mountain dressed as a rich aristocratic king.

The mythical function of the kingship operates on at least two levels of subtlety in these stories. On one level, the monarch is a godlike theatre for information, meaning, wealth and power. The nobles communicate on his magic. His words, signs and deeds are numinous, and sometimes omniscient. Royal effects are seen in the scenery, the castles, the provisions and even a defrocked cleric. On this level, the king is associated with oral custom. Custom is seen as an established avenue of Divine approval. Custom also measures the extent of victories such as the surprise fall of Damietta. The king is alive with the success of conserving custom willed by God. These oral sources exhibit a certain timeless quality through this oral heritage.

The king is more than the body natural and the body politic which Kantorowicz brilliantly describes, the king is a body mystical. The figure of the Crusading king integrates events in spiritual mystery. People, objects, disputes and encounters are judged and completed in his kingship. Royal functions are not analyzed nor distinguished as in the seneschal's borrowed monastic written material. This is an oral king, a spoken king. He belongs to the nobles' oral communication system where all is part of one schema of social experience.

The king is more than a military leader, more than a chivalrous "prud-homme", more than an ascetic saint. He belongs to the popular religion of his knights. He is a folk-image, a legend of old, a beloved custom. He is part of the land, part of the castles, part of the dread, part of the expected, part of the troubled, part of the abundant, part of evil, part of good, part of the ordinary, part of the hero. His knights share him, recreate him, exchange his heritage. They celebrate his

deeds and words around their fires in the evening. They speak of him
within a <u>genre</u> of royal tales. His sacred function is a social
celebration as well as a religious myth.

   The king possesses a second level of differentiation which gives
him certain nuances. The greatest test of the royal myth is the
Crusade disaster. Was it possible that God was frowning on this
Crusading movement? It is in defeat that perhaps more than at other
times that the power of the royal myth is revealed. Its intensity is
unrelenting. Louis becomes a self-fulfilling prophecy.

   In times of success, the king represents God. He is invested with
divinelike power, chivalrous courage, military prowess. In times of
failure, it is the king who causes it. He has disobeyed God's oral
customs. The king's sins against this heritage break the Crusading
covenant with God. It is at this point that we see the emergence of
a second pattern upon the dualism of the basic motif.

   With the fall of Damietta on their side, the Crusaders are the
Chosen People, hierarchically structured from God through the king
and his knights under the law of oral custom. In the gaping failure
after Mansurah, the Crusaders are represented as a Mystical Body.
They are united with their human Christlike king through the fragility
of suffering and the tenacity of principles.

   In the manner Joinville utilizes his oral sources concerning the
captivity experience, the king's Suffering Servant motif is glossed with
a familiar script. While Joinville leaves it to the king's words to
express the mystical meaning of suffering in defeat, he uses the
Saracens' words to extol the political advantages of this Suffering
Servant theme. The king's attitude shows the vicarious nature of his
suffering. However, the theme of conquest enters strongly through the
Saracen oral reports on this suffering. These Moslem attitudes express
admiration for the moral victory of this beaten Crusader. The moral of
these oral reports is almost that the Christian death on the Cross
is the next best victory to military triumph. This implication leaves
a rather one-sided interpretation of the king as a figure of Christ's
Redemption. This theme deserves further research in other oral sources
of the period to see if it as widespread during peace as during a

Crusade. We may surmise that Louis' Suffering Servant theme was less natural to the Crusading mentality than was conquest and conversion.

In Louis IX's birth, coronation and death, a special God-man relationship is implied through the king. This relationship heightens all that is human in birth and death yet it separates the king from the laity by his coronation.[64] Through Joinville's embellishments on these rituals of passage, we see the theme of Crucifixion strongly attached to the meaning of Louis' birth and death. In these events, the providential destiny of his Crusades is reconciled. Christ's Redemption is associated with redemption from the guilt of falling from God's graces of success. Heavenly joy at the eternal meaning of failure is contrasted with earthly failure.

Joinville's oral sources reveal that the sacred nature of the kingship was still a living force in thirteenth century aristocratic mentalities and Crusading beliefs. As a bond among the Crusading knights, the kingship reached beneath the legal, political or canonic aspects of Louis IX's reign to ancient vital roots. A stream of magic barbarism is tied to the dualistic interpretation of good and evil in the world and heavens. There is a superstitious element attributed to the permanency of oral custom, especially in the event of failure, symbolizing God's disfavour. A new alliance with God is worked out through the king figure whose sufferings expiate guilt and open paths to other forms of victory.

We see a rather politicized accent on the religious dimension of Louis' kingship. These oral sources dwell in a demi-light of magic which externalizes evil onto the other, sees Divine Will in failure and success and expects punishment for broken custom. These oral sources look for reparation through some Christian content of the kingship. At times, it is as if the Christianity of the kingship is a function of this anthropology, this dualist world-vision, this magico-religious attitude.

What we particularly note in Joinville's oral sources is the contradictions contained within the figure of the king. In him, there is a mysterious reconciliation of opposites, victory and defeat can live side by side in the same king. This ambivalence of his function is the

heart of the king as myth. He is the lone God-Warrior as well as
the corporate suffering Christ.[65] He is the theocratic monarch as well
as the feudal suzerain.

Walter Ullmann has shown the fundamentally divergent functions of
the theocratic and feudal monarchs.[66] Jean-François Lemarignier has
traced the historical evolution from sacral to suzerain to sovereign
monarchy in France. He has masterfully illustrated Louis IX's reign
as a time of change from feudal towards sovereign monarchy. Jean de
Joinville's oral sources reveal the simultaneity of ancient beliefs
with newer accretions within the mentality of the aristocracy.

It is possible that during the trying time of war and Crusade,
more primitive layers of royal beliefs surfaced among the knights of
the seventh Crusade. Joinville's oral sources suggest that the
sacral and feudal conceptions of the king were still very vital to the
lay aristocracy on Cruade. The theocratic and feudal stages of the
monarchy were present within the minds of the fighting Crusaders.

Unlike Joinville's written sources which define, then list what
the king accomplished with clear categories and sovereign conceptions
of governments and sanctity, Joinville's oral sources reveal the
ambivalent, contradictory world of the nobles' emotions and beliefs.
This is a world in which the king himself participated as a lay noble.
While Joinville's written sources reveal <u>Historie</u>, the world of facts
and deeds, his oral sources reveal <u>Geschichtlichkeit</u>, the meanings
of facts and deeds as these were experienced by the Crusaders themselves.

CHAPTER TWO
NOTES

[1] R. Bouthoul, Les Mentalités (Paris, 1966), pp. 54-58. On the school of History of Mentalities and its influence in North America see: P. Hutton, "The History of Mentalities: The New Map of Cultural History", History and Theory 20 (1981), pp. 237-259; on the origin and composition of the school in France see: T. Stoianovich, French Historical Method: The Annales Paradigm (Ithaca, New York, 1976); A. Burgière, "The Fate of the History of Mentalités in the Annales", Comparative Studies in Society and History 24 (1982), pp. 424-427; and H. Coutau-Begarie's critical study, Le Phenomène "Nouvelle Histoire" stratégie et idéologie des nouveaux historiens (Paris, 1983). Paul Ricoeur has written an excellent introduction to the work of the school in The Contribution of French Historiography to the Theory of History (Oxford, 1980).

[2] Bouthoul, Les Mentalités, pp. 38-41.

[3] Jean-Louis Flandrin, Le Sexe et l'occident- évolution des attitudes et des comportements (Paris, 1981), p. 21. On this question see the foundational works of Lucien Febvre: "Man or Productivity", Rural Society in France, Selections from the Annales, ed. R. Forster and O. Ranum (London, 1977), pp. 1-6; A New Kind of History and other essays, ed. P. Burke, tr. K. Folca (New York, 1973); Le Problème de l'incroyance au XVIe siècle. La religion de Rabelais. (Paris, 1942).

[4] Bouthoul, Les Mentalités, pp. 66-69.

[5] Ibid.

[6] B. Lacroix, L'Historien au moyen âge (Paris, 1971), p. 50.

[7] Jeannette Beer, Narrative Conventions of Truth in the Middle Ages (Geneva, 1981), p. 31.

[8] Beer, Narrative, pp. 36-45.

[9] Lacroix, l'Historien, pp. 50-54.

[10] E. Le Roy Ladurie, Montaillou - the Promised Land of Error, tr. B. Bray (New York, 1979), p. 241.

[11] L. Levy-Bruhl, Le Surnaturel et la nature dans la mentalité primitive (Paris, 1931).

[12] HSL 28.128,129, p. 72. The procession, a ritual to cope with impending trouble, was a moral lesson passed on by oral report. There is evidence in Joinville's work that such moral lessons were a favoured topic of conversation in Crusading circles. For example, in Joinville's first section, he recalls a teaching of the king to the seneschal on their experience of a severe storm at sea while returning to France: "Seneschaus, ore nous a moustrei diex une partie de son grant pooir; car uns de ces petiz venz, qui est si petiz que à peinne le sait-on nommer, deut avoir le roy de France, ses enfans et sa femme et ses gens noiés." HSL 7.40, p. 22. Joinville, in turn, uses this lesson as a way of teaching Philippe, Louis' grand-son, to mend his ways, as if his book served an end similar to oral report: "Si y preingne garde li roys qui ore est; car il est eschapez de aussi grant peril ou de plus que nous ne feimes: si s'amende de ses mesfais en tel maniere que diex ne fiere en li ne en ses choses cruelment." HSL 7.42, p. 24.

[13] HSL 38. 180, p. 98.

[14] M. Bloch, Feudal Society (Chicago, 1964), v. 1, p. 83. Two other religious forms for giving events their eternal meaning were the prophecy and the miracle. Joinville records the authoritative prophecy of the Legate, fulfilled in the subsequent fall of Acre in 1291: "'Nulz ne sait tant de desloiaus pechiez que l'on fait en Acre, comme je faiz: dont il couvient que Diex les venge, en tel maniere que la cités d'Acre soit lavée dou sanc aus habitours, et que il y vieigne après autre gent qui y habiteront.'" HSL 613, p. 334. Joinville also mentions one miracle in his work. It comes from the oral report of the squire of "mes sires Dragonés, uns riches hom de Provence." HSL 79. 650, p. 356.

[15] J. Le Goff, La Civilisation de l'occident au moyen âge (Paris, 1964), p. 381.

[16] Bouthoul, Les Mentalités, p. 62. J. Huizinga, in his work Homo Ludens (Boston, 1955), describes the cultural and sacred significance of representation in ritual forms in his introductory chapter: "Nature and Significance of Play as a Cultural Phenomenon." According to Huizinga, cultural changes in mentalities can be detected through changes in forms of play.

[17] For a good introduction to the oral traditions of noble medieval families see Bloch, *Feudal*, v. 1, pp. 97-99. The tales of other kings and rulers which Joinville recounts in his work highlight the symbolic character of oral tales and the values with which noble circles endowed their rulers. What appears most evident in these stories is that good and evil rulers were dramatic symbols of a war between the divine and the diabolical, and furthermore that they represented the harmony which existed between the human and the supernatural orders. For tales of evil rulers in Joinville's work see: HSL114.585, pp. 320-322; HSL 31.143, pp. 80-81.HSL 56. 280, pp. 154-158.

[18] Myths surrounding medieval kings have been brought to the foreground by Georges Duby and Marc Bloch in *L'Adolescence de la Chrétienté occidentale, 980-1140* (Geneva, 1967), p. 15. For treatment of royal ritual and myth in the Ancient Near East and Israel see: *Myth, Ritual and Kingship*, ed. S.H. Hooke (Oxford, 1960). For the role of myth in Mesopotamian, Egyptian, Israelic and Hellenic culture see: C. Loew, *Myth, Sacred History and Philosophy* (New York, 1967). For the classic study on magical and religious myths of kings consult: J.G. Frazer, *The Golden Bough* (London, 1922). Apart from the work of Marc Bloch on medieval kings, mentioned above as *Les rois thaumaturges*, no comparable work exists on medieval royal myths. However, in his work *L'Adolescence*, Duby states: "Modèle des perfections terrestres, la figure royale s'établit au sommet de toutes les représentations mentales qui entendaient alors montrer l'ordonnance de l'univers visible. Arthur, Charlemagne, Alexandre, David, tous les héros de la culture chevaleresque furent les rois... Il faut mettre en évidence cette permanence du mythe royal et voir en elle l'un des caractères les plus marquants de la civilisation médiévale...", p. 15.

[19] The popular custom of utilizing the king's name as a substitute for the presence of God had its theological counterpart. In the treatises of Pseudo-Denis on the Divine Names, one chapter is devoted to God as King of kings: *De Divinis Nominibus* 1.1 PG 3, p. 385. Aquinas gave the name of king to God in many of his theological passages: e.g. *Summa Theologica* 1. q.39, a. 4. The Cheminon tale in Joinville is found in HSL 27. 120, p. 68.

[20] HSL 26. 115, p. 66.

[21] HSL 26. 118, pp. 66-68.

[22] HSL 136, pp. 370-374; 13, p. 36.

[23] HSL 30. 138, p. 76.

[24] See Paul Ricoeur's excellent treatment of the king-figure's significance in dualistic cults: The Symbolism of Evil (Boston, 1967), pp. 191-206.

[25] M. Benvenisti, The Crusaders in the Holy Land (New York, 1970), pp. 147-150.

[26] HSL 90.463, p. 254.

[27] HSL 89. 454, p. 248; messages, messengers and embassies are a recurring motif of the chansons de geste: e.g. Le Couronnement de Louis, ed. E. Langlois (Paris, 1925), vs. 322, 452, 1384, 1777; Raoul de Cambrai, ed. P. Meyer and A. Longnon (Paris, 1882), vs. 140, 2135, 3202. Exchange of gifts in courts of foreign kings and rulers is a familiar motif in the Crusade cycle of the chansons de geste: e.g. La Chanson du chevalier au cygne et de Godefroid de Bouillon (Geneva, 1969, reprint) 2.5, p. 268. In that Jean de Joinville belonged to the Champagne court, a centre for literary activity in the thirteenth century under Thibaut de Champagne, Joinville's lord, and an accomplished lover of the arts and poetry, we may presume some knowledge on Joinville's part of the chansons de geste tradition. To know the extent of Joinville's knowledge, we would need to understand more of his education and exposure to Champagne literary traditions. See Jean Rychner, La Chanson de Geste (Geneva, 1955), for an interesting treatment of the oral method found in the chansons de geste based on the research of M. Parry and A. B. Lord. For the court of Champagne literary activity see: M. F. Benton, "The Court of Champagne as a Literary Centre", Speculum 36 (1961), pp. 551-591; R.R. Bezzola, Les Origines et la formation de la littérature courtoise en occident (Paris, 1944-1963).

[28] S. Runciman, A History of the Crusades (New York, 1967), v. 3, p. 280. Consult with profit the useful work of A. S. Atiya, The Crusade: Historiography and Bibliography (Bloomington, Indiana, 1962); and the revealing study of R. W. Southern, Western Views of Islam in the Middle Ages (Cambridge, Mass., 1962).

[29] HSL 95. 490, p. 268.

[30] Ibid. In crusading circles, oral tales also envisioned foreign rulers in courtly ideals of chivalrous generosity and courtesy. In speaking of Charlemagne and his friendly relations with Harun al-Rachid, Guillaume de Tyr recounts the caliph's generosity: "Diebus tamen illius admirabilis et praedicandi viri, Aarum videlicet, qui cognominatus est Ressith, qui universo praefuit orienti cujus liberalitatem et urbanitatem praecipuam, et mores singulariter commendabiles, universus etiam usque hodie oriens admiratur, et praeconis attollit immortalibus..." Guillelmi Tyrensis Archiepicopi, Historia rerum in partibus transmarinis gestarum, lib.1, cap. 3, Patrologiae cursus completus, series latina, ed. J.P. Migne (Paris, 1884-1885), v. 201, col. 216. The Crusade poems of the twelfth century are full of descriptions of the coveted treasures of Crusading and infidel leaders, giving us an idea of the popular curiosity concerning this theme: e.g. The Chanson d'Antioche describes in detail the famous tent of the Sultan Corbaran, La Chanson d'Antioche, pub. P. Paris (Geneva, Slatkine reprints, 1969), v. 2, ch. 39, p. 246. La Conquête de Jérusalem describes emir Turks with the same intriguing magnificence: La Conquête de Jérusalem, pub. C. Hippeau (Geneva, Slatkine reprints, 1969), v. 13, pp. 93-94. For informative discussion on the Crusading mentality see: P. Alphandery and A. Dupront, La Chrétienté et l'idée de croisade, 2 vols (Paris, 1954-1959). For a study of ritual patterns in oral literature see: A. B. Lord, The Singer of the Tales (Cambridge, Mass., 1960). Recent studies in medieval literature stress the folklore methods which help scholars understand the influence of oral traditions on literary works in medieval times: Oral Tradition - Literary Tradition - A Symposium, ed. H. Bekker-Nielsen et al (Denmark, 1977); E. Bahn and M. L. Bahn, A History of Oral Interpretation (Minneapolis, 1970).

[31] HSL 27. 124, p. 70.

[32] HSL 29, pp. 72-76; qualities of power and riches were also common in epic legends of kings: e.g. Le voyage de Charlemagne à Jerusalem et Constantinople, ed. Paul Aebischer (Geneva, 1965), p. 34, v. 73, 78, 83-84, v. 85.

[33] HSL 94, 484, p. 264. On God as a king in the medieval west, see the references at foot-note 19 above on Aquinas' and the Pseudo-Denis' use of the name of king for God. Also see Dom Jean Leclerq, L'Idée de la royauté du Christ au moyen âge (Paris, 1959).

[34] For the Germanic idea of lordship see: Otto Gierke, Political Theories of the Middle Ages, tr. F.W. Maitland (Boston, 1959), p. 33 and the survival of its Christian blend see: M. Bloch, La France sous les derniers Capétiens - 1223-1328 (Paris, 1958), p. 16.

[35] HSL 24. 106, p. 60 and 62. The scene is reminiscent of scenes in the chansons de geste: e.g. H. Pigeonneau, Le Cycle de la Croisade (Saint-Cloud, 1877), p. 89.

[36] HSL 24. 107, p. 62. As in the Crusading chansons de geste, women appear with the king as nursing aids to his sicknesses. See: Pigeonneau, Le Cycle, p. 89-90.

[37] This event is reported in many mémoires and chronicles. Coming from the mouth of a contemporary, perhaps an ear-witness from Louis himself, this anecdote should not be diminished. Etienne de Bourbon, for example, refers to it in his collection of exempla : "Item rex francie, laborans ad mortem et desperatus a medicis et positus in cinere, vocavit omnes astantes, dicens: 'Ego ecce, qui ditissimus eram et nobilissimus de mundo et potentissimus pre omnibus, diviciis et potencia et amicis, non possum extorquere a morte inducias vel ab hac infirmitate per unicam horam. Quid ergo valent ista omnia?' Et hoc dicens omnes auditores concitavit ad fletum. Ipse contra spem a domino curatus, cum crederetur mortus, resurgens et deo gracias exhibens, crucem accepit." Etienne de Bourbon, Anecdotes historiques, légendes et apologues, ed. A. Lecoy de la Marche (Paris, 1878), p. 63.

[38] HSL 24. 108-109, p. 62. The idea of a feudal hierarchy leading up to the king was the twelfth century dream of Suger, realized a century later in royal suzerainty. See: J.F. Lemarignier, "Hiérarchie monastique et hiérarchie féodale", Rev. hist. de droit, 31 (1953), pp. 171-174. Joinville's passage symbolizes a hierarchy which emanates down from the king as a sacred personnage, a less-structured, sacred counterpart to Suger's suzerain of structured authority: Suger, Vita Ludovici Regis, ed. A. Molinier   (Paris, 1887), p. 29. Villehardouin opened

his Crusade account as "le service Dieu" undertaken by chivalrous nobles inspired by the miraculous signs and the pious preaching of the priest, Foulques de Neuilly: Villehardouin, <u>La Conquête de Constantinople,</u> ed. and tr. E. Faral (Paris, 1961), pp. 4-12. Joinville follows a similar sequence of sacred signs through the king, inspiring the chivalrous mission of his knights who enlist in a hierarchy of order from God's instrument, the king. Duby and R. Mandrou in, <u>Histoire de la civilisation française</u> (Paris, 1968), p. 151, comment on this notion of hierarchy: "C'est dans l'entourage du roi que s'est formée, au début du XIIe siècle la notion, très fausse d'abord, mais à laquelle on s'est efforcé d'ajuster la realité d'un système féodal en forme de pyramide, dont le roi serait le sommet et qui le relierait par échelons successifs à tous les chevaliers de France, jusqu'aux plus humbles."

[39] W. C. Jordan, <u>Louis IX and the Challenge of the Crusade - A Study in Rulership</u> (Princeton, 1979), p. 65. Jordan's thesis that it was the Crusade of 1248-1254 that led Louis to deal imaginatively with his administration and that finally, it was the failure of the Crusade which produced a profound crisis in him, leading to his creation of an "ideal" medieval monarchy, is instructive and enlightening.

[40] HSL 35. 165, p. 90.

[41] Ibid.

[42] HSL 48.236, p. 130. An early indication of this interest in the persons of the great as a centre for historical interpretation of events can be found in the work of Raoul Glaber, an eleventh century chronicler: "Sicut quispiam igitur peragrans quamlibet vastissimam orbis mundani plagam, seu spatiosum remigando aequor penetrans, saepius altitudini montium aut proceritati arborum scilicet respectans, dirigit aciem oculorum, ut videlicet illorum a longe reperta agnitione, absque errore quo disposuerat valeat pervenire. Ita quoque erga nos fore contingit, qui utique, dum cupimus praeterita ostendere futuris, obtutus nostri sermonis pariterque animi frequenter in relatione porrigimus magnatorum virorum personis, quibus videlicet fiat ipsa relatio clarior et appareat certior: <u>Historia</u>, 2,1 <u>Patrologiae cursus completus</u>, <u>series latina</u>, ed. J. Migne (Paris, 1884-1885), v. 142, pp. 627-628.

[43] Ibid. The person of the king represented a secure centre in the midst of insecure oral communication. Joinville's oral reports reflect this. They also indicate the precedence of the king as a functional personnage, over kingship as a principle, in this custom of oral report. While general works on King Louis IX have sometimes stressed the importance of his sacred paternity over his feudal suzerainty, the question has not been thoroughly treated, e.g. J. Dahmus, Seven Medieval Kings (New York, 1967), pp. 271-272.

[44] HSL 36. 166, p. 90. This is an Old Testament prototype for the king. This prototype is also seen in medieval sculpture and liturgical prayers. L. Brehier, Les sculptures de la façade de la cathédrale de Reims et les prières liturgiques du sacre (Paris, 1915), p. 157: "Ce n'est évidemment pas par une simple coincidence que ces sculptures rappellent justement les paroles qui accompagnaient l'acte essentiel du sacre et plaçaient l'autorité des rois de France sous la protection divine que David et Solomon eurent en partage. Elles exaltent ainsi la légitimité de leur pouvoir en le rattachant à celui des rois de l'Ancien Testament."

[45] Ibid. Joinville's oral report represents the feudal king subject to unwritten customs. The history of the Assizes of Jerusalem amply illustrates this important theme. The authors of the Assizes collected and selected the customary laws of the various national societies from which the Crusaders came. When Saladin conquered Jerusalem and it was thought the Assizes were lost, the Crusaders fell back on unwritten custom. Carlyle cites the text of Jean d'Ibelin, 111, to clarify this: A History of Mediaeval Political Theory in the West (London, 1963), v. 3, p. 45. The origins of medieval monarchy in Germanic beliefs and customs that the king is below the law and subject to unwritten custom is well presented in Fritz Kern, Kingship and Law in the Middle Ages (Oxford, 1939), pp. 70-79.

[46] HSL 36. 168-169, p. 92.

[47] HSL 108. 557, p. 304. For the influence of oral opinion as a shaping force in medieval history see: L. C. MacKinney, "The People and Public Opinion in the Eleventh Century Peace Movement", Speculum 5 (1930), p. 181.

[48] Ibid. It is typical of medieval oral anecdotes that Etienne de Bourbon attributed this same story to Philippe-Augustus: Anecdotes, p. 341. Similar forms are found in Jacques de Vitry and St. Pathus.

[49] See foot-note 45.

[50] HSL 62. 306, p. 168. Mathieu de Paris quotes words from Louis IX which identify him as Head of a Mystical Body in Christ when sighting Damietta. These words were cited in an officer's letter from the house of Melun: Grandes Chroniques (Paris, 1840), 6, p. 554. De Pange in Le Roi très Chrétien (Paris, 1949) refers to the king's sacred person and anointing as a uniting factor of his people in a common cause: "Les Français sont un dans le roi comme les chrétiens sont un dans le Christ", pp. 30-33. Medieval sermons on the theme of Ecce rex were frequent in thirteenth century France: Leclercq, L'Idée, p. 113.

[51] HSL 42.311, p. 170.

[52] HSL 42. 309, p. 168.

[53] Ibid.

[54] HSL 67. 341, p. 186.

[55] HSL 67. 342, p. 186.

[56] HSL 67. 343, p. 186.

[57] HSL 71. 363, p. 198.

[58] HSL 71. 365, p. 198.

[59] HSL 72. 366, p. 200. These oral reports from the captivity illustrate the mystical aspects of Louis' kingship. Walter Ullmann discusses the fundamentally divergent functions of the theocratic and feudal king in the The Individual and Society in the Middle Ages (Baltimore, 1966), pp. 66-67. It is noteworthy that in Joinville's tales of the captivity, the two aspects of the king co-exist in these crisis circumstances. E. Mura in his theological work Le Corps mystique du Christ (Paris, 1937), pp. 108-109, refers to the kings of France, particularly King Louis IX, as representatives of Christ the King. This sacral heritage of the French king played a large role in the motifs of these captivity tales. See J.-F. Lemarignier, "Autour de la royauté française du IXe au XIIIe siècle," Bibliothèque de l'Ecole des Chartes (Paris, 1956), pp. 5-25 for the distinctions of the sacral from the

feudal and sovereign character of the evolving French monarchy.

[60] HSL 15.69, p. 40.

[61] HSL 15.70, p. 40. Joinville's use of the liturgical words of the Advent Mass re-enforce the sacred character of the king. Marc Bloch, in La France p. 16, comments: "Que le roi fût un personnage sacré, que sa fonction mettait à part du monde des simples laiques, c'était au XIIIe siècle, une idée déjà vieille. Mais une idée qui conversait encore toute sa force." The oldest and best known of the sacred legends which developed around the French kings was that of "la Sainte Ampoule": at the baptism of Clovis a dove descended from heaven with sacred oil to anoint him. This sacred unction was kept in its original container at Rheims, in the abbey of Saint-Rémi. It was used for all the coronations of the French kings. Hincmar of Reims in his Vie de Saint Rémi, composed in 877 or 878, is the oldest author to acquaint us with the legend, which survived and created an atmosphere of pious veneration around the French kings. Saint Louis was the culmination of this popular collective reputation which had grown up around the French kings and their coronation rite. Since the thirteenth century, it was recounted that the level of the liquid never changed although several drops were added at each coronation. See Philippe Mousket, Chronique rimée (Bruxelles, 1836-1838), v. k, verse 24221.

[62] HSL 146. 756, p. 406. On rituals of death and dying in the medieval period see: Philippe Ariès, l'Homme devant la mort (Paris, 1977), pp. 21-26. Recent works studying rites surrounding kings are: B. Guenée and F. Leheux, Les entrées royales française de 1328-1515 (Paris, 1968); the excellent article of Elizabeth A. R. Brown, "The Ceremonial of Royal Succession in Capetian France: The Funeral of Philip V", Speculum, 55(April 1980), pp. 266-294.; and Jacques Heers, Fêtes, jeux et joutes dans les sociétes d'occident à la fin du moyen âge (Paris, 1971). On rituals of the royal coronation see: Percy E. Schramm, "Coronation Ritual and Festivities", in A History of the English Coronation, tr. L. Legg (Oxford, 1937), pp. 31-94. Also consult with profit the classic works of: T. and D. Godefroy, Le céremonial françois 2 vols., folio 1649, where the French ordines of coronation rites are treated; Dom E. Martene, De antiquis Ecclesiae ritibus, 2 vols., 1736-1737; Dewick, The Coronation Book of Charles V of France

(London, 1899); P. Thurston, The Coronation Ceremonial, 2nd ed., (London, 1911); L. G. W. Legg, Three Coronation Orders (London, 1900); and for treatment of royal liturgical acclamations see: E. H. Kantorowicz, Laudes Regiae, A Study in Liturgical Acclamations and and Mediaeval Ruler Worship (Berkeley & Los Angeles, 1958). Also see M. David, Le Serment du sacre du IXe au XVe siècle (Strasbourg, MCMLI).

[63] Ricoeur, Symbolism, introd. For a provocative discussion of sacred space with its blend of the profane see: M. Eliade, The Sacred and the Profane, tr. W. R. Trask (New York, 1959), pp. 20-65. The razed castle of Joinville's Rhone voyage blends this sacredness of space with the profanity of power, something repeated in Joinville's battle scene of Mansurah.

[64] David, Le Serment; and G. Duby and R. Mandrou, Histoire, p. 150, discuss the enduring aspects of the king's "privilège d'avoir été sacré ...".

[65] See Joseph R. Strayer, "France: The Holy Land, the Chosen People, and the Most Christian King,", orig. pub. 1969, reprinted in Medieval Statecraft and the Perspectives of History: Essays by Joseph R. Strayer ed. J. F. Benton and T. N. Bisson (Princeton, 1971), pp. 300-314.

[66] Ullmann, The Individual, pp. 66-69; Lemarignier, "Autour", pp. 5-25.

CHAPTER THREE
THE KING IN JOINVILLE'S VISUAL SOURCE

INTRODUCTION

Because of the knowing eye-witness of Joinville, Louis IX is the only Capetian king we know well.[1] Moreover, his testimony is the first comprehending lay account of a lay lineage. Finally, his eye-witness is his only source which is not an eclectic montage of others' views.

The seneschal's oral sources describe Louis within popular Crusading tradition, something of which the king was a part. This was a collective caste tradition which attributed sacred and feudal myths to the monarch. Joinville's written sources depict the king as the literary fulfillment of official hagiography and dynastic biography, both institutionally pertinent to a monarch who became a canonized saint and moved the Capetian monarchy towards sovereignty. As we shall see, these written sources also represented collective caste traditions of the clergy.

Against this setting, how original were Joinville's own recollections? Were his royal perceptions distinct from these collective traditions? If so, in what manner? From what traditions did Joinville's eye-witness speak? These are the questions we ask of Joinville's first-hand account.

Through comparative source-analysis, salient features of the seneschal's story become apparent, features not previously analyzed in studies on Joinville or St. Louis. Joinville's visual account of Louis illustrates a cultural transition from the collective perceptions of his caste towards an individualized perception of a thirteenth century king.

THE MEDIEVAL EYE-WITNESS

The medieval world was one of sights and sounds experienced directly and almost exclusively through the undiluted senses. Much of our contemporary society is relayed to us through the printed word or some extension of the senses, mechanical or electronic. This makes a qualitative difference between the modern and medieval eye-witness which must be kept in mind. There was a keenness of visual perception in the medieval spectator which is lost to most of us today. The absence of research, the vivacity of impressions, the clarity of exposure, the warmth of sentiment, all are characteristics of the medieval eye-witness.

Jean de Joinville is the medieval eye-witness *par excellence*. His vivacity, immediacy and honesty as a participant observer is successfully translated into his prose style. As Marc Bloch says of his work: "Joinville est un pur chef-d'oeuvre, peut-être le premier chef-d'oeuvre de prose de toute la littérature européene."[2]

We can read a medieval eye-witness' account as we might appreciate a medieval artist's painting. The medieval eye-witness description of events and the medieval artist's products were both pictorial spectacles.[3] While we are trained to read printed books with the logic of words, we must adjust ourselves to assimilate the scenes of the medieval eye-witness with the harmony of vision. As there is anthropology in medieval costume, so there is in the medieval spectacle.

People and events were seen didactically in a religious civilization such as the Middle Ages. Medieval people believed in a supernatural world which was made manifest in the natural events of their day. The social role of a person and the rituals of that role played a symbolic part of this revelatory process. The visual description of a person in medieval times defined his social status in the hierarchy as if it were a religiously significant event.

In particular, the space around important personnages, like the king, was perceived symbolically. As in a medieval painting, the relative spatial dimension surrounding a person of important status told something of his social role, and his relationship with the

symbolic world of the supernatural. As in Gothic illuminations,
tapestries and stained glass, the chronicled medieval king was a
pictorial allegory of the Divine presence immanent in the regal role.
Usually, the monarch was portrayed stylistically, as a <u>tableau vivant</u>
of the sacred world he represented. His actions and words, his central
placement in a scene demonstrated a ritual rather than a real space
because a divine drama was being enacted. In the medieval chronicle as
in Gothic art, this portrayal of the king as a revelation gave his
presentation a two-dimensional quality.

Through his role, a medieval monarch was generally chronicled in
images of royal ritual, much like the medieval saint was shown in
familiar holy gest and garb. We may see this as a stilted <u>tableau</u>, or
clumsy illusionism. Rather than inexpert imitations of the visible,
these representations manifested the world of Truth lying latent in the
universe. To the medieval eye-witness, each action and word had a
natural disposition to become a supernatural sign, especially the deeds
and conversation of a pious king.

The thirteenth century monarch was a spectacle, both official and
popular. Eye-witnesses recorded their memories according to those
royal rituals which corresponded to their caste traditions: clerical,
chivalrous or popular. Chronicled by an elite according to their
official customs and purposes, he was also loved by the illiterate and
celebrated by his peers in enduring popular fashion.

On the whole, royal chroniclers were not necessarily concerned with
recording something new or innovative about a particular king. Rather
they attempted to find signs of continuity with rites and doings of the
golden past. They looked for scenes and events which would display
the moral meaning of a royal life. Had this king lived out his role and
reign successfully or dismally, morally or immorally, justly or
unjustly? What was new was often chronicled as a continuity with the
past or as a moral application of God's laws.

As an archetype of custom, the medieval king was also a Biblical
event, the leader of a new Chosen People under God. Like a King of
Juda, he was a public ritual of God's disposition to His People. The
king's moral life was a public concern. Morality meant success for the

for the kingdom. Royal immorality could lead to God's punishment on not only the king and his family but the entire kingdom. As visible exemplum, a monarch's every illness, piece of bad luck, lost battle or thwarted plan became the occasion for an omen.

The royal cult was also interpreted through more specific social and political interests. Each chronicling caste depicted the king from within the social and political values of their place in the caste hierarchy. The early Capetians were recorded by the clergy and cloaked in their values. With Joinville in the thirteenth century, their witness was augmented by an increasing number of lay aristocratic chroniclers. Finally, towards the end of the medieval period, a third caste's perceptions recorded the king: the bourgeoisie.

Along with general cultural values, caste codes of chivalry framed Joinville's royal portrait. The paragon of the lay aristocracy was the chivalrous knight: courageous in battle, succouring of the needy, generous to his peers, polite to the lady, diplomatic with rivals and loyal to his God and his lord. This was the moral ideal of the lay Christian knight to which both Joinville and his king aspired.

The medieval eye-witness noted the royal cult-objects of a king. These helped to externalize his eternal majesty and identify his allegorical function in a scene. These visual symbols were the throne, the crown, the helmet, the standard, the banner, the sceptre, the staff, the shield and the ring. Joinville, like other medieval chroniclers of monarchs, utilized these objects in his royal descriptions.

Royal cult-events were medieval chroniclers' daily bread. The king's birth, coronation, marriage, processions, feasts, visits, ceremonies, Crusades, treaties, arrivals, departures, processions, illnesses and death were edifying and instructive occasions worthy of record. These events were affirmations of God's presence in the royal life.

In medieval annals, the king was surrounded with royal cult-people. These people were exemplars more than individuals. They served to illustrate God's communion with His People through His king. The council, barons, rebels, loyal confidantes, knights, clergy, merchants, peasants, ladies, fools, queen, wizards, prophets, hermits, preachers, bishops and even the Emperor and Pope were part of the extended royal family. Joinville, like his chronicling predecessors, depicted the king in functional relationships with royal cult-people.

THE PLACES, THE PEOPLE, THE WORDS AND THE DEEDS

Joinville saw Louis at court and on Crusade. Before the Crusade, he witnessed the monarch at the great feast of Saumur. It was held on June 24, 1241 to celebrate the knighting of the king's brother, Alphonse of Poitiers. At this time, Joinville was a sixteen year old squire of the count of Champagne and Navarre. He carved his lord's meat at the splendid affair, carefully observing the guests and the monarch. It is possible that Joinville also witnessed the king at the battle of Taillebourg of 1242. There, Louis proved himself a military tactician and king of his barons. In order to defend Alphonse of Poitiers from the powerful coalition of lords which had formed against him, the king gathered a force of approximately 4,000 knights and 20,000 foot soldiers to soundly defeat the rebellious lords.

On Crusade, Joinville spent six years with Louis from 1248-1254. He also shared the sea-voyage with the king upon his return to France. When the young seneschal from Champagne embarked on Crusade, it was at his own expense. Only in Cyprus, did he enter the king's service receiving a determined sum of money for a fixed period of time so that he could continue to support himself and pay his men.[5] Joinville accompanied the king to Limassol, Cyprus; Damietta and Mansurah in Egypt; and Acre, Sayette, Caesarea and Jaffa in the Holy Land. It was not until the Crusaders reached Jaffa that Joinville became the king's man, receiving a perpetual annual grant of 200 pounds from Louis.

After the Crusade, the seneschal divided his time between his Champagne fief and the royal court. He saw the king at Paris, Soissons and Corbeil. Although he returned to the royal court as a close and respected confidante and lord, Joinville was never an official member of Louis' Paris court.

These geographical and feudal facts of Joinville's relationship to King Louis played a large role in the kind of memories he had of the king.

At court, Joinville witnessed the monarch with the noble élite of the kingdom, lay and clerical. He saw Queen Blanche of Castille; the young Herman, son of St. Elizabeth of Hungary; the great barons of France; the king's brothers, Robert of Artois and Alphonse of Poitiers; the recalcitrant count of La Marche; the fiery widow of King John of England; Louis' arrogant young brother, Charles of Anjou; the papal legate; the Duke of Burgundy; the chamberlain of France; Master Robert of Sorbonne and Louis' long-suffering wife, Margeret who bore him eleven children. In this setting, the king and Joinville's peers are viewed as a centre of meaning for the whole kingdom.

On Crusade, the seneschal witnessed the king with other Crusaders, pilgrims, prisoners of the 'devil's men', the Moslems, legates, the great Crusading barons and dukes, members of the Shi'ite sect of Moslems, messengers from the Genoese and Pisans, leading prelates, Templars, Hospitallers, sultans, serving-people, renegade Moslems, knights from the Morea in southern Greece, Frankish barons of Outremer, priests and friars. In the Holy Land, the king and Joinville's noble acquaintances were seen as a <u>plenitudo temporum</u>. The Holy Land was described as the centre of the world with the French king and his entourage as a centre for cosmic meaning.

In the opening remarks of his 'third chapter', Joinville says he is dividing his work into words of teaching and deeds of chivalry:

> Et avant que je vous conte de ses grans faiz et de
> sa chevalerie, vous conterai-je ce que je vi et oy
> de ses saintes paroles et de ses bons enseignmens
> pour ce qu'il soient trouvei li uns après l'autre,
> pour edefier ceuz qui les orront.[6]

Perhaps the seneschal wished to make the traditional division of secular royal <u>vitae</u>, into private <u>conversatio</u> and <u>res gestae</u>. This division of Joinville's work into words and deeds is similar to a Roman history which was popular during the thirteenth century: <u>Factorum et dictorum memorabilium libri ix</u> (c. A.D. 31) by Valerius Maximus, a champion of Caesarism. While Louis' words are treated with some hagiographic style of <u>exemplum</u>, his Crusading deeds acquire some epic narrative form. The king's deeds are referred to as "grans chevaleries et

... ses granz faiz d'armes."[7]

JOINVILLE AS A MEDIEVAL EYE-WITNESS

Joinville's eye-witness account of King Louis was both narrative and didactic. It was narrative in the sense that it was a tale, a story, a recital of what happened to the king king and Joinville at court and on Crusade. It was a story without distinct literary *genre*, full of vivid scenes, simple people, symbolic *tableaux*, anecdotal digressions, crisp dialogue and even dreams.

It was didactic in that the seneschal saw the monarch and recorded him for the purpose of teaching others some of the human lessons of his experience. His visual memory was disposed to concretely paint a moral contained in a situation without intrudicng too much of his own reflection. He selected those visual effects best disposed to shadow a fault or highlight a virtue. He also wished his official work to influence the dynasty and provide worthy examples for King Louis' heirs to follow. For this purpose, Joinville included a number of seemingly irrelevant royal scenes, simply because they illustrated a specific quality or moral.

In his visual recital, Joinville sees the king in three distinct spatial settings:
1) sacred, above and apart from his men and people;
2) corporate and engaged with groups;
3) individually related to Joinville.

The first two spatial environments intermingle throughout most of the seneschal's eye-witness account. The third environment appears for the last half of the Crusade tale, during the years 1250-1254. During this period, Joinville became the king's confidante and a king's man.

The first two kinds of spatial settings see the monarch in one type of visual focus. The king appears as a Gothic functional monarch. He plays traditional public roles as saint, *prud'homme,* suzerain, relative, Crusader, judge, teacher and monarch. In this milieu, ritual objects, events and people abound.

The last kind of spatial setting is culturally new to thirteenth century chronicling. It presents the king as an individual personality.

In this environment, Joinville contrasts and compares his own feudal chivalry to the king's more lofty religious chivalry. This occurs in a concrete anecdotal way. Through the human interchange between the king and his chivalrous confidante, each figure is humanized. Louis ceases to be shrouded in awesome mystery and allegory. He can now be approached and loved through the intermediacy of Joinville.

In all three kinds of spatial settings: aloof, corporate and individually related, sights and sounds combine to illustrate the narrative and didactic meaning. The king is shown in an order of typical rituals: a milieu, a robe, a river-crossing, a battle, a throne-room, a débat. These objects and events surround the king's actions in an order of relationships: the king and his God, the king and his council, the king and the evil sultan, the king and his trusted knight. It is true to the medieval style, that nowhere in his collection of anecdotes, not even the more personal ones, does Joinville give a visual description of Louis' features.[4]

Dialogue also plays a major role in presenting Louis both as a stylized type and a personalized individual. As a type, the king's conversation is authoritative. His words determine the dialogue. He has no equal. In the last kind of individualizing setting, where Joinville is alone with Louis, the dialogue develops into a débat or disputatio between two equal but different aristocrats. The king and his knight joust with their words and their feelings over different social interpretations of chivalry. In this focus, the king is not the final authority. He is vulnerable. He is limited.

In the first two kinds of visual settings, where Louis is either alone or incorporated with a group, there is a resemblance of Joinville's motifs to those of his oral sources. Moreover, the visual focus is two-dimensional. The king lacks solid depth . He appears in mythical forms and ritual gestures.

In the third kind of visual setting, Louis loses divine mystery and gains humanizing depth. Joinville allows his audience to intensely feel the human drama involved between himself and the king. The seneschal reveals his own private thoughts and feelings about the king. More surprisingly, he exposes the shy king's own feelings and internal reserves. Their talk emerges from internal feelings or private thoughts rather than typical roles or public rituals.

The action arises around Joinville's way of responding to the world as a practical feudal prud'homme. The closer the seneschal comes to Louis, the more his way of doing things contrasts with the king's approach to life as a religious prud'homme. Joinville's honest integrity and friendship with Louis draws him into dialogue. It is not an elegant court-game. The monarch cries, gets angry, thinks, laughs, loses face, gets taught and teased. Within this close visual focus, we come to behold a king of depth and solidity, inner thoughts and feelings, apprehensible individuality. This is a three-dimensional monarch.

The two-fold purpose of Joinville's eye-witness tale: to laud both himself and the king led the seneschal to a double theme. On the one hand, there is the personal heroic story of Joinville. It is conditioned by the oral traditions of the Champagne nobility which formed his perceptions and experience.[8] The glories of the seneschal's Crusading lineage, Champagne's proud heritage and knightly chivalry, all shaped this theme and Joinville's presentation of it.[9] His story is saturated with the air of Champagne.[10] Alongside this theme of self-praise runs Joinville's official theme of Louis' royal words and deeds. In this parallel theme, Louis is the Christian king par excellence.[11]

Although Joinville and Louis are both portrayed as types of oral tradition, the growing interaction of their distinct forms of chivalry renders them each a partiality, a limitation, a relativity which is humanizing. By the end of the Crusade story, we are faced with a genre of literature approaching that of Memoirs, something which Joinville's work anticipated, without consciously attempting.[12]

Joinville's presentation of two heroes - the ascetic, mystical king who surpasses the heights of religious chivalry, and the more practical, worldly yet religious knight of a chivalry which stops short of sanctity - leads to a dramatic conflict of two kinds of traditional Christian prud'hommie, two ways of life.[13] Through this conflict developed in action and dialogue, there is a perceptual development of both characters. This metamorphosis goes beyond the precedents of stylized medieval portraiture into the late medieval portraiture of individuals. Joinville's eye-witness memories may be considered as a transitional point between these two kinds of literary portraiture.

PERCEPTUAL DEVELOPMENT IN CONTEMPORARY ART OF THE PERIOD

The seneschal's visual perceptions of the king reflect the contemporary emergence of individualizing portraits in late medieval art. While the medieval art subject is usually shown in humble relation of dependence upon some transcendent figure or God, the later medieval and Renaissance subject is seen in a stance affirming himself with some independence from authority. Attitudes of self-affirmation abound: a hand on a hip, a shoulder raised, the head forward, a stance affirmed with a leg advanced.[14]

Joinville's first visual focus on Louis as aloof or corporate, sees the king in a medieval stance: a symbol of his sacred office, a myth of abundance and power, a military hand of God, a religious sword of the world. In the seneschal's second focus, Louis' holiness, chivalry and royal justice are realistically assessed and even criticized. The practical mettle of the Champagne prud'homme tests the limits of Louis IX. Joinville could be portrayed as a late medieval portrait with his head thrust forward, shoulder raised and hand on hip. From out of dependence upon the French king, he asserts himself on an equal plane.

The seneschal's passage from a collective to an individual mode of perception also parallels the royal iconography of his period. The art historians, Maumené and Harcourt, find that the idea of copying a royal image from a living individual does not appear in royal iconography until the end of the thirteenth century, the time when Joinville was composing his memories for a book.[15]

In cathedrals, tomb effigies and illuminated manuscripts, the kings are presented in the heroic symbols of their office until the end of the thirteenth century. Along with the Eternal Father, Christ, the Virgin, the saints and the kings of Holy Scriptures, the kings of France are carved in the silent symbolism of royalty on cathedral walls and portals. They are represented through the rituals of their office.

Their sculptured effigies on tombs show their crowns, sceptres, swords, crests and shields but not their individual faces. Illuminated miniatures are colourful, costumed but anonymous replicas of a king. Only in the late thirteenth century does there emerge some tentative individualizing artistic representations of monarchs.

According to Brécy who has thoroughly studied the royal iconography of the time, the head of Louis IX which appears in the vault of La Chapelle du Château de Saint-Germain-en-Laye shows little resemblance to the real king.[16] However, the statue of Saint Louis which was placed in Rheims cathedral does bear some resemblance to the monarch. By the end of the century, the statue of Philip III in the same cathedral demonstrates real likeness to the man it honors. During the reign of Philip III, Louis IX's son, the custom began of doing a sculpture of the dead king from a mortuary mask.

In the Bible moralisée done for Louis IX's personal use, we find the only contemporary likeness to the king in an illuminated miniature. It seems to have been executed between 1226-1234, before Louis went on Crusade. This tentative attempt to capture the personal likeness of Louis echoes the developing perceptions of Joinville's eye-witness portrayal.

Like the art and royal iconography of the period, Joinville's portrait of Louis IX reflects a cultural anthroplogy. From teaching saint to sacred spectacle, from barbaric warrior to religious myth, King Louis IX gradually appears with a distinctive personality. In Joinville's eye-witness account, Louis IX emerges from collective myth to individual man.

THE PERFECT PRUD'HOMME OF THE COURT

Prud'homie was the knight's hagiography. In Joinville's introductory section, Louis is the paragon of prud'homie. The seneschal's aim is to show that the king "se gouverna tout son tens selonc Dieu et selonc l'Eglise, et au profit de son regne".[17] Joinville claims that prud'homie was the king's highest ideal. He proves this with the king's words:

> Je vourroie bien avoir le non de preudome, mais que je le fusse, et touz le remenans vous demourast; car preudom est si grans chose et si bons chose que, neis au nommer, emplist-il la bouche.[18]

Prud'homie involves a whole range of chivalrous virtues in a lay aristocrat: military courage, justice, piety and social graces. It is this aspect of aristocratic idealism which comes closest to summing up Louis' attributes. Perhaps only another lay aristocrat could seize this truth about the royal nobleman.

In Joinville's introduction to his book, he spins out one story after another on the virtuous words of the king. His presentation is reminiscent of the exemplum style still popular in the seneschal's day. Kings and saints were the favourite subjects of the exempla. Etienne de Bourbon's collection of exempla compiled in the thirteenth century describe Charles Martel, Charlemagne, Roland, Oliver, Rainouart, Philip Augustus, Henry III as well as Louis IX in exemplary anecdotes. Exempla served as a popular way to educate illiterate people about moral models for their daily conduct. Exempla were repeated through sermons, popular preaching and informal story-telling. Originating in Biblical, ancient and early European history, contemporary events, fables, legends as well as popular bestiaries, exempla spoke of a divine order revealed in the lives of extraordinary people.[19]

As Alfred Foulet illustrates, Joinville turned the formal exempla style of dramatizing virtue fighting vice into a realistic comparison between two worthy consciences responding to different views of prud'homie.[20] In contrast to the proto-exempla form of Etienne de Bourbon or Philippe de Novare, Joinville did not describe absolutes of good and evil. Rather, he presented nuanced versions of two different sides of one ideal embodied in the persons of Louis and Joinville. On

the one hand, there was the saint who aspired to a prud'homie which
accented a relationship to God above all others, on the other hand,
there was the good knight who aimed to live by the values of his caste
in being charitable to others.

According to Frederic Tubach, the socially oriented exemplum style
emerged in the thirteenth century. It was the first illustration of a
breakdown in an absolute ethical norm shown in the earlier proto-
exempla. Joinville's anecdotes on the holy teachings of Louis illustrate
this kind of socially oriented exemplum style. He showed how one ideal
of prud'homie could be lived out decently in two socially distinct ways
within the same caste. However, in Joinville's opening section, the
king is always the superior to Joinville. He is always the teacher.

In the introductory section, Joinville portrays Louis primarily in
a corporate space. As teacher, his role is dependent upon his
communication with other people: his sons, Joinville, his barons, his
clerk, his knights. However, there is also a sacred spatial quality
to the monarch which sets him above and apart from his peers, his
prelates and Joinville.[21]

a) King of Justice

Who can forget the captivating image of Louis IX as the last court
of appeal in his kingdom, leaning his back against an oak tree in the
woods of Vincennes with Joinville and his men of note around him?[22]
This pastoral scene of justice has endured throughout the centuries.
Louis' feudal and corporate concern with good government is vividly
conveyed as is the familial flexibility of his inner judicial council.

Joinville also recalls that he sometimes saw Louis go to the public
gardens in summer in order to administer justice. He would be dressed
in only a plain woolen tunic, a sleeveless surcoat and a hat of white
peacock feathers. The good seneschal stresses his moderate justice,
dress and behaviour. The people who had a suit to present could
approach him without hindrance and speak to him directly. The king
would say to the crowd: 'Keep silent all of you, and you shall be
heard in turn, one after the other.'[23]

The raconteur from Champagne remembers the intimacy of the king's
majestic justice in his royal bed-room. After Mass, the monarch would

call his Council to him, seat himself at the end of his bed and ask his advisors to bring in appellant subjects. From his royal bed-post, Louis would ask of his subjects: "Pourquoy ne prenez-vous que nos gens vous offrent?" [24] The familial nature of the grouping strikes us as does the fatherly counsel between monarch and subject.

Corporate as it evidently was, the king's justice is also shown to be above the views of his Council. Joinville recounts how Louis' peace with England in 1259 was not liked by his Council members. They thought that the land-settlement to England was humiliating. Although the French gained more than they lost and Henry III, the English king, relinquished his claims to Normandy, Anjou, Maine, Touraine and Poitou, he was also granted the reversion of Agenais, Quercy, Saintonge and became a peer of France for Bordeaux, Bayonne and Gascony. Louis' Council found it inconceivable that a king could legalize the ownership of French land, no matter how inconsequential, to an English monarch. Joinville quotes Louis' defense of his peace to his Council lords: "' Il m'est mout grans honnours en la paiz que je faiz au roy d'Angleterre, pour ce que il est mes hom, ce que il n'estoit pas devant.'"[25]

Joinville also makes plain that Louis' justice surpassed the claims of his own clergy. The knight records the occasion when the French prelates came to the king with a request to have his provosts and baillifs seize all goods of those subjects under sentence of excommunication for more than a year and a day. In this case, Louis was faced with the question: what is the extent to which the king is obliged to act as a secular arm to the church? The position of the crown, expressed by Louis, was that if the matter of excommunication had not been reviewed in a secular court, the crown had no jurisdiction of support.

By the thirteenth century, the papacy had developed a substantial administration of papal intervention in secular affairs through such spiritual weapons, and excommunication and interdicts were over-used.[26] Excommunications occurred over such things as taxes, diocesan efforts for autonomy from Rome and the backing of rival candidates to a benefice. Joinville records that Louis reiterated to the prelates that he would not seize the goods of excommunicates without certain proof of guilt: "' ce seroit contre Dieu et contre raison, se il contreignoit la gent à aus absourdre, quant li clerc lour feraient tor.'"[27]

Joinville represents Louis as traditionally feudal and corporate in his judgments. But before the extra-territorial powers of the papacy and the English crown, Louis IX was above and beyond his feudal peers.

b) King of Holiness

In Joinville's introduction, the monarch moves sacred and alone in the religious rhythm of his day. The seneschal says that every day the king heard prayers chanted, a mass of requiem, and then the service of the day according to what saint the day was dedicated. After eating, he rested on his bed where he prayed with one of his chaplains, and every evening he heard complines. This was the duty of his office:

> Li gouvernemenz de sa terre fu teix que touz les jours
> il ooit à note ses heures, et une messe de Requiem
> sanz note, et puis la messe dou jour ou dou saint, se
> il y chèoit à note.[28]

Louis governed his land by the liturgy of the day.

The seneschal recounts the incident of the Crusaders' ship accident off the island of Cyprus, an incident he represents later in the Crusade story. He illustrates how, in the middle of the disaster, late at night, the scantily dressed king, roused from his bed, throws his body before the Holy Eucharist in the form of a cross: "se ala mettre en croiz devant le cors Nostre-Signour..."[29] Meanwhile, the sailors tear their clothes and beards in despair. The knight observes that shortly after Louis' solitary prayers, the weather clears.

On the morrow of the storm, the king calls Joinville to him and reflects upon the event. He says that God has shown him a part of his immense power. With a trifling wind, God could have seen to it that the King of France, his queen, his children and family were drowned. Louis asks: why would God so threaten a king? God would not be richer by his death. Louis interprets this wind as a threat. If he has the most trifling thing within him which displeases God, he should rid himself of it immediately. He should do all that he can to please God. The king concludes that in this manner, he and all who follow his words will gain more in this world and the next.[30]

In this text, we observe the monarch's complete and solitary submission to His God. His self-understanding is one of sole responsibility for the fate of his people collectively before God. This sublime and terrifying task of the king is one of salvation of his kingdom through his personal holiness. This literal prud'homie is unique to the monarch and leaves him alone, above and apart from his peers. This understanding of the kingship makes Louis the central interpretation of all events in the kingdom. This sacred role of the king as central interpretation and interpreter of history is familiar to Joinville's oral sources. The oral myth of the king is alive within Louis himself.

In the introductory section, the king also debates his holiness with Joinville. A charming series of exempla develops between the two men in which the monarch instructs the reticent aristocrat in the higher reaches of sanctity. There is not the slightest sign of criticism from Joinville as appears later in the Crusade story. In this exempla of social orientation, Joinville is instructed by the king. He readily admits he is not up to the monarch's level but he never casts doubt on its worthiness.

Louis tells Joinville that no matter what is done against him personally, he must never act or say anything contrary to God's law. He warns the knight that the subtle powers of the devil can intrude on a person's intentions at any time. A Christian should constantly be on guard against anything which could shake his faith in any article of the Catholic religion.[31]

The king asks Joinville if he knows the name of his own father. Joinville answers that he knows it well because his mother told it to him several times. His father's name was Simon. Louis draws an analogy between believing his father's name from his mother and believing the articles of the faith on the word of the apostles in the Creed. The testimony of his mother is like the testimony of the apostles in the Credo of the Mass.

In these social <u>exempla</u>, Joinville is the common-sense foil to the king. The monarch asks Joinville if he would rather be a leper or commit a mortal sin. The knight frankly answers that he would certainly prefer to commit thirty deadly sins rather than be a leper. Louis is horrified. He asks Joinville to sit at his feet and receive a lesson. He instructs Joinville that when a leper dies, he is cured of that illness. However, when a mortal sinner dies, he runs the risk of perpetual punishment. The king entreats Joinville to retain in his heart this important lesson. As he says: "' l'ame qui est en pechié mortel est semblable au dyable..'" 32

Another dialogue ensues between Louis and Joinville on the topic of washing the feet of the poor on Holy Thursday in memory of Christ's action before his Crucifixion and Resurrection. The knight expresses his aristocratic reserve for such an act: "' Sire... en maleur! les piez de ces vilains ne laverai-je jà...'" 33 The monarch begs his noble who stands by the values of his caste to consider the example of Christ as paramount: "' Si vous pri-je, pour l'amour de Dieu premier, et pour l'amour de moy, que vous les acoustumez à laver.'" 34

The ceremonious pleading of the king conveys his stern but loving role as a moral teacher to Joinville. The seneschal's frank disavowal of Louis' daring holiness establishes the charm with which these <u>exempla</u> unfold. It is evident that the monarch's close allegiance to God's laws establishes the nature of his corporate conversations. In the practice of his holiness, the king is first and foremost sacred, alone and apart. Only secondarily is he a part of a feudal hierarchy incorporated with his peers and people. In both instances however, we observe a king who is a collective type: he is a holy man for the collective welfare of his people and his kingdom.

c) King of Chivalry

The seneschal tells of the time that Louis engages his clerk, Robert Master of Sorbon and Joinville in a debate over the superiority of a <u>prud'homme</u> to a devout man. The monarch gives his own judgment on the problem by saying that he would prefer to have the name of a <u>prud'homme.</u> If he could earn this title they would be certainly welcome to the rest. 35

Included in the ideal of prud'homie were the social graces of chivalry, those noble codes of honour and behaviour with peers. Louis' grand-father, Philippe Augustus, had described the prud'homme as one who is both brave in body and a faithful servant of Christ.[36] The Christ-like qualities of a noble included courtesy, generosity, protection for the poor and the helpless, moderation in dress, drink, food and talk. Joinville selected certain examples to illustrate the king's social graces of moderation, courtesy and abstinence.

Joinville demonstrates royal chivalry in Louis' words concerning moderation in word and dress. The occasion occurs at Corbeil. First, the king is seen alone emerging from the sacred space of the chapel, above the crowd of his eighty knights gathered in the court below. Then, in the presence of the monarch and his company, Master Robert of Sorbon advances towards Joinville, takes hold of his mantle and asks him a daring question: 'Would you not be blameable if you seated yourself above the king?', asks Robert. Joinville agrees. 'Why then do you not think yourself blame-worthy for being more richly dressed than the king?', queries Robert.

The Champagne knight defends himself by saying that he has not had his dress made on his own authority. It has descended to him from his ancestors, and hence, is worthy of his established rank. The seneschal turns the argument on Robert by reminding him that Robert has risen above the dress and rank of his parents. His clothing rivals that of the monarch himself. This is his own doing.

At this point, Louis intervenes. He defends the honour of Robert, and reminds the audience of Robert's humility and kindness. Later, Louis calls to him his son, his son-in-law and Joinville. Within this corporate and familial grouping, the monarch admits to Joinville that he had been in the wrong to defend Master Robert against Joinville. He says he did not agree with Robert at the time but he defended him out of mercy. Louis bids Joinville to sit closer to him, so close that their gowns touch in symbolic equality. Louis supports Joinville's argument that everyone should dress in a manner appropriate to their familial heritage, neither too grandly nor too poorly. He reminds his sons of this admirable moderation in dress:

> 'Car, aussi comme li seneschaus dist, vous vous devez
> bien vestir et nettement, pour ce que vos femmes vous
> en ameront miex, et vostre gent vous en priseront plus.'[37]

Louis concludes that dress should be moderate enough so that a *prud' homme* would not judge one extravagant.[38]

The *exemplum* illustrates that the king's function set him apart from his knights and even his own chivalrous views as a *prud'homme.*

Joinville also includes a tale which demonstrates the king's chivalrous teaching on moderation in drink. At Cyprus, Louis asks Joinville why he did not water down his wine at table. Joinville answers that his physician has assured him of a cold liver and a large head against which no strong wine could do him harm. The wise monarch replies that Joinville has been deceived:

> 'car se je ne l'apprenoie en ma joenesce et je le
> vouloie tremper en ma vieillesce, les gouttes et
> les maladies de fourcelle me penroient, que jamais
> n'auroie santei..'[39]

According to the king, a chivalrous gentleman should not run the risk of gout or intoxication.

In another *exemplum*, the noble of Champagne recommends the king's teaching on the chivalrous virtue of courtesy. One day when Master Robert of Sorbon and Joinville are dining at the king's table, they are conversing together in so low a voice that no-one else at the table can hear them. The monarch reprimands them saying that in a group, they should speak out so that their companions will not think they are speaking ill of them:

> 'Se vous parlés, au mangier, de chose qui nous doie
> plaire, si dites haut; ou se ce non, si vous taisiés.'[40]

As the king of chivalrous behaviour, Louis appears as the teacher. In the spatial setting of separation from or incorporation with his noble peers, the king is superior, unquestioned and the final authority. He has no rival in his chivalrous words.

d) Conclusion

In the seneschal's introductory section, he recounts the good king's words. The monarch appears mainly at court as a didactic sign of justice, holiness and chivalry. He is the teacher of prud'homie. His relationship with the supernatural world is vividly portrayed through both his verbal philosophy and his spatial settings. He is set above his peers in his unrivalled words whether he is aloof or incorporated with them. This is a king who consorts with the divine for the collective benefit of his people. Corporate, he is a feudal father and suzerain who mingles with his peers as almost as an equal, yet is always called to represent his sacred function as judge, as holy man, as prud'homme beyond the function of his noble peers. Joinville learns from the words of Louis, the typical embodiment of religious chivalry which gives service to God alone for the sake of his kingdom.

Louis is presented through a pattern of roles. The personality of the king is always contained within the role he is playing, be it, father, monarch, holy man, judge, prud'homme or peer. Close enough to Joinville to touch his gown, this monarch is always a royal personnage in these scenes. We see no imperfections in his holy words.

Joinville's form of socially oriented exempla demonstrates two sides of one coin: prud'homie. Louis plays the lead role as religious prud'homme while the seneschal plays the secondary role of limited feudal prud'homme. The Champagne knight builds up his portrait of the king by showing him in a variety of relationships with a contrast in oral dialogue. Each scene stands as a stratum all its own.

The visual effect is similar to a medieval painting where painters often repeated the main figure many times in the same series of pictures. "Their purpose was to represent all possible relationships that affected him, and they recognized this could be done only by a simultaneous description of various actions."[41] Joinville's representation of Louis in his introductory section showed a connectedness in meaning rather than a logic of written development.

This section visualizes Louis IX as a collective and public saint. He plays various aspects of his role as a king and fulfills the rituals of his office exactly and ardently. Joinville's relationship with Louis is differentiated only through contrast. There is no comparative development of the two figures.

THE STYLIZED CRUSADING KING

In the first years of his Crusade account, Joinville sees Louis as a public spectacle. Louis appears as a distant visual pivot surrounded by people and events, Crusading rites and customs.[42] He could be almost any king. Socially, militarily and politically, King Louis moves through a series of public, functional and anticipated actions with little oral exchange. He is sometimes too far away from the observer to be overheard. He is a monarch a passerby might see or hear about from others.

As in the introductory exempla, Louis is visualized in two spatial settings: alone, above and apart from the Crusaders or in corporate consultation with them. Solo battle power, wondrous wealth; corporate spaces of feudal counsel move with this monarch across the face of Joinville's memories. As in the seneschal's exempla, the visual focus gives a two-dimensional effect of a stylized king of collective images and traditions.

a) Military Might and Aristocratic Abundance

Joinville's visual memory of the Crusaders' departure from Cyprus for Damietta recalls the king as a central figure of expansive power. With wine and food, Louis embarks on the Friday before Pentecost, ordering his barons to follow him in their ships for Egypt.

The Champagne knight describes the departure as the launching of a sacred space into the unknown and ominous region of the Saracens. The seneschal remembers it as a spectacle of space almost infinite in its scale: it seemed as if the whole sea was covered with cloth from the quantity of sails which were spread to the wind:

> qui mout fut belle chose à veoir; car il sembloit que toute la mers, tant comme l'on pooit veoir a l'ueil, fust couverte de touailles des voiles des vessiaus, qui furent nombrei à dix-huit cens vessiaus que granz que petiz.[44]

John of Beaumont, the chamberlain of France, estimated that the fleet consisted of 120 big ships and 80 smaller ones. With provisions for his men and orders to his barons, Louis sails like a king of God. He ends in a space which is corporate and protective with his men's ships anchored around him off Damietta shores.

Joinville sees Louis IX as a bolt of God's power at the Damietta landing, ensuing battle and the Good Friday fray. The king is a spectacle of epic proportions at his landing on the Damietta banks. Before Louis on the shore stretch the Sultan's forces, with arms of gold shining in the sun, and trumpets and horns terrifying to hear. Rejecting his barons' advice to wait for some Crusaders who had been swept away in a wind, and wishing neither the risk of giving heart to the enemy nor the danger of another storm, the monarch orders the invasion of the Damietta shores for the Friday before Trinity Sunday.

In the tale, Louis lunges waist-deep into the water before his Council and his legate as soon as he sights the Saint-Denis ensign blowing from the Damietta beaches. Urgently, he pushes with his shield and sword up to the sands to fight the Saracen enemies assembled in his face.[45]

We sense the sacred foolhardiness, the warrior's ardour, the tribal force of the monarch. The epic qualities of a Roland, the religious emotions of earlier Crusaders are celebrated in Joinville's images of Louis on the attack. At the later battle of Mansurah up the Nile from Damietta, similar images ripen in the king-figure. Joinville pictures Louis ride from a hill into the disassembled ranks of his men dehorsed or fighting for their lives upon their raging beasts of battle. His German helmet shines in the sun, his sword glints with glory as he descends to his troops and saves the day.[46] Sacred, savage, swift, he brings divinity to battle, like a new Charlemagne. The Good Friday battle is no exception: Louis is imagined as a warrior of old.

> il feri des esperons parmi les batailles son frere, l'espée ou poing, et se feri entre les Turs si avant que il li empristrent la coliere de son cheval de feu grejois.[47]

Lit with fire from the Saracen engines, this redeeming warrior suffers
the flames of the enemy for the sake of his people.

The seneschal says that with the king goes "Diex li touz puissans".[48]
His is a sacred space. The visual vivacity, clear impressions and warm
sentiments of Joinville attach themselves to the Crusading mission
through the sacred function of the monarch. Courageous, alone and
apart from his men, Louis is the sign of salvation for his Crusaders.
This is a king of theocratic power, reminiscent of Joinville's oral
motifs.

b) Solo and Corporate Spaces

After the successful fall of Damietta, Louis decides to head
towards Cairo. The aim is to destroy the massive Saracen concentration
of strength under Ayub, the sultan of Egypt. If Egypt can be taken and
its armies reduced, the Holy Land is a feasible conquest for the
Christians.

The Crusaders fight their way up the Nile with Joinville recording
each serious obstacle. The most insurmountable of the obstacles is
a branch of the Nile which must be crossed near Mansurah. The Christians
find the Saracens ranged on the opposite shore of the canal with their
Greek-fire weopanry prepared for attack. Greek fire had been adapted
by the Moslems from the Greeks. It was a highly inflammable mixture,
including sulphur, tow, pitch and naptha or petroleum.

Camping on the corner of land between the Nile and the canal of
Bahr as-Saghir, the Crusaders look for a way to cross the outlet and
fight their opponents. Joinville describes the king as the centre of
the decision, the collective point of the Crusaders' solution. The
decision is reached to build a cat-castle to protect the passage of
the Crusading troops across a constructed causeway over the canal.
All the knights bring wood to the king's pavilion for the construction
of the castle, a moveable fortified tower of several stories. It will
house several layers of bow-men to shoot arrows into the Saracen ranks
while the troops cross the canal.

Just as the solution was centred in the king, so is its failure.
Joinville describes how the castle was burnt by the bolts of searing
Greek-fire. A crisis develops. The seneschal depicts the monarch in

a closer focus with a corporate grouping. Louis consults his Council of war: "Quant li roys vist ce, il manda touz ses barons pour avoir consoi." [49] The Greek-fire which Joinville describes as a 'vinegar barrel of fire with a tail as long as a spear', has done its work. Another solution must be found. Humbert of Beaujeu suggests that a stray Bedouin's offer to show the Crusaders a good ford down-stream could be accepted for 500 bezants.

Leaving the Duke of Burgundy in charge of the camp to arrange for a pontoon bridge to be built for the bowmen, Louis and his troops go down-stream to cross the ford. As the crossing is arduous and slow, the king's brother, Robert of Artois finds he and his men alone upon their successful crossing. Contrary to the king's orders, Robert goes off without the remaining Crusaders to attack the sleeping Saracens. His surprise attack wreaks havoc on the Moslems by the river-bank. Drunk with the glory, Robert rushes his men into the nearby town of Mansurah and there he is killed.

The Christian cavalry make their crossing and engage the Moslems who rush out of the town. Joinville recalls the dramatic scene in three visual environments. First, the king appears in the seneschal's account: distant, powerful and beautiful; then he is identified with the knights of his household and his Crusading cavalry; finally, after the battle is won, he is presented for the first time during the Crusade, in an individual setting with Joinville, his comrade-in-arms.

Gravely wounded by Saracen lances, Joinville sees Louis' magnificent entry into the battle of Mansurah. He sees the king in a daring aloof space above his men, leading their chivalrous feats into the midst of the enemy. The monarch is a formidable figure of strength, urging Crusaders into "très biaus fais d'armes". [50]

The remainder of the battle is described in fixed corporate hierarchical spaces. In Joinville's eye-witness report, the battle proceeds through static consultations between Louis and his barons. This consultation becomes the ritual centre for interpreting the action of the battle, The seneschal was no military expert.

> Li roys commanda à ses serjans que il li alassent
> querre ses bons chevaliers que il avoit entour li
> de son consoil, et les nomma touz par lour non. [51]

    The description proceeds in a series of staccato decisions and movements. Louis asks his Council if they should move forward or backward. His Council decides to move forward. The Counts of Poitier and Flanders send messages begging the king not to move at all. The king reconvenes his Council to explain that they are not going to move at all. John of Waleri returns to the monarch to protest his delay in moving forward. Louis and his reconvened Council again decide to move forward. A messenger then arrives with urgent word that Robert of Artois is cut off in the town of Mansurah and is in desperate need of help. Louis immediately departs to aid his brother trapped in the town.

    Joinville recalls the battle as a daring feat of royal bravery, individual and symbolic on the one hand, and on the other hand, as a static series of consultations between the king and his Council. The king and the battle are stylized into a feudal pattern of hierarchical movements, heroic acts and feudal rituals, centred in the king as a type.

    The knight from Champagne credits the day to Louis. He says he never saw such gallant deeds performed by anyone else in battle from that day forward. If it had not been for the king's chivalrous example of gallant bravery, the whole army might have been destroyed. His valiant fighting off six Saracens from the bridel of his horse, his caring defense of his men, his corporate consultations for the common good won the day.

c) An Intimate Space

    The last setting in which Joinville recalls Louis at Mansurah is an intimate one. It is the first Crusade arena in which the king is individualized.

    The day falls on the battle and about sunset, Joinville is relieved of his post defending the bridge. The knight recalls how the monarch's constable congratulates him for his admirable job. He invites Joinville to join the king. The wounded knight joins the king as he is returning to his pavilion from the battle-scene. Joinville recounts the honourable interchange.

When the king takes off his helmet, Joinville valiantly offers him his iron skull-cap because it is lighter and provides more air than a helmet. On the road back, Louis is met by Father Henry, prior of the hospital of Ronnay. He kisses the monarch's hand and inquires if the king has heard the tragic news of his brother's death. Louis acknowledges that he knows that his brother is in paradise. Robert of Artois has been his great loss of the day's battle. When the Father compliments Louis on the honour he has reaped that day, great tears fall from the king's eyes. Joinville comments that this caused great anguish among the men who witnessed his emotion. Louis says that God is to be adored for the good He has granted the Crusaders that day.

This third spatial setting captures Louis with internal feeling, something rare in royal portraiture. The stoic role of the typical warrior is dissolved in tears. Louis, the human mourner, rides beside Joinville and reveals his inner disposition amidst dignity and a prayerful attitude. The stylized Crusader of God becomes human and vulnerable. It is a privilege for Joinville to be present on such a occasion and he shows how the emotional, the practical and the spiritual were intertwined in Louis at a deep level.[52]

In this intimate moment, we also hear from Joinville his comments on the feelings of those surrounding the king at this mourning. He describes the anguish of Louis' companions on that road from Mansurah. This is also the first time, Joinville has mentioned the private feelings of the king's entourage.

d) Conclusion

In these early images of Louis on Crusade, he is a divine spectacle of power and expansiveness. We see him opening the departure from Cyprus, opening the Damietta landing, opening the battle of Mansurah, opening the battle of Good Friday to symbolic proportions of God's prowess. He is also a ritual corporate space through which God descends hierarchically to his Crusaders: the king's brothers, the knights of his household, his barons, his troops, his infantry and Joinville. Joinville places himself at the base of the king's noble hierarchy, until the poignant reward of the road from Mansurah.

ONE IN ONE THOUSAND

At first the royal observer from within 1,000 Champagne men who fought with the approximately 15,000 Crusaders, Joinville becomes the one in 1,000 Champenois to gain privileged access to the person of the king. From within his own contingent of Champenois, the seneschal aspires not only to Louis' financial aid and military protection but to his personal recognition. Joinville traces this desire in his second theme throughout the Crusade account.

At first, Joinville's self-portrait develops parallel to that of the king's. In contrast to the expected meaning of the monarchy on Crusade, Joinville must prove his glory. Recognition for his prud'homie on Crusade comes from the king. This is Joinville's proof before his peers. Royal recognition is gained through his deeds of chivalry: brave, generous and loyal acts.[54]

When the author first meets Louis, he is outside the monarch's immediate entourage. For example, after Damietta's capture, Joinville approaches the monarch and his Council as an outsider:

> Je, touz armez, alai parler au roy, et le trouvai
> tout armei séant sus une forme, et des preudomes
> chevaliers qui estoient de sa bataille, avec li
> touz armés.[55]

Gradually, through steadfast courage and valiant deeds, Joinville becomes a part of this royal entourage.

Joinville's earlier story of his Crusading adventures build the audience up to this finale. In contrast to the king's majestic opening gests, Joinville's acts bristle with uncertainty. However, Joinville appeals to ideals comparable to those of the king. His landing at Damietta is depicted with a courage which rivals that of the monarch. He tells of his troubles in securing a landing galley for his men despite the king's insistence that two of his men settle their quarrel and swear on the Gospels before landing on the Damietta shores. Like King Louis, Joinville lands contrary to the advice of the king's men, even arriving on the beaches before the king himself.

While the seneschal does not wait for the king, he does wait for a native Champenois noble, Lord Baldwin of Rheims who sent a message

to Joinville requesting that he wait for him.[56] Although an
'all-powerful God' does not land with Joinville as He did with the
king, it is clear that Joinville also lands with God on his side:

> ... et soiés certains que, quant je arivai, je
> n'oz ne escuier, ne chevalier, ne varlet que je
> eusse amenei avec moy de mon pays; et si ne m'en
> lessa pas Diex à aidier.[57]

The landing was a significant ritual in oral Crusading tales. It
illustrated the nobility of the knight. The finest landing mentioned
by Joinville is that of a native Champenois, the count of Japhe, a
member of Joinville's lineage. The seneschal comments: "ce fu cil
qui plus noblement ariva..."[58]

In following Joinville's self-descriptions carefully, it becomes
evident that the Champenois knight wishes to prove that he is better
than the other knights on Crusade. After the Crusaders take Damietta,
when the sultan lays seige to the city on the land-side, Joinville
goes to the king. He requests permission to attack the sultan with his
Champenois men. However, Sir John, a member of the royal Council,
orders him in the king's name to stay in his quarters until the king
commands. Joinville obeys.

The seneschal recounts that another knight was not so obedient.
Walter of Autrèche rides out alone from his tent that very day.
Surrounded by cries of "Chatillon!", he falls from his horse and is
trampled to death. When Louis is told of this man's tragic death, he
replies that it was his own fault because he did not listen to the
king's orders. Joinville comments that the king reminds his nobles
that he does not wish for the services of any knight who will not
attend to his words.[59] The king sees the danger of chivalrous heroes
who do not act in the common good he directs.

While Joinville does not make himself into a major figure in the
ensuing action of the Nile campaign, he continues to insert examples
of his loyal gallantry. At the canal of Bahr as-Saghir, Joinville
recounts how he saves two knights from the Saracens. The Moslems had
attacked these knights' camp and captured them on Christmas Day. In
the same location, the seneschal fights beside the Count of Poitiers,

the king's brother, to successfully ward off a Saracen manoeuvre. Joinville notes that while great numbers of Moslems are slain, few Christians lose their lives in this escapade.

At the battle of Mansurah, the Champenois knight describes how he is wounded in five places, his horse in fifteen. Nonetheless, the task he has set out to do is accomplished with bravado and skill. The bridge beside the king's side of the battle is admirably defended from the Saracens. It is after this victory, that Joinville wins the merit of accompanying Louis back to his pavilion from the battle.

The monarch's recognition for Joinville's bravery and good sense endures for the rest of the Crusading venture. As a result, the Champenois contingent is highly valued by the king. That very night after Mansurah, Louis sends special protection to their forces. Joinville tells how at daybreak, the Saracens break into the Champenois camp to seize the engines stolen from them during the battle. Joinville rouses himself and his men. Wounded and without armour, they come out to defend the engines. Joinville says that Louis sees their movement and their danger. He commands Sir Walter de Chastillon to protect their tired and damaged contingent.

The seneschal proudly records that one of his priests becomes known as the hero of that dawn. John de Waysy, Joinville's priest, rushes out and attacks six Saracen leaders with such fury and surprise that they take flight. The other Moslems follow them. The priest becomes known as 'the priest of Joinville who singlehandedly defeated Saracens.' The heroic valiance of Joinville and his Champenois men is obedient to the king in any display of individual gallantry.

Beginning as a poor knight who leaves Champagne at his own expense with nothing more than a pilgrim's staff, Joinville finishes as the favoured protector of Louis after their first big battle. [60] As a representative of Champagne, its traditions and his family, Joinville appears as a worthy exemplar of noble prud'homie. Moreover, he emerges as superior to other Champenois knights, close enough to perfection to win royal tribute. His prowess is a feudal prud'homie which respects the hierarchical order of obedience, loyalty, consultation and protection of his superior. Although not yet a king's man, he is loyal.

ROYAL ALLIANCE

In the early Crusade account, Joinville describes the king in the Gothic mode. He respects his limits of perceiving the monarch and does not translate him beyond traditional imagery. King Louis belongs to the roles of his royal majesty, and like a Gothic painting retains the characteristics of a single plane. Gothic art respected its material, and rarely went beyond its limits, whether it was a wall or a window, a miniature or a tapestry. Joinville rarely obtrudes in this visual presentation of the king.

In this first group of Crusading images, the king is like a stained-glass window. What he visually lacks in dimension, he gains in translucency. The king appears as a figure through which Divine Light comes. He is like a Gothic painting, welcoming the natural day with unfinished quality, incorporating it into a flat space, sometimes through transparency, sometimes by bold highlights. [61] Louis is presented as not merely a symbol, nor merely a mediator, he evokes the mystery of what lies behind him. In this sense, Joinville's early Crusading monarch is always more than one particular king. Yet he also belongs with his feudal vassals, his Council of war and his Crusading men in a physically corporate way which is best expressed in a two dimensional translucid image. It is this unfinished quality to Joinville's images of the king which evokes his mystery.

Contrary to the images of the public sacred king and the corporate feudal king, the second group of Joinville's royal images begin to individualize both the king and himself. These images belong more to the form of sunlight painting which increased in the thirteenth and fourteenth centuries and became associated with portraits of individuals. These portraits were modelled in depth, striving to give an illusion of complete space with its dark and light shades in imitation of the sun. Through more internalized exchange with Joinville, the king gains in depth dimension. Sometimes, it is at the expense of his sacred image to the benefit of Joinville's prud'homie. [62]

Distinct from the first group of Crusade images which usually show Joinville and the king in separate tableaux, there begins to emerge a pattern of regular encounters between the seneschal and the monarch. In contrast to the opening court exempla, these meetings go beyond a contrast in styles of prud'homie which favour the king's superlative authority. During the latter half of the Crusade story, Louis is not a teacher of prud'homie. Joinville challenges the king's prud'homie, illustrates its limitations and demonstrates his own qualities which rival those of the king. The Gothic symmetry of epic images, sacred roles and feudal rituals begins to change.

a) The Payment of Ransom

After the gruelling captivity of the Crusaders, Joinville describes how Louis negotiates a ransom of a million bezants or about 167,000 tournois pounds with the Saracens for the release of himself and his army. Louis' bargaining point is that the queen, his wife, has managed to hold Damietta. It is agreed that half of the ransom will be paid to the Saracens from Damietta over the week-end of the 7th and 8th of May, 1251. We know from other sources that since the vast sum was calculated by weight, it took the whole week-end to weigh the ransom. Joinville recounts that by Sunday night, it becomes evident that the Crusaders are 30,000 pounds short.

Word is sent to the king. Joinville suggests to Louis that the Crusaders should borrow the remaining sum from the wealthy Templars. When the Commander of the Templars balks at such a daring plan, the seneschal suggests that the money be seized forcibly from the Templars' deposits. This was a pro forma theft since the Templars knew they would be compensated by the royal moneys held at Acre where the queen had escaped. [63] With the king's permission, Joinville accomplishes the mission himself.

The Champenois knight goes into extensive detail to illustrate the boarding of the Templar galley and the seizing of the moneys for the ransom. The autobiographical nature of this passage, its length, detail, narrative and description could still be concerned with any typical Crusading king. In the standard material of chivalrous deeds, the seneschal portrays himself performing something noble, daring and necessary for his royal master. But the alliance between Joinville and Louis is strengthening. Joinville is now acting in the personal service of the king.

b) A Tap on the Toe

A note of new individuality in Joinville appears once the ransom is paid. Louis asks his knights if all is in order concerning the ransom payment. Sir Philip de Nemours proudly asserts that they have cheated the Saracens out of ten thousand pounds. The king is furious. Joinville quickly intervenes by stepping on Nemours' foot to silence him. The quick-thinking seneschal explains to the king that Nemours had spoken in jest. Nemours immediately agrees. In his strict conscience, Louis takes the matter very seriously and has to be convinced that his enemies had received every last pound.

In this interchange, Joinville reveals his inner perception of the king's tender conscience. As on the Mansurah road, Joinville is not completely alone with the king. He is included in the royal entourage. However, the scene illustrates something more than the inner emotions of the Mansurah road. Joinville establishes his judgment of the king and acts on it to forestall further difficulties. Joinville takes an individual stance with a tap on the toe. This is not an act of obedience, nor of contrast. Joinville acts subtlely but separately in this scene based upon his independent evaluation of Louis.

c) A Familial Dinner

Joinville makes it evident to his audience that he has won the trust of the king. This trusting favour is solidified when the Crusaders are freed and arrive at Acre. The setting opens through contrast. Whereas Louis enters Acre joyfully with people surrounding him, like Christ entering Jerusalem, Joinville enters sick and alone, riding on a pony.

Four days later, Joinville visits the king and he is greeted like a brother. The monarch insists that the Champenois knight become his regular dinner guest:

> et me commanda, si chiere comme j'avoie s'amour, que mangasse avec li adès et au soir et au main, jusques à tant que il eust aréei que nous feriens, ou d'aler en France ou de demourer. [64]

This familial embrace of Louis puts Joinville on a par with the king's own brothers. One is brought to the point of wondering if Louis may have been looking for a replacement for his dead brother, Robert of Artois.

This close embrace of Joinville builds to a public acknowledgement of Joinville's privileged status before the royal Council. This transition is accomplished by the personal bond of conscience which is established between the seneschal and the king. As the seat of his person, a bond of conscience was nothing transient for Louis. This bond brought Joinville beyond the familial king to the private man.

d) A Bond of Conscience

Joinville's alliance with Louis comes to its climax when the king summons his men of note to a Council. He asks their advice about returning to France or staying in the Holy Land.

The seneschal spends a fair amount of space in his story detailling how he came to special stature with the king through these Council meetings. It has been debated whether he may have exaggerated his part in these meetings.[65] Whatever the case, the private alliance which develops between Louis and the seneschal is so strong in the remaining tale that we can rely on its basic truth in the psychological sense. Furthermore, since Joinville proves his reliability on every other source, there is no good reason not to trust his report of these key meetings.

Joinville says that at the first Council meeting, the king presents the options to the members. Either they remain in the Holy Land or they return to France as Louis' influential mother, Blanche of Castille has requested. For the first time, Joinville appears solidly within the inner sanctum of the royal Council. Once an outsider to this body of deliberation, Joinville becomes an integral part of its consultations. Now, they are no longer ritual.

After the first meeting, the seneschal reflects on the decision to be made. Joinville speaks to the papal legate and recalls to him the words of the knight's cousin, the Lord of Bourlemont, when he left Champagne for the Crusade:

> ... vous prenés garde au revenir; car nulz chevaliers,
> ne povres ne riches, ne puet revenir que il ne sait

> honniz se il laisse en la main des Sarrazins le peuple
> menu Nostre-Signour, en laquel compaingnie il est alez.[66]

Joinville's cousin had warned him of the disgrace he would find upon
his return if he left fellow-Crusaders imprisoned with the Saracens.
Joinville appeals to his family and Champagne honour in explaining how
he comes to making his decision.

As he tells it, when the seneschal returns to the second meeting
of the Council, he does not have many supporters. He and one other
Council member wish to stay in the Holy Land. Moreover, Joinville
receives the ire of the papal legate for his divergent views. The
Champenois knight responds with an eloquent plea to his fellow-members
to stay and save the prisoners. He says that his speech made other
men cry:

> Il n'avoit nul illec qui n'eust de ses prochains amis
> en la prison; par quoy nulz ne me reprist, ainçois se
> pristrent tuit à plorer.[67]

The seneschal remembers that many of the barons attacked him as
they came out from the Council meeting. They called him crazy:

> Or est fous, sire de Joinville, li roys, se il ne
> vous croit contre tout le consoil dou royaume de
> France.[68]

How dare this new incomer to the Council hold so dangerous a view, a
view which could keep these tired defeated barons in the Holy Land!
The king has delayed sharing his views or making his decision until a
third meeting.

At dinner that evening, silence reigns. The king's brothers are
absent and Joinville is alone with Louis. The monarch says absolutely
nothing to the knight. Joinville concludes to himself that Louis is
angry with him. He thinks that because he mentioned the king's personal
money as an argument of feasibility for staying in the Holy Land,
Louis thinks he has intruded on his private life too much. Joinville
had argued that more Crusaders could be hired to stay in the Holy Land
because of Louis' private funds.

In this frame of private mind, Joinville develops his new
individual style of describing both the king and himself.

Joinville speaks of himself going to a window overlooking the city after dinner. He commiserates with himself. He tells how he privately and bleakly considers his future alone in the Holy Land. He confides in us that he thinks about enlisting in the services of the prince of Antioch. He leans against the window-frame in contemplation of his lone but noble future. For the first time, the seneschal speaks from an inner dialogue to his audience. We hear his thoughts as he alone knows them.

In this attractive spatial setting by a window-frame, Joinville establishes himself as a person separate from the king's Council and from his function as a Champenois knight. His stance of leaning at a window in thought would become more familiar to Renaissance portraits of art and literature.[69] This signals his individualization and with this scene, Joinville departs from medieval collective typology.

Joinville tells the climax of this honourable and lonely fate. Someone comes up behind him and puts his hands on the knight's head. Thinking it is one of the Council members, Joinville asks the person to leave him in peace. Then he notices the emerald ring. It is the ring of the king. Joinville records Louis' tender words of praise and support for the young knight:

> 'Tenez-vous touz quoys; car je vous vueil demander
> comment vous fustes si hardis que vous, qui estes
> uns joennes homs, m'osastes loer ma demourée,
> encontre touz les grans homes et les saiges de
> France qui me looient m'alée.'[70]

How could so young a knight be more noble and courageous than all the barons of France who had come to the campaign as the king's men?

Louis confides what is in his heart. Although he could say nothing at the last Council meeting, he also wishes to remain in the Holy Land to free the imprisoned Crusaders. Louis asks Joinville:

> ' se je demeur, demourrez-vous?' Et je li dis que oyl.
> 'se je puis ne dou mien ne de l'autruy.' 'Or soiés touz
> aises, dist-il, car je vous sai mout bon grie de ce que
> vous m'avez loei; mais ne le dites à nullui, toute cette
> semaine.'[71]

A personal alliance is formed between the inner conscience of Louis and his knight from Champagne. Joinville's Champenois honour is upheld and he is alone in a secret alliance with the king of France. Unlike the earlier Corbeil court scene, the private thoughts of the king which agree with those of Joinville will be publically acknowledged at the next meeting of the Council.

At the third and final Council meeting, the king announces to his assembled advisors that he has decided to stay in the Holy Land against both the wishes of his mother and his barons. He will stay until all the prisoners-of-war are released by the Saracens. All is now changed. Joinville and his chivalrous beliefs are the quiet victors over all his rivals before the king. Joinville is the truest son of Champagne and his family honour. He is also superior in prud'homie to all the barons assembled at the meeting due to the king's decision.

This alliance between Joinville and the king constitutes a departure in French medieval historiography from collective towards individual perceptions of a French monarch. Louis breaks the mold of his Council's corporate advice and becomes an ally of conscience with Joinville. This occurs on the basis of principled judgment which places prud'homie above security. The two prud'hommes of differing social values meet on a deeper level of moral conscience. Theirs is an inner alliance.

Joinville had been taunted by Council members that he was a colt, or poulain, a word for a half-French, half-Syrian native. He had replied that it was better to be a colt than a broken down old horse like his critics. Now Joinville was to reap the rewards of his noble but unpopular opinion. The king's brothers and many French barons returned to France. Joinville and Louis remained. If he was a poulain, Joinville had chosen royal company. The importance of the quality of their bond cannot be stressed more strongly. It had been formed on the basis of two individual judgments around the facts of an issue which were unpopular but which corresponded to each of the men's evaluation of their respective moral duties.

A HUMAN PRUD'HOMME OF THE HOLY LAND

With the rituals of the court and Crusade campaign behind him, Joinville adopts a familial and personal attitude towards Louis between 1250-1254. The king is slightly displaced as an accepted centre of sole meaning for the action of those years in Outremer. Often, it is Joinville who occupies the other half of the stage. Without tearing down the epic, sacred or feudal qualities of the king he had earlier depicted, the seneschal quietly finds the occasion to question some of their excesses within Louis' personality and attitudes. Occasionally, this takes the form of familial mocking.

The interchange which is described between Joinville and Louis evolves around issues, events, occasions of dialogue. It is Joinville's point of view which determines the development of both characters. This takes its origin in the knight's opinions, principles and approaches which distinguish themselves from those of the king. The ensuing years are ones of friendship and mutual interdependence. In effect, the Crusade Campaign was finished. Its military feats of epic and sacred images lay in the dust of Mansurah. The feudal grouping of barons and Council of war had vanished. This was a situation of new circumstances without many oral precedents, familiar forms or heroic traditions. It was within these new circumstances, that Joinville developed a new way of portraying a medieval monarch.

a) Perfect King of Holiness?

The anecdote which best introduces the tone of contrast and comparison in the latter half of Crusade tale makes the monarch's holy reputation an occasion for some humour. Even Louis is amused.

It is the secret of Joinville's reliability that he never pretends with the king. Perhaps it is also the secret of the knight's bond with him - his realistic forthrightness is a foil of integrity for the other-worldly monarch. When Joinville keeps Louis in the dark about his thoughts, he does so with a sense of play or protection, never disloyalty. Most of what the seneschal shares with his audience, he has first shared with Louis. The result is convincing in its integrity. Through these two admirable people in close contact over demanding issues, two living <u>prud'hommes</u> emerge in full spatial dimension.

When a group of pilgrims come to Joinville at the royal camp on the sands of Acre, they ask if they can see the holy king: "il me firent prier que je lour monstrasse le saint roy." In going to announce the pilgrims' visit to the king, Joinville discovers Louis in a state of monkish contemplation, sitting on the sands within his tent without a rug or anything around him:

> Je alai au roy là où il se séoit en un paveillon,
> apuiez à l'estache dou paveillon; et séoit ou
> sablon sanz tapiz et sans nulle autre chose
> desouz li.[73]

Joinville addresses his royal confidante with profane humour and a play on the word "os". He explains that the pilgrims wish to see the "saint roy" but says "je ne bé jà à baisier vos os".[74] Joinville jokes affectionately with the monarch about his holy reputation and plays on the royal archetype whose bones were sitting so incongruously in the sand. Perhaps the seneschal was also appealing in his book to a nobility who frowned slightly on the special status of the sacred Capetian monarchy.

The king's laughter at Joinville's joke assures the friendliness of the interchange: "Et il rist mout clerement, et me dist que je les alasse querre; et si fis-je."[75]

This current of humour is carried one step further in three other anecdotes which Joinville relates. With slight irony, Joinville contrasts and compares his deeds to Louis' prayers. Joinville comes off favourably in the comparison. The king's holy devotions, while not found wanting, appear somewhat inappropriate to the occasion. The juxtaposition of Joinville's concrete and appropriate responses to the same situation place him in an active role. The king represents the contemplative life of chivalry, while Joinville plays the active role of chivalry.

The seneschal contrasts sacred formality with social chivalry in the liturgy which he and the king attend at Sayette. Having risen early in the day for his customary Mass which Joinville also attended, Louis asks his trusted companion to ride into the open fields of the local country-side with him. Crossing the land, Louis spies a small church named in honor of a miracle in which the devil had been successfully expelled from a little girl. There they see a priest offering Mass. The king suggests that they participate.

When it comes time for the sign of peace to be shared by the congregation members, Joinville decides to protect the king. The sign of peace asks of the participants a personal greeting as members of Christ. A large, dark and suspicious looking man helping to sing the Mass approaches the king to personally offer him the sign of peace. Feeling this may be dangerous for the king, Joinville moves to take the greeting for the king from the large man. Louis does not appreciate Joinville's chivalrous gesture during the liturgical celebration.

After the Mass, the seneschal and monarch ride out from the little church. They meet the papal legate in the surrounding fields. Drawing up to the legate, the king complains to him about Joinville. He says his knight would not allow him to receive the sign of peace during the Mass. The seneschal gracefully explains the situation to the legate. Louis is incensed and continues to argue. "'Vraiement non fist'", he says.

Joinville's comment on the ensuing argument is a quiet ironic remark. While the king continues in disaccord, Joinville stays quiet and as he says: "en paiz".[76] While Joinville was living the sign of peace, Louis was arguing it.

The seneschal's peaceful pun turns to direct criticism on another occasion. The king celebrates the liturgy in such a way that he escapes greeting his wife and new-born daughter when the queen rises from birth. His wife, Margeret arrives at Sayette from Jaffa to join her husband for the first time after the birth of her child. When she arrives, Louis is at Mass. Moreover, he has left instructions that he is not to be interrupted under any circumstances. While Louis stays attentively worshipping in the chapel, Joinville excuses himself from the same liturgical celebration to greet the queen.

The king is so ardently fixed on following each part of the liturgy that he asks the celebrant to have the sermon delayed until Joinville returns. He believes that the sermon will be a fitting reward to Joinville's courtesy to his queen:

> Et quant je reving au roy, qui estoit en sa chapelle,
> il me demanda se la royne et le enfant estoient
> haitié; et je li diz oil. Et il me dist: 'Je soy
> bien quant vous vous levates de devant moy, que vous
> aliés encontre la royne; et pour ce je vous ai fait
> atendre au sermon.'[77]

In this paradoxical situation, Joinville forms his critical view of the king's family attitudes. In his book, Joinville openly states the harshest criticism he is to make of the king. He says that during his five years with the king, Louis never once spoke to him of either his wife or his children. Joinville finds this a questionable state of affairs: "... ce n'estoit pas bons manière, si comme il me semble, d'estre estrange de sa femme et de ses enfans."[78]

The third and last time on which Joinville compares his chivalrous deeds to the king's prayers occurs on the ship-journey home to France from Outremer. In the middle of the night, their ship strikes a shoal off Cyprus. Joinville recalls how he awakens to a great cry. He rises quickly from his bed to join the crowd of worried passengers. His aim is to see what can be done to practically remedy the situation.

While he is inquiring about the concrete realities of the grounding, one of his men does him a chivalrous courtesy. He brings a furred surcoat to put over his shoulders in the cold night air. The seneschal asks what he would do with this surcoat if they were all to drown. His man replies that he would prefer to drown than to see Joinville sick with cold:

> 'Par m'ame! sire, je averoie plus chier que nous
> fussiens tuit naié, que ce que une maladie vous preist
> de froit, dont vous eussiez la mort.'[79]

The feudal loyalty of his man to him is as touching and real as the seneschal's protection of the king during the liturgy at Sayette. In Joinville's world of prud'homie, these are the active gestures which count. His man sees that Joinville could just as easily die of a bad cold as die of drowning. He performs his duty with alert devotion. Joinville appreciates the gesture and records it as a tribute to his authoritative presence on the ship-decks.

By comparison to Joinville's practical presence, marked by the protective loyalty of his man, the king again appears in another world. This is the world of devotional contemplation. Louis is nowhere to be seen during the danger. Once the ship is moved off the shoal, the king makes his appearance.

Joinville says that Louis had spent the anguished hours in solitary prayer before the Sacred Host exposed in the ship's chapel:

> Et lors frères Remons le ala dire au roy, qui étoit
> en croiz adenz sur la pont de la nef, touz deschaus,
> en pure cote et touz deschevelez (devant le cors
> Nostre-Signour estoit en la nef), comme cil qui bien
> cuidoit noir.[80]

Alone and dischevelled, the king spreads himself in the form of a cross before the Holy Sacrament, imploring his Maker for his men's safety. Evidently, Louis believes that it is his superior duty to fight the danger with prayer. Joinville tells his audience this same anecdote in his introductory *exempla*. However, in this section of his tale, Joinville does not exalt the king's actions of prayer.

His treatment invites comparison between his caring deeds and that of his man to the obvious absence of the monarch. Joinville faces the danger directly with the loyalty of his man and a furred surcoat. The king deals with the danger by storming the heavens alone and dischevelled. Louis' lack of stoicism, appropriate garb and active participation are subtlely suggested by Joinville's presentation.

These three anecdotes, complemented by the joke about Louis' holy bones, illustrate that Joinville believed in an active *prud'homie* which charitably responded to the realities of a situation. By comparison, Louis' *prud'homie* seeks God's word in a way which appears excessive because he sacrifices other important duties to this. The king appears indifferent to husbandly support, familial celebration, stoic presence with his ship-wrecked men, personal danger to his body during the liturgy and appropriate regal appearances before curious pilgrims. By comparison, Joinville pursues the peace of his king's physical safety even though it is not appreciated, greets Louis' wife for him with *politesse* despite the king, faces a ship-wreck

directly and stoically, showing appreciation for his own man's loyal
protection and finally, he maintains a peaceful relationship with the
king even while the king ignores or disputes his feudal form of
prud'homie.

It is evident in these four anecdotes which show the limitations
of Louis' pursuit of holiness that Joinville is his own man. He
responds to inner principles for his action just as steadfastly as he
did at the Council meetings of Acre. It is not through submission to
a king-figure that he makes his prud'homie. He is loyal, he is res-
pecting, he evidently loves this king. But first and foremost, this
Champenois knight is a man of duty to those chivalrous principles he
has learned from his family and his homeland of Champagne. Moreover,
Joinville is steadfast beyond Champenois collective heritage. He
establishes himself through acts of conscience and charity in a new
land with little support, not even from the king he so diligently
serves.

In these anecdotes, we may presume that Joinville had honed their
telling to a Champenois audience before the composition of his book.
They appeal to the kind of prud'homie which would be understood and
admired by his lay aristocratic peers of Champagne. By never exceeding
his bonds of respect for the king, by always attempting and succeeding
eventually to keep the alliance of Louis, Joinville proves himself a
most moderate narrator.

b) Perfect King of Chivalry?

Another area which Joinville opens for lay aristocratic scrutiny
is the king's severe application of chivalrous moral principles. The
monarch appears uncompromising in his literal and emotional
interpretations of moral matters and in his excessive zeal to impose
his views on others. Joinville goes so far as to illustrate that the
consequences of such zeal sometimes had an opposite effect to that
intended.

Unlike the hagiographic exempla of his introductory section,
these anecdotes deal with actions not words. These actions affect
others with their consequences. By word, Louis' religious prud'homie
stands superior to Joinville's feudal prud'homie. But by deed

it leaves something to be desired. That something appears in the seneschal's steadfast feudal chivalry.

It is as if the monarch's stern ideals did not take account of needs in specific situations. Perhaps Louis found it difficult to see the implications of human motives at work in others when he had long controlled them within himself.

Joinville recalls that the king hears that his brother, the Count of Anjou, is playing at dice while on board their ship from Damietta to Acre. Louis reacts immediately with fury. He goes to the game and seizes the dice, throwing them into the sea:

> Et il ala là touz chancelans pour la flebesce de sa
> maladie; et prist les dez et les tables et les gata
> en la mer; et se courouça mout fort à son frere de
> ce que il s'estoit si tost pris à jouer aus deiz. [81]

The scene connotes Christ overturning the moneychangers' tables in the temple. Joinville shows, however, that while the king rages with indignance against his brother's gambling, thievery is committed. A shrewd observer of the emotional scene makes off with all the money:

> Mais mes sires Gautiers en fu li miex paiez; car il
> gata touz les deniers qui estoient sus le tablier
> (dont il y avoit grant foison) en son geron, et les
> emporta. [82]

The monarch's immoderate anger leads to a sin worse than dicing.

Another time, Joinville makes a joke about Louis' anger. Temper was apparently easily identifiable with Louis' personality. At Caesarea, the monarch asks the seneschal if he wishes to renew his royal contract for one more year. Joinville makes a bold request. He says he would prefer the king's abstinence from anger to more money. The knight asks for the monarch's promise to reply moderately and peaceably to his requests throughout the coming contract year:

> Et je li dis que je ne vouloie que il me donnast plus de
> ses deniers que ce que il m'avoit donnei; mais je
> vouloie faire un autre marchié à li: 'Pour ce, fis-je
> que vous vous courrouciés quant l'on vous requiert
> aucune chose, si vueil-je que vous m'aiés couvenant,

> que se je vous requier aucune chose toute ceste année,
> que vous ne vous courrouciés pas; et se vous me
> refusés, je ne me courroucerai pas.'[83]

Louis receives the critical query with grace and humility. Joinville recounts how he laughs "mout clerement". Later, the king related the incident to the legate and members of his Council as a humourous instruction. By finding the chinks in Louis' armour and daring to confront him with them, Joinville reveals a more human king but also a more humble one. In reverse to the earlier exempla of his court scenes, it is now Joinville who is the teacher.

The seneschal's realism chafes the sacred event of death itself. While at Sayette, Louis receives word of his mother's death. This was the mother who had exercised so much influence over Louis' early formation and even his adult life. The king goes into deep mourning for two entire days of silence. Then he calls Joinville to him. When Joinville enters the royal chamber, Louis holds out his arms to his companion and says with a moan: "A! seneschaus, j'ai pardue ma mère." Joinville, the courtly stoic, is not impressed. He is not even sympathetic. Rather than consoling his lord, he takes a firm line with him and chides him for his excessive emotional demeanour. This is not fitting for a wise man, says he. Moreover, do you wish to give heart to your enemies by showing your suffering?

> 'Sire, me ne m'en merveil pas, fis-je me merveil
> que vous, qui estes uns saiges hom, avez menei si
> grant duel; car vous savez que li Saiges dit, que
> mesaise que li om ait ou cuer, ne le doit parer ou
> visaige; car cil qui le fist, en fait liez ses
> ennemis et en mesaise ses amis.[84]

Once more, Joinville is the antidote to royal passion. Once more, he is the sane counterpart to this holy private man.

Joinville advises Louis to listen to the wise words of the Bible and hide his grief so that he will not discomfort his friends and delight his opponents. He recalls the king to stoic prud'homie. In this intimate spatial setting, Joinville has virtually switched roles with the earlier monarch of his introduction who taught the seneschal good lessons.

In Joinville's later Crusade tale, the king needs him. He needs the seneschal as more than a knight, a vassal or a companion. The king needs Joinville as a counselling friend. In this expression of need, Louis becomes a whole person with limitations, emotions, blind spots, and excesses. But it is the test of his sincerity, that Louis can receive from Joinville what he also gives him: good advice. This moral partnership was the beginning of their bond and it is the centre of its continuity. As Joinville was vulnerable to the superiority of Louis' ideals in the <u>exempla</u>, now Louis is vulnerable to the fortés of Joinville's practical wisdom. Within their very human dialogue at times of death, familial argument and serious making of contracts, the two men acquire internal depth, personality development and separate identities. Their medieval cast is transformed into new cultural forms of portraiture.

c) Perfect King of Justice?

Joinville dares to point out certain failings in the traditional function of the king as a judge. Once again, Joinville's chivalrous order of feudal values and social charity demonstrates the limits of Louis' royal justice.

While the king awaits the release from the Saracens of his brother, Count of Poitiers, a well-dressed Moslem visits him. He arrives before the monarch with a present. The king learns that this complimentary visitor is a fallen Christian who has converted to the Moslem religion. Without further ado, Louis expels his guest from his presence with the uncompromising words: "'Alez-vous-en, que à vous ne parlerai-je plus.'"[85] The king was not known for his tolerance in the best of circumstances but for heretics, Jews and fallen Christians, he reserved his undying disdain. His response was, within his time, the conventional response of strict Christians to those people considered worse than heretics: converts away from Christendom.

By his behaviour, Joinville indirectly questions Louis' curt dismissal. As the man hurriedly departs from the royal chambers, Joinville entertains a polite and curious conversation with him. He asks the Saracen what occasion brought him to this present condition. He learns from the Moslem that he has originally come to Outremer from his native Provence. He had arrived in the Holy Land with King John and married in Egypt where he became a rich Moslem.

The seneschal goes further. He attempts to convert the man back to the Christian religion. He asks him: "'Ne savez-vous pas bien que se vous mouriés en ce point, que vous seriez damnez et iriez en enfer?'"[86] The Saracen from Provence replies that he knows well that he could go to hell and suffer when he dies. However, he does not want to return to France now for fear of certain reproach and poverty. Joinville warns the Saracen convert that the Day of Judgment will be far worse for him than reproach or poverty if he does not repent. They exchange "mout de bones paroles... qui gueres ne valurent."

In the end, the two men part. However, the comparison to the king is that Joinville has taken the same kind of time and effort with a retrograde convert to Mohammed that the king would take with Joinville himself. The seneschal has played a different role than the king. He has tried to convert him to Christ, while the king has dismissed him outright. Joinville appears as the one who will go the extra mile in the ways of social charity, a charity which exceeds justice.

The seneschal openly reproaches some formal judgments of Louis at Caesarea. While in this city, one of the monarch's knights is found in a brothel. Louis orders the knight to forfeit his horse and arms to the king and quit the camp for good. When Joinville requests Louis to give the horse to another poor knight, the king refuses because the horse is worth too much. The seneschal reminds Louis of his pact to treat Joinville without anger:

> Et je li respondi: 'Comment m'avés-vous les couvenances rompues, quant vous vous couruociés de ce que vous ai requis?' Et il me dist tout en riant: 'Dites quant que vous vourrez, je ne me courouce pas.'[87]

The king laughs at Joinville's reminder of their contract and his weakness. However, Joinville has to admit he does not win the horse for the poor knight. The monarch's justice rules over his charity.

However, Joinville's chivalrous intentions of generosity compare favourably to the king's unyielding strictness.

On another occasion, Joinville forces a judgment from the recalcitrant monarch. A royal man-at-arms had laid hands on one of Joinville's knights from Champagne. The king believes the incident is too small to concern him. Louis' lack of attention to concrete matters of concern to others seemed to be one of his weaknesses. However, Joinville does not let the king get away with his indifference to the incident. He poises his moral strength against that of the king.

Joinville threatens to leave the services of the king if Louis does not do something. This threat convinces the king. Louis then requires his man-at-arms to kneel before Joinville's knight and apologize. The royal man-at-arms is required to say to the Champenois knight that he can wound him with the sword he presents to him if he so desires:

> 'Sire, je vous ament ce que je mis main à vous;
> et vous ai aportée ceste espée pour ce que vous
> me copez le poing, se il vous plait.' [88]

The seneschal wins a point for Champagne in this interchange and forces the king to declare himself. His honour is intact and he is victorious over the monarch's indifference to matters of knightly honour. This anecdote must have been fully appreciated by his Champenois peers upon his return from Outremer. Joinville's firm defense of his principles in the name of knightly chivalry is convincing as is his testing of the king's need of his services.

In these three tales, Jean de Joinville pits his knightly sense of honour against the monarch's high role as judge above the aristocracy. He dares to call the royal justice into question when it comes to knightly codes of chivalry to fellow aristocrats, even fallen ones.

CONCLUSION

Joinville's eye-witness account of King Louis IX's words and deeds illustrates a cultural transition in French royal historiography. In his introductory section on the holy king's words and during his report of Louis' heroic deeds on the Egyptian Crusade campaign, the seneschal depicts King Louis in traditional collective images of the monarch, saint and Crusader. Like a translucent Gothic king of stained-glass or a tapestried monarch in allegorical cartoons, Louis is identified with ritual roles, objects, events and people. However, within the bond of conscience which cements Louis' and Joinville's alliance during their last four years in the Holy Land, a growing interchange develops between the knight's autobiography and the royal biography. This shapes personal features in the king's portrait. With their increasing closeness in unfamiliar circumstances, through the comparative background of their respective familial and geographical traditions of Joinville's Champenois feudal prud'homie and Louis' Parisian religious prud'homie, the seneschal relates a developing dialogue between two internal human beings. In this more intimate setting, Louis emerges from the public king of collective rituals to a private person with individual emotions, thoughts, beliefs and humour. This personal dimension of Joinville's later Crusade tale creates an illusion of depth and solidity in the king's portrayal approaching late medieval historiography and three-dimensional painting of sunlight and shadow.

CHAPTER THREE
NOTES

[1] R. Fawtier, The Capetian Kings of France, tr. L. Butler and R.J. Adam (London, 1964), p. 4-5.

[2] M. Bloch, La France sous les derniers Capétiens, 1223-1328 (Paris, 1958), p. 123.

[3] Consult F. P. Pickering, Literature & Art in the Middle Ages. (London, 1970), for selected studies on the relation of medieval art, architecture, drama and literature.

[4] Just as Dante nowhere supplies a physical description of Beatrice's features, this is very medieval. See H. O. Taylor, The Mediaeval Mind. (London: 1938), passim.

[5] Henri François Delaborde, Jean de Joinville et les seigneurs de Joinville suivi d'un catalogue de leurs actes (Paris, MDCCCXCIV), no. 341.

[6] HSL 3.19, p. 10. Also see: HSL 1.2, p. 4. This parallels the words of kings collected as exempla in the late thirteenth century by Etienne Bourbon: J.T. Welter, La Tabula Exemplorum (Paris, 1926), pp. 38-39.

[7] HSL 3.19, p. 10; HSL 1.2, p. 4.

[8] We get some idea of the Champagne courtly circles as a centre for oral tradition and chivalrous literature in Les Chansons de Thibaut de Champagne, roi de Navarre, ed. A. Wallenskold (Paris: 1925) and Les Oeuvres de Guiot de Provins, poète lyrique et satirique, ed. J. Orr (Manchester, 1915). The court of Champagne was more influenced in its literary style by the Norman-Angevin traditions of England than by the French royal court.

[9] For the literary traditions of the court of Champagne see the study of M.J.F. Benton, "The Court of Champagne as a Literary Center", Speculum, t. XXXVI (1961), pp. 551-591.

[10] For all that concerns the history of the house of Blois-Champagne see d'Arbois de Jubainville, Histoire des ducs et comtes de Champagne (Paris, 1869-1871). As Bezzola points out, feudal literature such as the chansons de geste did not find its centre at the French royal court but rather in the châteaux of the great barons. It was the clergy who

created the genealogical ideals of official kingship which protected the Church with the consent of the great vassals. See R.R. Bezzola, Les Origines et la formation de la littérature courtoise en occident (Paris, 1963), p. 349. The dynastic ecclesiastical image of a Capetian king is well-represented in Suger's Vita Ludovici VI, and is renewed with the ethical ideals of Carolingian heritage by Guillaume le Breton's De Gesta Philippi Augusti Francorum regis.

[11] For early general works on chivalry see: L. Gautier, La chevalerie (Paris, 1891); E. Prestage, Chivalry (New York, 1928). For more recent treatment of the subject see: R. Barber, The Knight and Chivalry (London, 1970); N. Denholm-Young, "Feudal society in the thirteenth century: the knights", History, v. XXIX (1944), pp. 107-119; G. Duby, "Une enquête à poursuivre: la noblesse dans la France médiévale", Revue historique, t. CCXXVI (1961), pp. 1-22; F.B. Ganshof, "Qu'est-ce que la chevalerie?" Revue générale belge (1947), pp. 77-86; L. Genicot, "La noblesse dans la société médiévale", Le moyen âge, t. LXXI (1965), pp. 539-560; S. Painter, French Chivalry (Baltimore, 1940).

[12] Joinville's familiar descriptions of himself and the king reflect the modest rather than the brilliant courtly tastes of chivalry. In this way, his portraits correspond to the more prosaic chivalrous themes of Jehan et Blonde and Castelain de Couci, two late thirteenth century romans d'aventure. For an informative discussion of the evolution of chivalrous literary portraits see: Faith Lyons, Les Eléments descriptifs dans le roman d'aventure au XIIIe siècle (Genève, 1968).

[13] The use of a foil to a central character was not unprecedented in medieval literature. See for example, Barber's discussion of: 'Roland is fierce and Oliver is wise', in The Knight and Chivalry, ch. 3.

[14] Henri Van Lier, Les Arts et l'espace (Tournai, 1963), p. 27.

[15] Charles Maumené & L. d'Harcourt, Iconographie des rois de France (Paris, 1973), 1: p. 1.

[16] René Brécy, Portraits des rois et reines de France (Monaco, n.d.), p. 7. Also see: Edgar de Bruyne, Etudes d'Esthétique médiévale, III, Le XIIIe siècle (Brugge, 1946); H. Focillon, Moyen âge, survivances et réveils (Paris, 1943); Emile Male, L'Art religieux du XIIIe siècle en France (Paris, 1948); Guy de Tervarent, Les Enigmes de l'Art du moyen âge (Paris, MCMXLI).

[17] HSL 1.2, p. 4.
[18] HSL 5. 32, p. 18.
[19] F.C. Tubach, "Exemplum in Decline", Traditio, v. XVIII (1962), p. 415; Lecoy de la Marche, in La Chaire française au moyen âge (Paris, 1886), pp. 302-304 gives the classic definition of exempla in four categories: "Les exemples employés par nos sermonnaires sont de quatre sortes. Les uns sont extraits de l'histoire ou des légendes, particulièrement des historiens de l'antiquité, des chroniques de France, des vies de saints, des livres historiques de la Bible. D'autres sont pris dans les événements contemporains, les anecdotes du domaine publique ou les souvenirs de l'auteur... Les fables composent une troisième catégorie... Le dernier genre d'exemples consiste en descriptions ou en moralités tirées de ces signuliers bestiaires si communs au moyen âge." Joinville's anecdotes in the opening section would fall into the second category of exemplum. Also see Baudoin de Gaiffier, "Mentalité de l'hagiographe médiéval d'après quelques travaux récents", Analecta Bollandiana, v. 86 (1968), pp. 391-399.
[20] Alfred Foulet, "Notes sur la Vie de Saint Louis de Joinville", Romania 58 (1932), p. 553.
[21] HSL 6. 35, pp. 18-20.
[22] HSL 12.58, p. 34. Guillaume de Saint-Pathus, Vie, p. 142, records how Louis administered justice in person but it is only mentioned in general.
[23] Hallam, p. 205.
[24] HSL 12.58, p. 34.
[25] HSL 14.65, p. 39.
[26] Hallam, pp. 234-6.
[27] HSL 13.61, p. 36.
[28] HSL 11.54, p. 32. This was a traditional hagiographic form for representing King Louis, e.g. see: St. Pathus, Vie, p. 37; Beaulieu, Vita, p. 13 e, pp. 54-55.
[29] HSL 7. 39, p. 23.
[30] HSL 7. 39, pp. 23-5.
[31] HSL 8. 43, p. 24.
[32] HSL 4. 27, p. 14.

[33] HSL 4.29, p. 16.
[34] HSL 4.29, p. 16.
[35] HSL 5.32, p. 18.
[36] Labarge, p. 249.
[37] HSL 6.38, pp. 20-22.
[38] For a good discussion of the differences between Joinville's more feudal and social chivalry and Louis IX's religious and mendicant form see: Painter, French Chivalry, chapters on "Feudal Chivalry" and "Religious Chivalry". The moral of this anecdote, that the king took the side of the weaker against the stronger is mentioned in general by St.Pathus, Vie, 20: 78.
[39] HSL 3. 23, p. 12.
[40] HSL 5. 31 and 32. pp. 16-18.
[41] Kepes, The Language of Vision, p. 96.
[42] The king as a majestic spectacle was a favourite epic theme. Le voyage de Charlemagne à Jerusalem et à Constantinople, ed. Paul Aebischer, (Genève, 1965), p. 31, opens with the picture of Charlemage, crown on his head, sword at his side, in the midst of his noble lords at Saint-Denis.
[43] Henri François Delaborde, Jean de Joinville et les seigneurs de Joinville suivi d'un catalogue de leurs actes (Paris, MDCCCXCIV), no. 341.
[44] HSL 32.146, p. 82.
[45] HSL 35. 162, p. 88.
[46] HSL 47.229, p. 126.
[47] HSL 54. 267, pp. 146-148. Also see the earlier scene of the battle of Taillebourg, HSL 22. 101, p. 58.
[48] HSL 35. 165, p. 90.
[49] HSL 45. 214, p. 116.
[50] HSL 47. 229, p. 126.
[51] HSL 47, 231, p. 126.
[52] William Chester Jordan, Louis IX and the Challenge of the Crusade - A Study in Rulership (Princeton, 1979), p. 105.
[53] Jordan, p. 65.
[54] Richard Barber, The Knight and Chivalry,pp. 189-208.
[55] HSL 37. 172, p. 94.
[56] HSL 157, p. 86.

[57] HSL 34. 157, p. 86.

[58] HSL 34 158, pp. 86-88. A good summary on the importance in the growth of rivalry and individual prowess among knights during the thirteenth century may be found in L.T. White, Medieval Technology and Social Change (Oxford, 1965), pp. 31-33.

[59] The emphasis on individual glory was very strong in thirteenth century warfare. It had been the downfall of the Frankish troops in the East again and again. In 1250, at Mansourah, Robert d'Artois, the king's brother, nearly brought disaster to the entire army by disobeying specific instructions not to attack. See Barber, The Knight and Chivalry, pp. 189-208. HSL 37. 176, p. 96.

[60] HSL 50. 243, p. 134. Sidney Painter discusses how the decrease of noble economic, political and military power led to the chivalrous art of being courtier to kings and princes: French Chivalry, pp. 25-29. Joinville's self-portrait stands between the feudal chivalry of the "preudome" and the social chivalry of the courtier. Also see: HSL 25,112,p. 64.

[61] H. Focillon, Art d'Occident: le moyen âge roman et gothique (Paris, 1947), p. 236.

[62] Guillaume de Tyr's Historia rerum in partibus transmarinis gestarum, Patrologiae cursus completus, series latina, ed. Migne (Paris, 1849), v. 201, is a good example of the new expression of the ideal knight, a man of honesty and character shown in his immediate milieu, rather than imagined in a far-away world of ideals based on bravery, devotion to the church, his suzerain and piety. Guillaume de Tyr created his heroes and individualized them through their witnesses and their immediate ancestors, rather than through the traditions of Charlemagne and his sons. See R.R. Bezzola, Les Origines et la formation, v. 11, p. 485. It is in a similar manner than Joinville depicts himself in this cluster of images. The heroic biography played an important part in the cult of chivalry. For example, the biography of William Marshal, regent of England during Henry III's minority, was written largely at his dictation: L'histoire de Guillaume le Maréchal, comte de Striguil et de Pembroke, ed. Paul Meyer (Paris, 1891-1901.)

[63] HSL 75. 381, p. 208. Also see Labarge, p. 130.

[64] HSL 60. 411, p. 224.

[65] Joinville's statement that he and William of Beaumont were the only two knights from France who favour the stay in Palestine, appears to conflict with the king's report that the majority of barons were in favour of his staying. See Delaborde, Jean de Joinville, pp. 106-108 who suggests that Joinville's lone position may have been taken before the barons knew that the emirs had broken the treaty regarding the prisoners-of-war captured from the Christians after the Good Friday battle. Foulet thinks there need be no real contradiction: "Joinville et le conseil tenu à Acre en 1250", MLN 49 (1934), pp. 464-468.

[66] HSL 82. 420, p. 229.

[67] HSL 83. 427, p. 232.

[68] HSL 84. 430, p. 234.

[69] This motif of Joinville at the window begins to appear in chansons de geste, in which one person approaches another at a window. See Jean Rychner, La Chanson de geste (Genève, 1955), passim, and for specific examples see: Raoul de Cambrai, pub. P. Meyer and A. Longnon (Paris, 1882) v. 183; La Chanson de Guillaume, pub. Duncan McMillan, 2 vols.(Paris, 1949-50), v. 932; v. 1241.

[70] HSL 84. 433, p. 236. This relationship between the king and Joinville evolves from the new chivalry of the thirteenth century. Bezzola in Les Origines et la formation, t. 11, p. 366, describes this new development: "La littérature courtoise, où le lien de fidélité du vassal à son roi-empereur de la chanson de geste avait fait place à la réalisation individuelle d'un idéal chevaleresque et courtois, commun à un groupe d'hommes placés, pour ainsi dire, sur le même échelon, autour d'un roi plus symbolique que réel, était bien plus faits pour plaire à ses grands barons, toujours plus indépendants du pouvoir royal."

[71] HSL 83.433, p. 236.

[72] Joinville's self-portrait reflects the ideals of the knight developed in the late twelfth and early thirteenth centuries in the courts of Champagne. Except for the notions on courtly love, the De Amore of André le Chapelain composed at the Troyes court of Marie de Champagne describes the good customs of the knight in terms which correspond to those of Joinville. The good knight should: "Révérer son seigneur, ne blasphémer ni dieu ni les saints, être humble envers tous et

servir tout le monde, ne dire du mal de personne, parce que les médisants ne peuvent demeurer dans la demeure de courtoisie, ne pas louer les méchants, avec des mensonges, mais les corriger, si possible, par des admonitions secrètes et, s'ils ne s'améliorent pas, les exclure de sa compagnie. Le vrai amant ne doit se moquer de personne et surtout pas des misérables. Il doit éviter les querelles et tâcher de réconcilier les litigants... Qu'il fréquente les cours des grands. Qu'il joue aux dés avec modération, qu'il lise, étudie ou écoute, réciter les faits héroïques des anciens. Qu'il soit courageux dans la bataille, et contre les ennemis, hardi, intelligent, prudent et ingénieux... Qu'il veille à l'ornement de soin corps d'une façon modérée. Qu'il soit sage, aimables et doux envers tout le monde..."c.f. Drouart la Vache, traducteur d'André le Chapelain, li Livres d'amours, ed. R. Bossuat (Paris, 1926), p. 62.

[73] HSL 110. 565, p. 308.

[74] HSL 110. 565, p. 308.

[75] HSL 110. 565, pp. 308-310. G. Duby and R. Mandrou, in their Histoire de la Civilisation française (Paris, 1968), v. 1, pp. 170-173, discuss "l'esprit critique" which developed in the thirteenth century among all society castes. "Vue positive du monde, volonté de n'être pas dupe: Tous ces gens sont croyants sans la moindre fissure... mais à l'égard du monde ils ont gagné, progrès majeur, le sens de l'ironie. Tout ce qui est excessif est critiqué...", p. 170. While Joinville was not a man to mock, he did have this critical spirit for the excessive.

[76] HSL 115. 588, p. 322. G.G. Coulton, Five Centuries of Religion, 4 vols. (Cambridge, 1923-1950), v. 1, pp. 495-499, has an appendix on "Good and Bad Masses".

[77] HSL 116. 594, p. 326.

[78] HSL 116. 594, p. 326.

[79] HSL 122. 620, p. 340.

[80] HSL 122. 622, p. 340.

[81] HSL 79.405, p. 220.

[82] HSL 79.405, p. 220.

[83] HSL 98. 499-500, p. 274.

[84] HSL 119. 603, p. 330. This incident is remarked upon by Gustave Cohen, La vie littéraire en France au moyen âge (Paris, 1949), p. 194.

[85] HSL 77. 395, p. 216. The good feudal knight's courtesy extended even to non-Christians: see Freidrich Heer, The Medieval World: Europe, 110-1350 (Cleveland, 1962), pp. 148-152.

[86] HSL 119. 603, p. 330.

[87] HSL 99. 506, p. 278. As Count Geoffrey of Anjou says of some unkempt knightly prisoners: "If we are knights, we ought to pity knights." Historia Gaufredi ducis Normannorum et comitis Andegavorum, ed. Louis Halphen and René Poupardin (Paris, 1913), pp. 195-196.

[88] HSL 99. 510, p. 280. R.R. Bezzola in Les Origines et la formation, v. 2: p. 366, analyzes "la réalisation individuelle d'un idéal chevaleresque et courtois".

CHAPTER FOUR
THE KING IN JOINVILLE'S WRITTEN SOURCES

INTRODUCTION

The written sources of Joinville have not been fully clarified, nor has the manner in which he utilized his written sources and incorporated them into his work. Joinville seemed to use his written source material as a supplement to his primarily oral and visual sources.

It has been established with some accuracy that Joinville's major written source, as he describes it himself, was a "romant", that is to say, a book written in the French tongue.[1] This book has been identified by Natalis de Wailly in his 1874 edition of Joinville's work as the Vie de Saint Louis by Guillaume de Nangis. This was an official dynastic biography, compiled in Latin as the Vita Sancti Ludovici and translated into French. A compilation of various sources on Louis IX, this work formed part of the official chronicles on the French kings edited by the monks of Saint-Denis, a Benedictine monastery just outside Paris. Named after the abbey where they were housed, these chronicles were known as the Chroniques de Saint-Denys or Les Grandes Chroniques de France.[2] The abbey was considered a royal monastery with special links to the Merovingian kings. It was also the burial ground for many of the Capetian monarchs.

LATIN WORKS OF THE TWELFTH CENTURY

Historiography in the kingdom of France took on an official character in the twelfth century when a body of historical works composed in Latin were collected in the abbey of Saint-Denis. This collection was completed in 1250 under the direction of Mathieu de Vendome, abbot of Saint-Denis.[3] Preserved in the Latin MS. 5925 of the Bibliothèque Nationale, it contained the Historia Francorum of Aimon, the Gesta Dagoberti, the Annales of Lorsch, the Vita Hludovici by l'Astronome, Histoire des ducs de Normandie by G. de Jumièges, the Gesta Philippi II Augusti regis Francorum by Rigord and the Vita Ludovici VI Grossi sive Crassi regis Francorum by Suger.[4]

Latin historiography was accessible to only a fraction of the population, mostly clerks. The ordinary people with an interest in their history had at their disposal long poems, fiction mixed with fact, and the familial tales of their ancestors. The wars of Troy, the adventures of Aeneas, Wace's history of Brittany and Normandy, poems of the first Crusade, this formed the stuff of history in the vulgar tongue.[5]

During the thirteenth century, public curiousity about the Crusades provoked eye-witnesses such as Geoffroi de Villehardouin in l'Histoire de la Conquête de Constantinople and Robert de Clari, with his account of the same events, to dictate their memories into book-form. Oral and visual experience became an expanding basis for literary works in the French language. As we find in the life of Guillaume le Maréchal, verse-form was not entirely abandoned, but as we find in the chronicle by William of Tyr - prose grew increasingly popular. This movement of vulgarisation among the lettered public which included the laity, did not fail to touch the monks of Saint-Denis.

TRANSLATIONS BY THE MONKS

Towards 1260, a minstrel in the service of Alphonse de Poitiers translated into prose the Historia regum Francorum, sometimes taken mistakenly for the prototype of the Grandes Chroniques. What is probable, according to Robert Bossuat, is that the success of this translation encouraged the monks of Saint-Denis to undertake a work of the same nature.[6]

It was in 1274, four years after Louis XI's death, that Primat, a monk of Saint-Denis, completed the translation of these Latin chronicles up until 1223. In the same year, he presented the translated collection to Philippe III, Louis IX's son. Being familiar with the work of the ministrel of Rheims, Primat borrowed part of his preface from this composition.

A fruitful source for investigation of the political attitudes of the time, the Grandes Chroniques added what has come to be considered a telling innovation to the original text. There is a new stress on Capetian royal lineage contained in the prologue. In documenting the growth of Capetian dynasticism during the thirteenth century, Andrew Lewis utilizes this addition to buttress his argument. He maintains that it was in part to publicize the Capetian royal descent that the collection and translation were made.[7]

THE WORK OF GUILLAUME DE NANGIS

The success of this translation led the monks of Saint-Denis to continue the French collection. It was in the spirit of this continuation that the monk Guillaume de Nangis compiled the lives of Louis IX and Philippe III. In their first form, the Grandes Chroniques included a direct translation of Guillaume de Nangis' Latin biography of Louis. This can be found in the MS. fr. 2610, 2615 of the BN and MS. 16 G VI of the British Museum.

Later, however, for reasons we do not know, modifications were made to the French version of Guillaume de Nangis on Louis IX. Certain parts were developed while other sections were reduced. This revised French version is found in the MS. fr. 2813, 17270 of the BN and the MS of the Sainte Geneviève library.[8]

Little is known of Guillaume de Nangis. He was a monk of the abbey of Saint-Denis. He fulfilled the role of official historiographer of the crown and custos cartarum of the abbey in charge of the charters. He composed his work on Louis IX sometime before 1297, the year of Louis IX's canonisation. He dedicated the work to Philippe III and encouraged him to follow in the footsteps of his illustrious father. It is estimated that Guillaume de Nangis died between 1300 and 1302.[9]

GUILLAUME DE NANGIS AND THE GRANDES CHRONIQUES

The Grandes Chroniques have been described by Robert Fawtier as the work of churchmen "as interested in hagiography as in the story of the dynasty."[10] Guillaume de Nangis' biography of Louis IX was no exception to this tradition. The work from which Joinville borrowed his written sources was both a biography of a secular ruler and a hagiography of a saint. Both literary genres had established medieval traditions.

The mentor of Christian biographers of secular rulers was Suetonius. His use of vivid detail to illustrate the character of a ruler set a pattern in medieval biography.[11] Einhard in his Vita Karoli, Thegan in his Vita Hleudovici Imperatoris, the monk of Caen in his sketch of William of Conqueror, and William of Malmesbury in his portraits of

English kings utilized Suetonius as an exemplar for their works. Medieval chroniclers rarely achieved physical descriptions of their heroes without the authoritative words of a prototype. Suetonius' historical work on the twelve Caesars provided a suitable model. Two other models also utilized were: Eusebius' portrait of Constantine and Sidonius Apollinaris' description of the Gothic king: Theodoric II. Medieval monarchs were described by their biographers in terms which linked them to the lofty political lineages of the past.

While Suetonius was the literary authority for many medieval lives of rulers, Sulpicius Severus was the model for lives of saints. His The Life of St. Martin of Tours was known to almost every medieval hagiographer.[12] Southern calls this type of ecclesiastical biography heroic, displaying "an overwhelming concern with the impact of the supernatural power on the natural world."[13] The example of Severus sometimes inspired lives in which the human element scarcely entered, like the eleventh century Lives of the Welsh saint, full of miraculous folklore. The conversation was usually visionary and sometimes, as in the Life of St. Wilfred, it did not even offer a clue to the personality of the saint.

A new style of hagiography was developed at Cluny. It subordinated the display of supernatural powers to activity directed to a practical end. In the Life of Saint Odo for example, exorcisms and miracles were replaced by virtues associated with the spiritual and temporal prosperity of Benedictine monasticism, such as the reconciling of kings, pacifying of churches, care of the poor, the young and the aged. These commemorative hagiographies were more concerned with action than with thought or speech.[14] Guillaume de Nangis' life of Louis XI fell into this line of hagiography.

Compiled in a comprehensive style similar to the contemporary summa form of Vincent de Beauvais and Thomas Aquinas, Guillaume de Nangis' biography of King Louis constituted a public defense of the monarch as saint and sovereign. On the monarch, the custos cartarum brought forth civil, legal, political and military facts. On the saint, he assembled those deeds which brought temporal and spiritual well-being to the poor, the royal entourage and the Church.

Guillaume de Nangis elaborated a new <u>genre</u> within these traditions of historiography. He was one of the first medieval royalist biographers to produce history as a <u>speculum</u> in order to furnish examples to the new king to live from his family's past.[15] In dedicating his work to Philippe III, he wanted the monarch to keep the praiseworthy deeds of his father before his eyes like a mirror for a model of virtue.

His life on Louis IX reflects the association of at least two major medieval traditions on the monarchy: royal legitimacy through bloodright from ancestor to heir, father to son; and royal legitimacy through worthiness or sanctity. Whereas Lewis interprets the latter as a succession within the office which attributed some of the sacred aspects of the kingship to the entire line, he interprets the former as a succession within the family.[16] Contradictory as the two notions were according to Herbert Rowen, many royalist texts of the thirteenth century suggest that the conceptual distinctions were not made.[17] In the work of Guillaume de Nangis, we see the two notions fused.

HOW HE WROTE HIS LIFE OF THE KING

Guillaume de Nangis' work on King Louis is a collection of diverse texts which he gathered together and arranged in chronological order. The assemblage touches on the public, civil, legal, political and military aspects of the reign as well as on the private and pious side of the king. Thanks to the recent edition of the <u>Grandes Chroniques</u> by Jules Viard (1930-1937), we know something of the major source-material of Guillaume de Nangis.

The beginning of his work is a likely copy of the unfinished biography by Gilon de Rheims, a fellow-monk from Saint-Denis. Following this are direct selections from his major source: Geoffroi de Beaulieu's <u>Vita et Sancta Conversatio Piae Memoriae Ludovici Regis</u>. Vincent de Beauvais was likely Nangis' principal source for the king's first Crusade. Primat, another Saint-Denis monk originally considered a mere translator, was his source for the end of the reign. Nangis also used letters, diplomatic documents, the <u>Chronicon Ecclesiae Sancti Dyonsisii ad Cyclos Paschales</u>, the <u>Chronicon Pontificum et Imperatorum</u> and the <u>Chronicon ab Initio Mundi Usque ad Annum</u>.[18]

THE USE OF GEOFFROI DE BEAULIEU'S HAGIOGRAPHY

The majority of Nangis' texts on the saint came from the work of Geoffroi de Beaulieu, Louis IX's Dominican confessor.[19] The Dominican had composed a hagiographic eulogy on Louis in 1272, two years after the monarch's death, at the request of Pope Gregory X. The request was made as an initial step in Louis IX's canonization process. Its material was directed towards the requirements for the canonic procedure.

During the eleventh and twelfth centuries a tendency had developed to refer most canonizations to the Pope who could consult synods of various kinds for his decision. By 1234 after the two lawyer Popes, Alexander III and Innocent III, the canonization procedure had grown clearer and more regular. By the time of Beaulieu's hagiography, the criteria for sanctity had been quite firmly established.

In canonizing St. Homobonus in 1199, Innocent III had said that although the grace of final perseverance alone was required for sanctity in the Church triumphant, proof of the virtue of morals and the virtue of signs must be demonstrated for sanctity in the Church militant.[20] Geoffroi de Beaulieu presented canonic evidence on Louis' virtue of morals and virtue of signs. He disregarded his political and military accomplishments and emphasized Louis IX's private and pious life. Louis IX is compared to the Old Testament king, Josias. Beaulieu used the ancient form of _exempla_, illustrative apologues for moral edification first used in the Christian tradition by Gregory the Great in his _Dialogorum_ written before 604 A.D. In Beaulieu's _exempla_, Louis IX appears as an accomplished saint of heroic virtue.

WHAT WRITINGS JOINVILLE BORROWED

The traditions and origins of Joinville's borrowed writings are illuminating. It is likely that when the seneschal added this official supplement to his work, he was aware of their impeccable credentials in royalist and church circles.

Of the fifteen chapters in his concluding section, seven were borrowed at least in part from Guillaume de Nangis. The subject matter of four more chapters was probably suggested by Nangis' work. These chapters were augmented with anecdotes from Joinville's personal experience.[21] Only four of the fifteen chapters were direct accounts of the king's life from Joinville's eye-witness.

It is estimated that when the seneschal added these written sources to his work, he was nearly eighty years old. After his Crusading experience with the king, Joinville had not had many opportunities to frequent royal company. The Saint-Denis chronicles supplied credible evidence on Louis' life after the first Crusade. This evidence was blessed by the very crown the courtly knight hoped to address in the person of its young and future king, Louis le Hutin. In 1305-1306, this evidence would have gained in prestige.

With scholarly acumen, Natalis de Wailly has analyzed the chapters in Joinville's life of King Louis which were either borrowed from or inspired by Guillaume de Nangis' compilation.[22] In fact, he has also traced most of these borrowings to their original sources. These findings may be enumerated as follows:

Ch. CXXXVIII: De Wailly establishes a direct link between this chapter and an anecdote in Guillaume de Nangis[23] taken from Geoffroi de Beaulieu.[24] It relates how the king, upon his return from Crusade, branded the lips and nose of a blasphemous Parisian bourgeois. The monarch's works: "Je vourroie estre seigniez d'un fer chaut, par tel couvenant que tuit vilein sairement fussent ostei de moy royaume", corresponds exactly to the words in Nangis.

Ch. CXXIX: The end of this chapter in Joinville concerning the collation of benefices is a textual passage from Nangis,[25] also found in Beaulieu.[26]

Ch. CXL: This chapter comes entirely from Nangis.[27] Its elements are also found in many other compilations of the time, notably the collection of the Trésor des Chartes. The chapter is a direct quote from the ordonnances concerning the correction of the king's new system of administrators: the baillis, prevôts and maieurs.

Ch. CXLII: This chapter corresponds completely to that in Nangis[28] who took it from Geoffroi de Beaulieu.[29] It treats the king's generosity to the poor and the monasteries of the French kingdom.

Ch. CXLV: The text of this chapter deals with the Enseignements de Saint Louis à son fils, Philippe le Hardi. This also is found in Nangis[30] and was probably translated from the Latin version of Geoffroi de

Beaulieu.[31]

Ch. CXLVI: In reporting details which the comte d'Alencon had told him of the king's death at Tunis, Joinville introduces and concludes with passages from Nangis,[32] who in turn had borrowed them from Beaulieu[33]

Two more chapters which Natalis de Wailly (presumably using the earliest MSS. 2610, 2615 BN) cannot match to the original text of Guillaume de Nangis, correspond exactly with the modified text of Nangis in the Viard edition of the Grandes Chroniques. Natalis de Wailly attributes these two chapters to a manuscript of the Chronique de Saint-Denis: MS. 2813 of the BN which reproduces the later manuscript of the bibliothèque Sainte-Geneviève.[34] These two chapters are:

Ch. CXLI: This chapter concerns the prevosté de Paris and Etienne de Boileau. It matches Ch. LXXIII "de la prevosté de Paris" in Nangis (Viard edition) except for the last sentence which comes from another part of Nangis.[35]

Ch. CXLIII: This chapter treats the religious orders in France and completely corresponds to Ch. LXXX of Nangis (Viard edition): "comment le roy fist plusseurs religions."[36]

The original source of these two chapters in Joinville is not clear. However, because of their complete correlation with the content of the revised and modified text of Nangis appearing in the Viard edition, we can tentatively conclude that Joinville had recourse to the official modified manuscript of Nangis in the Grandes Chroniques (MSS. 2813, 17270 BN). This manuscript was likely retouched by a clerk in the service of Philippe III.

NANGIS AS A SUPPLEMENT TO JOINVILLE

De Wailly sees these borrowed chapters at the end of Joinville's work on Louis IX as supplements to the author's personal testimony. For medieval and Renaissance writers of history, the authority of the eyewitness carried more weight than written documents, the touchstone of modern research. Intimacy with events, not objective distance from them was the medieval historian's best qualification.

As a spectator and listener, Joinville observed and participated in the life of his subject King Louis. Within the mentality of his age, this testimony carried his personal guarantee of credibility and was related to his reputation, his knowledgeability and his key participation in the events he described. Joinville considered that his own eye-witness and oral reports were his responsibility. De Wailly shows that the seneschal wished to make this distinction clear to his audience:

> Après les avoir signalès, je dois faire observer qu'il ne faut pas y voir des interpolations, mais un supplément qu'il a voulu faire ajouter à ses propres récites, et qui mérite à tous égards la confiance de lecteur, quoique Joinville en décline la responsabilité. La phrase où il a voulu exprimer cette réserve (768) est omise dans le manuscrit de Bruxelles, et probablement altérée dans les deux autres; mais la pensée de l'auteur était certainement d'etablir une distinction entre les faits qu'il garantissait personnellement comme les ayant vus ou entendus, et ceux qui étaient écrits dans son livre d'après une chronique française où il les avait simplement lus et empruntés...[37]

On the one hand, Joinville maintained that his written source merited the confidence of his reader but on the other hand, he declined direct responsibility for the material.

We agree with de Wailly that these texts were supplementary to Joinville's personal record. It seems fairly evident that in using Guillaume de Nangis, Joinville had recourse to an official document which supported the genealogy of the Capetian kingship and was recognized in the court circles to which Joinville was addressing himself.

THE COMPLEMENTARY PERSPECTIVE OF NANGIS

The perspective within which Nangis recorded the deeds and words of Louis IX was quite distinct from that of the rest of Joinville's book. Guillaume de Nangis recorded information on the king within established norms of an ecclesiastical institution beyond the temporal domain of France. Secondly, he compiled information on the king which illustrated his new administrative powers and moral sovereignty beyond the royal domain into all his kingdom. As such, Louis IX appears as a public and sacred cult. He is presented beyond the feudal ties and aristocratic perspective of Jean de Joinville.

These borrowed texts were complementary to Joinville's memories. While Joinville had shared the king's first Crusade with him, the occasions to participate in his administrative reforms and pious works after this Crusade were fairly infrequent. The texts taken from Nangis' compilation covered the time period following the Crusade. While Joinville's king fulfills the ideals of a knight's religious chivalry as a prud'homme, Nangis' monarch fulfills a monk's ideals of the religious life as a saint worthy of canonization. While Joinville's monarch is a feudal Crusader, Nangis' king is a superior administrator of a royal line worthy of exaltation. In the main body of Joinville's work, King Louis is represented in the visual and oral traditions of a knight's king. In the closing sections, Louis IX appears within the written traditions of a churchman's monarch.

Although Joinville selected certain passages which either blended with or compensated for his own view of the king as knight and Crusader, the over-all picture of the king in the written sources is more in keeping with a monk's ideals which were closely related not only to pious traditions of the religious life but to state traditions of a dynasty.[38] Guillaume de Nangis represents the king within the whole of his kingdom: whereas Joinville pictures the king within the feudal and courtly milieux. In the written sources, Louis is a royal saint of a dynastic lineage and a monarch who extracted the last iota of his royal rights.[39]

All the subjects treated in Joinville's written sources are of a binding or conventional nature: ordinances, traditional precepts and stylized hagiographic deeds. This is in contrast, on the one hand, with the royal-knightly tension of his visual sources and on the other, with the popular qualities of his oral sources. The written sources provide legally sanctioned evidence which exalt the king and the royal line. Joinville is no longer a participant in the king of his written sources.

In Joinville's oral king, we hear of the myths of kingship which were popular in knightly and Crusading circles. In Joinville's visual monarch, we see the king who belonged to his knights' rivalries, search for glory, courtly honour and feudal protection; a king whose hereditary character was tinged with divine motifs. In both these cases, Louis is presented within a relationship to Joinville and his functions. In both these cases, Joinville describes different layers of perception within his own milieu and from within his milieu's mentality.

By way of complementary contrast, Joinville's king in the written sources is further from the mouths of his lay-knights and people. He is a monarch of institutions: administrative and financial structures, religious orders and ecclesiastical courts. In his private life, Louis is depicted as a crowned monk, the monarch which the church traditionally sought.[40] In his public life, Louis appears as a ruler who strictly fulfills the written laws of his lineage and office.[41]

Joinville's written sources present a picture of documented dynastic and historical continuity in this king. This documentation is proof that Louis IX is beyond the heritage of Champagne knights. Informally, Joinville's book was a product of the Champagne nobility and their traditions, the result of a knight on Crusade with a king. In this sense, the book represented this world and addressed it. However, from a formal and official perspective, Joinville's book was destined for the royal court of Paris. The Grandes-Chroniques gave an official stamp of approval to his knightly testimony.

In utilizing the Grandes Chroniques, Joinville appealed to documentation which surpassed knightly and even baronial testimony to the king's dynastic superiority. The count of Champagne could trace his descent from Charlemagne. The king of France could only trace the Capetian family tree to Robert the Strong.[42] While Joinville's oral and eye-witness sources carried more weight than his written sources, his written sources proved something which no feudal knight's testimony could. Joinville's written sources proved that this monarch surpassed all feudal rivals, even those with superior genealogy. In Joinville's written sources, Louis IX is a ruler of a dynasty which produced a saint of superior merit and a monarch of superior prerogatives.

THE OFFICIAL SAINT

In Royal Succession in Capetian France: Studies on Familial Order and the State, Andrew Lewis documents the claim that royal sanctity was an element in the growth of Capetian dynasticism. He shows that "in a series of texts beginning in the last third of the twelfth century, terms indicating holiness were used as attributes of royalty."[43] The earliest certain reference to holiness in connection with Capetian royalty is the poem on the birth of King Philippe Augustus as "gaudia regia, plena deo." During the regency of Queen Blanche, Louis IX's mother, another epithet considers Louis and his brothers sure to be good because they come from "saint liu" or "pious loins":

> De biaus enfans i a, Dex les escroisse en bien!
> De saint liu sont venu, assés feront de bien
> Por le père est li fius qui a nom Looys...[44]

Such epithets imply that at least some writers in royalist circles believed that virtue was inherited by birth into the royal line.

Birth into an aristocratic house was associated with the monarchical ideal to produce a composite image of piety surrounding members of the Capetian dynastic monarchy. This mentality informing members of royal circles assumed a more developed yet eclectic form during the thirteenth century. Lewis estimates that it is probable that distinctions between succession within an aristocratic family and succession within a royal office were not clearly drawn. "In any case, partially under the stimulus of dynasticism, the two basic models of legitimacy - the blood-right and worthiness of sanctity - were brought into close association, and sometimes fused, in royalist circles before the end of the thirteenth century."[45]

When Louis IX's brother, Charles of Anjou testified in favour of Louis' canonization in 1280, he surrounds the Capetian lineage with an aura of holiness. He says that the "holy root put forth holy branches." These holy branches include not only the "holy king" but the Count of Artois who had died a glorious martyr and Alfonse of Poitiers who had died of the plague before Tunis.[46]

It is also important for an understanding of the mentality surrounding Joinville's written sources to point out the development of papal support for Capetian virtue. Explicit support can first be found in 1121 when Pope Calixtus II praised the reverence and obedience of the Capetians to the Roman Church. The French monarchs were said to pass on this devotion to their descendants "by a kind of hereditary right." [47] Lewis shows that comparable buttressing of Capetian virtue is found in letters from French bishops. By the time of Louis IX's succession to the throne, a large body of church literature supported the Capetian king as an hereditary and legitimate source of "aid and favour" to the Church.

Another related but distinct source of support for the notion of the holy Capetian monarchs can be found in royal historiography. As Fawtier shows, almost all these writers are churchmen up until the time of Joinville. As a result of this limitation, these authors came from outside the charmed circle of the nobility, the only caste which could criticize the king. The historiographical literature is largely filled with eulogy.[48] Louis IX's grandfather, Philippe Augustus had been called "Catholic in faith", "defender of the church", and "nourisher of the poor" by his most balanced chronicler of Tours. Its author, Payen Gâtineau, a canon of Tours had to admit that Philippe also loved wine, women and money but agreed with Philippe's standard eulogists, Rigord and William the Breton that this Capetian represented the major virtues of the monarchy.[49] Called 'Dieudonné' at his birth in 1165, he became known as 'Augustus' because he augmented the territorial domain of the Capetian monarchy. The French king's resounding victory over the count of Flanders and Otto of Brunswick at Bouvines on 27 July, 1214, was interpreted as God's sign of support for the monarchy: "thus by the victory which God had given, the Capetian monarchy found itself... truly consecrated."[50]

The historiographical tradition of seeing the monarch in a special relationship to God, anointed with oil at his coronation, protected by an intervening God of battle and equipped to cure the scrofula disease in his subjects was a fairly well-established heritage by the thirteenth century. This tradition attained a new height in the early part of the century when the dead king is depicted as either a saint or a man of signal piety.[51] For example, Vincent of Beauvais writing in the thirteenth century praised Louis VIII as "indubitably Catholic and of marvellous sanctity."[52] This is specifically new in its emphasis although it grows out of previous tradition. Vincent was a Dominican royal librarian and chaplain and had taught theology to the monks at Royaumont. His great *Speculum* was the best known encyclopaedia of the period. The accretion of extraordinary religious qualities to the Capetian kings is an important part of thirteenth century clerical perceptions of the monarchy.[53] These mingled with chivalric lay aristocratic ideals to create a community of values.

These three strands of tradition: epithets, Papal support and clerical historiography form part of the background within which Louis IX's proposed sanctity contained in Joinville's written sources can be understood. While the king's specific asceticism was his own achievement, he strove for sanctity and was perceived as saintly within a specific collective mentality. According to Lewis and his authoritative work, the proclamations of Capetian holiness which grew explicit during the thirteenth century were not empty eulogies but serious proofs offered for the legitimacy of a dynasty.[54]

a) King of the Poor and the Suffering

In Joinville's borrowed passages, King Louis is proven to be a Christian monarch who protected the poor and the suffering brethren of the Church. Guillaume de Nangis speaks glowingly of the number of poor the king fed at his own table, but this was an accepted obligation of the rich in the Middle Ages and those who failed to fulfill this duty were severely criticized by the preaching friars of the day. However, Louis put special effort into this duty and frequently fed the poor and served them himself with a dedication which surpassed his contemporaries.

> En quaresme et es auvens croissoit li nombres des
> povres; et plusours foiz avint que li roys les
> servoit, et lour metoit la viande devant aus, et
> lour trenchoit la viande devant aus, et lour donnoit
> au departir, de sa propre main, des deniers. [55]

By the multiplication of his good acts and the number of his deeds to a wide variety of people, Louis' generosity is carefully proven. His charity is extended to poor religious orders, hospitals, sick, colleges, prostitutes, widows, pregnant women and the elderly. The text claims that so many people felt the effects of his good charity "que à peinne porroit l'on raconter le nombre." [56]

This text which Guillaume de Nangis took in entirety from the
Dominican Geoffroi de Beaulieu, depicts King Louis as his confessor
wished to present him to Pope Gregory X in 1272 for the canonization
process. The Dominican composed a panegyric on Louis, comparing him to
the Old Testament King Josias, and to the Roman Emperor Titus. These
two models indicate the mentality of the friar's perceptions: this king
was as pious as a monarch of the Chosen People and as powerful as an
Emperor of Rome. Joinville's king was never so solemn nor so sovereign.
In these written sources, the human struggle of a king in relationship
to his peers and traditions is remarkably absent.

b) King of Religious Orders

In this same text from Geoffroi de Beaulieu, we glimpse the king
who lent his considerable benevolence to religious foundations and
orders. "Il commença à edefier moustiers et plusours maisons de religion,
entre lesquiex l'abbaye de Royaumont porte l'onnour et la hautesce."[57]
The passage enumerates the great number of religious institutions which
received his generosity: Pontoise, Compiegnes, Vernon, Abbey of le Lys,
Maubisson near Pontoise, a hospital and chapel for the blind near Paris,
the Vauvert monastery outside Paris, the hostel of the Daughters of God
and several houses of Béguines, women devoted to a life of chastity.

Beaulieu's illustration also demonstrates that Louis' generosity
to religious orders caused criticism from those who reproached his
priorities. However, the king responded with: "Je aim miex que li
outraiges de grans despens que je faiz, soit fais en aumosne pour l'amour
de Dieu, que en bobant ne en vainne gloire de ce monde."[58] The text
concludes by paying deference to the code of aristocratic chivalry. It
assures the reader that the king had sufficient chivalry to extend his
generosity to his barons and knights at court.

Another unidentified source in Joinville also emphasizes the king's
support of religious orders. "Li roys amoit toutes gens qui se metoient
à Dieu servir et qui portoient habit de religion ne nulz ne venoit à li
qui faillist à avoir chevance de vivre."[59] This passage states that
the king encircled Paris with religious orders: the Brothers of the
Sacks, the Friars of the White Mantels and the Brothers of the Holy
Cross.

c) A King Immune to Clerical Influence

King Louis was called king of the monks for his dedication to religious orders and his ascetic nature but he guarded the royal right to the temporal sword vis-à-vis the spiritual sword of the Church. Joinville takes a passage from Nangis which comes originally from Beaulieu. It completes a shorter selection from Joinville himself. In this text, King Louis appears as incorruptible in dealing with church benefices and the clergy. In seeking counsel before granting benefices, the king showed himself to be prudent and respectful of good persons of religion yet in giving only one benefice per person, he showed himself strict in his church dealings. "Ne il ne vouloit nul benefice donner à nul clerc, se il ne renonçoit aus autres benefices des esglises que il avoit."[60] The king wielded his temporal sword with justice but in matters of the spiritual, he subordinated himself to the Church.

The passage concludes with a short text which balances the main point by assuring the reader that wherever the king travelled in his kingdom he consulted Dominicans and Franciscans on spiritual matters.[61] Just as Beaulieu had payed his respect to chivalry in the earlier passage which stressed royal generosity to the religious orders, so he pays his respects to the opposite side of the coin in this selection.

d) A King Who Punished Blasphemy

One quick stark text illustrates the king's special anger for blasphemers. Once again, the passage is borrowed from Nangis who had in turn taken it from chapter 33 of Beaulieu. Blasphemy was a common and imaginative part of the medieval world. It was even common for men to swear by various parts of God's body or that of the Blessed Virgin and the saints.[62] The passage says that when the king returned from the Crusade he branded the nose and the lips of a Parisian bourgeois with a hot iron. The king is quoted as saying: "Je vourroie estre seigneiz d'un fer chaut, par tel couvenant que tuit vilein sairement fussent ostei de moy royaume."[63]

Joinville refers to this information as something he has heard: "Je oy dire que puis que je reving d'outre-mer..."[64], but de Wailly considers this another borrowing. The anecdote corresponds exactly with Nangis and Beaulieu and it is possible that Joinville heard about it as well as read it. This short passage, however, seems to be the only written borrowing which could have also been recounted to Joinville.

e) A King with the Grace of Final Perseverance

Final perseverance alone was necessary for sanctity in the Church triumphant according to Innocent III and since the vocation of any Christian was to be a saint in this sense, final perseverance was the lowest common denominator of a saint. King Louis' sanctity was being proven in the Church militant in both the texts of Nangis and Beaulieu. On this basis, the grace of final perseverance had to be demonstrated with an extra fervour and certitude.

In describing Louis' death on the 25th of August, 1270, Joinville begins and ends with formal phrases from Nangis, originally from Beaulieu. The text states that after instructing his son in the ways of public office and virtuous living, the good king asked for the sacraments of Holy Church, received them in sound mind and understanding, and after receiving the holy oils "on disoit les sept pseaumes, il disoit les vers d'une part." [65]

His burial is mentioned with tasteful aplomb. The miracles which followed upon his death offer final confirmation of signs that this king could be established as a saint of the Church militant:

> et enfoui à Saint-Denis en France, là où il avait eslue sa sepulture, ouquel lieu il fu enterrez, là où Diex a puis fait maint biau miracle pour li, par ses desertes. [66]

In these few hagiographic selections from Nangis, Joinville allows his readers to catch a glimpse of the documented saint through _exempla_ concerning Louis' post-Crusade period. These anecdotes supplement and complement Joinville's knightly portrait. The king's sanctity is highlighted within canonic traditions of Church canonization criteria.

THE OFFICIAL KING

When Louis IX returned from his first Crusade, his practise of legislating by virtue of his office increased. His legislative power was balanced by the advice he received from his barons, each responsible in their own barony. With royal domination of Normandy, part of Languedoc and Maçon, the king became the largest landholder in his kingdom and his administration developed to cope with these changes. It became impossible to summon the whole body of barons for consultation, and their consent was reduced to a formality. The monarch's conseil was deemed representative of such consent.

During Louis' reign, the king's feudal powers were extended to their full possibilities. Although Louis was not an innovator, he wished to push his suzerainty as far as possible in order to reform his kingdom and make its machinery of government as just as Christian conscience dictated. Coupled with his growing legislative and territorial powers, this reforming zeal led Louis IX to enact a series of ordonnances throughout his kingdom. Not only were these laws applicable in his royal domain but they were widely applicable beyond them. This modified the nature of royal authority in France and began to transform the monarchy from a suzerainty to a sovereignty.[67]

In Joinville's written sources, Louis IX appears as a monarch who strictly enacts the full legislative powers of his office over his entire kingdom. Joinville borrowed two lengthy texts from Nangis which set down the legal ordinances of Louis IX upon his return from Crusade. The moral justice of the private king is infused into the public order through the ethical concerns of his reforms. The moral nature of his growing administrative sovereignty is stressed. He is king of his kingdom in these texts beyond the customary limitations of the feudal ties within which Joinville had known and witnessed him. In this sense, the documents which Joinville included on the official laws of this reforming king filled a gap in Joinville's range of experience. The power and jurisdiction of the crown extends to every part of the kingdom in these laws.

a) The King's Legal Correction of Baillis, Prevôts and Maieurs

Perhaps the most striking example of Louis' expanding legislative jurisdiction appears in the first passage which Joinville cites on the official king. It was borrowed from Nangis and comes completely from Geoffroi de Beaulieu. The text gives a detailed description of Louis' severe moral correction of his crown officials: the baillis, prevôts and maieurs.

Many of the rules from these reforms are first found in the ordonnance of Beaucaire, declared by King Louis upon his return from Crusade with Joinville. Then in 1254 and 1256, these laws were widened and copied into texts such as the text of Nangis.

The bailli was an official of the French crown, not invented by the Capetians but borrowed by them from the Anglo-Norman monarchy. They were paid fixed stipends by the king to represent him judicially, financially and militarily in their respective bailliages. Although the geographical boundaries of these local administrators were never constant, their office represented the growing specialisation of royal officials employed by royal will alone. During the thirteenth century, these officials grew more royalist. The baillis were usually lower gentry or bourgeois laymen. Bringing the power of the crown throughout the kingdom with a zeal that surpassed the king's aristocratic peers, these officials helped the French kings of the late Capetian line to become sole head of justice, legislation and military forces in France. Louis IX's reign saw the start of this consolidation of power. During his reign, new officials were recruited from the crown's recently acquired lands in the south of France. These men brought with them the Roman concept of a prince whose will alone was law.[68] With these new baillis, the centralizing tendencies of the monarch's officials increased.

The second kind of official mentioned in these reforming laws is the prevôt. These were an older form of Capetian official administered by the baillis. Each bought his prevoté by auction. In return for an agreed farm, he administered the royal lands and collected the royal dues in his designated area. In the thirteenth century, these officials like the maieurs as minor officials, fell under the emerging powers of the newly established baillis. Appeals from the prevôts' courts, like all their accounts went to the baillis. In turn, the baillis presented these accounts to the Temple in Paris for audit. The baillis were also responsible for out-payments which from 1238 accounts onwards were divided into three broad categories: gifts, alms and pensions; the king's works; wages of officials such as judges and castellans.

From 1247 onwards, Louis IX sent around enquêteurs to collect complaints about the baillis. Records suggest that this was due to the fact that many of the royal officials were corrupt.

The bailliages formed the basic structure of royal administration under Louis IX. All of France, even the great independent fiefs, was divided into bailliages. For example, Brittany fell into the bailliage of Tours, Burgundy into that of Mâcon. However, in almost every bailliage, there were nobles with independent judicial and administrative rights of their own and the king's agents had to contend with this sort of rivalry for royal power.[69]

The borrowed text explains that when King Louis returned from the Crusade he turned himself devotedly to God and justly to his subject, deciding it was "belle chose et bonne d'amender le royaume de France."[70] The motif which appears most strongly in these reforms is that of a king literally applying machinery already in place in order to control his kingdom. The motive is moral control but the means is legal centralization.

The ordonnance of the king warns that all officials will be punished if they are disloyal, usurious or dishonest. Perjury, dicing and gambling, blasphemy, tavern frequenting and prostitution are forbidden to the king's officials. The law dictates personal morals as well as public standards for royal agents.

The use of the baillis' office for personal aggrandizement is forbidden, be it in the form of land purchase, the acquiring of Church benefices or any possessions or income beyond the strict limits of their office. The baillis are ordered to execute their judicial powers impartially and fairly. "Nous commandons que bailliz, ne prevoz qui soit en nostre office, ne greve les bones gens de leur justice outre droiture..."[71]

The king's legislative power is depicted above familial and and customary practices. The <u>ordonnance</u> insists on the abolishment of nepotism and favouritism under pain of punishment: "et deffendons que les diz offices il ne vendent à freres, à neveus et à cousins, puis que il les suront achetés de nous..."[72] The ethical purpose of these laws cuts through the period's customs. In so doing, the machinery of government around the king is brought under his control in a more effective fashion. The royal officials were given a series of oaths to swear and they were forbidden to behave in dishonest ways.

By prohibiting his royal officials from consorting with the conduct of the day, these instructions indirectly applied to society in general. Inn-keepers, prostitutes, gamblers, usurers and relatives were indirectly implicated by these laws if they were infringed by royal officials. By the end of 1254, this ordinance was promulgated in both the north of France and in Languedoc. Joinville comments that it greatly benefited the kingdom as a whole.

b) The King's Judicial Centralization

In Guillaume de Nangis' text, Louis IX also appears with increased judicial jurisdiction and centralization. Just as Paris becomes the permanent centre of the king's administration, so does one permanent place of residence within a <u>bailliage</u> become the judicial centre for the <u>bailli</u> to hear cases. Prevôts are likewise instructed:

> Nous défendons que baillif ni prevots ne travaillent nos sougiez. En causes que il ont par devant aus menées, par meument de lieu en autre; ainçois oyent les besoingnes que il on par devant aus, ou lieu là où il ont esté acoustumé à oyr, si que il ne lessent pas à poursuivre leur droit pour travail ne pour despens. [73]

Lesser agents could appeal against <u>baillis</u> within forty days of terminating their duties if their conduct had been wanting. This law also included <u>prevôts</u> et <u>maieurs</u>. In this way, the effects of these laws are given teeth.

c) The King Corrects the Corruption of the Paris Prevôt

Joinville cited another written source from Guillaume de Nangis which proves that the king took action against corrupt royal officials who disobeyed his laws. The original source of this selection is unknown.

The text shows that the bourgeois prevôt of Paris was misusing his office to reward his relatives and accept gifts from the rich to the disfavour of the poor. As a result, the little people of Paris were leaving it. The king is shown interceding on behalf of the little folk to rid the city of this corrupt official:

> Li roys, qui metoit grant diligence comment li menus peuples fust gardez, sot toute la veritei; si ne vout plus que la prevostés de Paris fust vendue, ains donna gaiges bons et grans à ceus qui dès or en avant la garderoient. Et toutes les mauvaises coustumes dont li peuples pooit estre grevez, il abati; et fist enquerre par tout le royaume et par tout le pays où l'on pourroit trouver home qui feist bone justise et roide et qui n'espargnast plus le riche home que le povre. [74]

In conclusion, Louis finds the good and worthy Etienne Boileau who does no misdeeds and abides by the duties of his office as prévôt of Paris. Joinville says that the land of the king improved so much as a result of his determined reforms that people flocked to it because of good laws and stable prices.

In his legislation, judicial centralization and direct intervention with corrupt officials, Louis IX is shown as king in his whole kingdom. He uses his rights to legislate for his entire kingdom with attention to the common good, reasonable cause against corruption and with the counsel of good men. This written source from Louis' ordonnances reflects a changing climate about the nature and legislative powers of the king. This was a monarch whose offices depended exclusively on royal legislation rather than on hereditary rights, past practices or unwritten custom. This was a monarch whose written public law could encroach on and limit the oral customs and feudal heritage of his government and its officials.

His role as legislator assured this king of rights which emerged from his suzerainty but grew into sovereignty. The king's essential function as supreme judge was strengthened as his jurisdiction was extended and centralized. Through his judges, the king became present almost everywhere in his realm. As Louis offered an appeal to the <u>parlement</u> against any denial of justice in his lower courts, he appeared above his representatives as the country's guarantee of justice.

This entire series of selections on the king's ordinances depicts Louis IX as a king of written law and justice, a king who extended his control through his moral reforms of his kingdom.[75] This is no longer a monarch of oral and visual sources and their relationships. This is a monarch who is seen above his feudal peers and almost beyond the perspective of his faithful counsellor and biographer, Jean de Joinville.[76] However, he is still defender of the oppressed and protector of the poor and this is a theme which corresponds to Joinville's chivalrous and feudal picture of him as a kingly father. Feudal father and new administrator in one breath, this king of the written sources is more than his knight's king, his officials' king, his clergy's king.[77] Louis IX is depicted as the king of all his people.[78]

THE OFFICIAL FATHER

The last written text which Joinville borrowed from Guillaume de Nangis is the famous one: "Les Enseignments de Saint Louis à son Fils." The lofty moral level of these precepts for his son combines blood-right with the theme of salvation. It illustrates the high-minded ideals with which noble children were to be taught through both inheritance and parental example. It also demonstrates the role of the monarch's lineage as a road for not only the salvation of the king and his family but for all his people. In this text, Louis IX appears as the official father of his son as future king and the official father of the people his son will rule. As father of the future king who is called to save his subjects, Louis IX appears as an official father.

It is likely that Guillaume de Nangis translated his version of the <u>Enseignments</u> from the Latin example of Geoffroi de Beaulieu. Louis is credited with having written these precepts by his own hand and while the precepts he wrote for his daughter concerned only private virtues, those for his son had far-reaching emphasis. Not only private virtues were advised but public peace, justice and reform. He instructs his son to preserve all good customs of his kingdom but to reform all those which are bad, to refrain from oppressing his subjects and to maintain the peace.

The <u>Enseignments</u> show Louis IX inspired with the monastic ideals which were popular with the order of friars during the thirteenth century. The ideals recommended by the king to his son are very similar to those praised in Vincent de Beauvais' <u>De Eruditione Filiorum Nobilium</u>. It remains open to question whether "Vincent modelled his ideal on his king, or whether the latter became so deeply imbued with the teachings of his mendicant friend that Vincent's very words flow from his lips in the rapturous story told by the Seneschal."[79] Certainly the Dominican emphasis on mortification of the flesh comes out in Beauvais' instructions for noble children and correspond to the virtues of the royal ascetic who wore a hair-shirt and deemed mortal sin a greater evil than leprosy.

Joinville set the scene for the king's precepts for his son by picturing the scene of the king's death on a bed of ashes in the pestilential heat of Tunis. Calling his son to him, Louis IX is attributed with these opening words:

> Biaus fiz, la premier chose que je t'enseing,
> si est que tu mettes ton cuer en amer Dieu;
> car sans ce nulz ne puet estre sauves. Garde-
> toy de faire chose qui à Dieu desplaise, c'est
> à savoir pechié mortel; ainçois devroies
> soufrir toutes manieres de tormens, que faire
> mortel pechié. [80]

The first theme evoked in these precepts is the high calling of the Christian noble who must place his priorities with God. The king advised his son that if God sent adversity, his son should receive it in patience and gratitude, thinking that he deserved it. If God sends prosperity, the son should accept it humbly as a gift without becoming proud. Virtue is seen as complete subordination to the fate of life's circumstances as if these circumstances were willed directly by God. Stoicism is the appropriate reaction of a nobleman to fate.

The advice given in the written <u>Enseignments</u> is irreproachable. The private virtue recommended is that of a saint. It is evident that the king believed that it was the calling of every Christian to aim for sanctity but in the case of a king, it was a duty of office. A kingdom of souls depended upon the king's virtue. The king advises his son to confess his sins frequently, to seek a trustworthy confessor, to be regular and devout in attending the services of the Church, to show compassion for the poor, to respect God's name, to hate evil and to honour his father and mother. These are not surface platitudes, they are serious injunctions to not only a nobleman but to a future king. These are the private virtues of a Biblical monarch. Primacy of faith and purity of heart are seen as the keystone to Capetian heritage. If the rewards and responsibilities of a king are greater than the average nobleman, so too are the punishments. Underlying this injunction to virtue is the common assumption of the period that loss of virtue in a king can lead to loss of the throne. [81]

These teachings convincingly demonstrate that Louis IX conceived of the royal mission as a religious vocation accountable directly to God. He advises his son that in public office he must keep good company and counsellors, to preserve peace particularly with other Christians, to be honest in retaining nothing which belonged to others, to respect persons of Holy Church even when they are in the wrong and to be diligent in maintaining good officials in his kingdom. The king enjoins his son to also play the role of saviour to his people. All vile sins are to be exterminated and all heresy erased in the kingdom. In these teachings, there is no distinction between private life and public affairs. The king is seen as responsible for the private lives of his Christian subjects and his non-Christian subjects are persecuted. He tells his son to fight swearing, games of dice, tavern-visiting and other sinful activities in his kingdom. His household and his royal officials should reflect these standards. He should avoid all evil and evil men.

This text's overwhelming religious tone shows Louis' own notion of the monarchy as a religious office. He recommends to his son to remember that he must be worthy of the oil of coronation, a holy unction reserved for the French kings. He asks his son to remember the special favour in which God has placed him as king. Louis closes by giving Philippe, his son, his father's blessing and commending him to God and God's service as king.

The text of the *Enseignments* reflect not only Louis' conception of the kingship but actually put his own behaviour into words. They repeat the laws of 1254 for his royal officials, they enjoin his own asceticism and religious patronage, his fighting the infidel, his wars against sin and heresy, his pious life of self-denial and prayer. The over-riding message is didactic. Royal virtue is spoken of as a professional business for his son. The *Enseignments* make little distinction between the private virtues and public good of the king, just as they make no distinction between the private lives and public doings of his subjects. For Louis IX in this text, the monarchy is an official paternity: both private and public. Royal virtue is a paternal duty to be passed down to his heir. It takes its origin with God and calls for thorough moral control of the king, his descendant and all his subjects in one eye of salvation according to the will of God.

Joinville's *Enseignments* reveal that the king thought of himself as an official father not only to his son as future king but to all his subjects.

CONCLUSION

Joinville's written sources document the spiritual, secular and paternal legist in the king. The monarch is seen as saint, moral sovereign and virtuous lineage. His moral, civil and familial jurisprudence are a tribute to the monarchy as an office directly responsible to God. All aspects of the king: his sanctity, his centralizing reforms and his familial paternity are part of his kingship. This is an untouchable king - set apart from the society around him by a halo, a crown and a dynastic lineage.

This is a king of the written traditions of the Church. He fulfills monastic ideals of personal virtue and churchmen's aspirations for the French monarchy. These sources recognize something in the king which Joinville could not share: this king saw himself as a crowned monk. This was also part of his ideal for the kingship.

In Joinville's written sources, Louis IX is an official representative of the Church, the Capetian crown and the paternity of his lineage and office. He is an official saint, worthy of canonization as proven in Beaulieu's <u>exempla</u> for the court. He is an official monarch fulfilling the Capetian thrust for a more centralized kingdom and sovereign dynasty as proven in his <u>ordonnances.</u> He is an official father fulfilling the calling of his lineage and office by teaching his son, as proven in his <u>Enseignment</u>s. In all three ways, the king of Joinville's written sources is superior to his aristocratic peers and proven as such.

As saint, king and father, Louis IX is also presented in didactic literary documentation: <u>exempla</u>,<u>ordonnances</u> and <u>enseignments.</u> This is a preaching king who takes his calling from God.

CHAPTER FOUR
NOTES

[1] HSL, CXLIX, 768, p. 412: "Je faiz savoir à touz que j'ai céans mis grant partie des faiz nostre saint roy devant dit, que je ai veu et oy, et grant partie de ses faiz que j'ai trouvez, qui sont en un romant, lesquiex j'ai fait escrire en cest livre." Robert Bossuat, in his article: "Jean de Joinville", Dictionnaire des lettres française, le moyen âge, ed. R. Bossuat, L. Pichard et G. Raynaud de Lage (Paris, 1964) p. 418, says of Joinville: "Il lisait en latin et en français et dit avoir utilisé le Livre de Terre Sainte, d'Ernoul et les Grandes Chroniques de France." It is possible that Joinville may have referred to the former written source (e.g. in his account of the tale told of King Richard of England: HSL, XVII, 77, p. 44). Joinville also mentions that he used a letter as a written source (HSL, XXX, 140, p.78) which concerned his promise to the Empress of Constantinople. Gaston Paris maintains that Joinville was influenced by Villehardouin (his eldest son married Mabile de Villehardouin) in his work. See G. Paris, "La Composition du livre de Joinville sur Saint Louis", Romania, XXIII (1894), pp. 508-524. On Villehardouin and his oral approach see: J.M.A. Beer, "Villehardouin and the oral narrative", Studies in Philology, LXVII (1970), pp. 267-277; and by the same author: Villehardouin, epic historian (Genève, 1968).

[2] HSL, Eclaircissements, XIII, "Sur quelques emprunts faits par Joinville à une chronique française", pp. 488-491. Also see: Natalis de Wailly, "Examens de quelques questions relatives à l'origine des chroniques de Saint Denys", Mém. Acad. Inscr., 17.1 (1874), pp. 403-407; A. Molinier, "Les Grandes Chroniques de France au XIIIe siècle", Etudes d'Histoire du moyen âge dédiées à Gabriel Monod (Paris, 1896), pp. 311-313. On the history of the abbey itself consult the classic by M. Félibien, Histoire de l'Abbaye royale de Saint Denys en France (Paris, 1706) and the more recent work by J. Formigé, L'abbaye royale de Saint-Denis. Recherches nouvelles (Paris, 1960).

[3] Robert Bossuat, "Les Grandes Chroniques de France", Dictionnaire des lettres françaises, le moyen âge, p. 193.

[4] The latest edition of Les Grandes Chroniques de France is that of Jules Viard, 10 vols (Paris, 1933). See his "Introduction" in volume 7, p. xvii on the composition of the work.

[5] Bossuat, p. 193.

[6] Bossuat, p. 193-5.

[7] Andrew W. Lewis, Royal Succession in Capetian France: Studies on Familial Order and the State (Cambridge, Mass., 1981), p. 115: "Primat, who directed the work, says... in the first sentence of the prologue: 'Because many people questioned the genealogy of the kings of France, from what origin and by what lineage they descended, he (Primat) undertook to do this work by the command of such a man that he neither could nor should refuse.' The man who requested the work is commonly taken to have been St. Louis; the date of his order should probably be placed in the 1260s."

[8] Viard, vol. 7, p. xvii-iv.

[9] H. F. Delaborde, "Notes sur Guillaume de Nangis", BEC, XLIV (1883), pp. 198-199.

[10] Robert Fawtier, The Capetian Kings of France (London, 1964), p. 3.

[11] Robert Southern, Saint Anselm and his Biographer: A Study of Monastic Life and Thought, 1059-1130 (Cambridge, 1963), pp. 325-327; G. Townsend, "Suetonius and his Influence", Latin Biography, ed. J. Dorey (London, 1967), pp. 79-113.

[12] Jacques Fontaine, "La composition: dessein et structure de la Vita Martini", Vie de Saint Martin par Sulpice Sevère (Paris, 1967), 1: 63-72.

[13] Southern, p. 320. For examples of this genre see Rosalind Brooke, "The Lives of St. Francis", Latin Biography, ed. J. Dorey, p. 180.

[14] Jean Leclercq, "Monastic Historiography from Leo IX to Callixtus II", Studia Monastica 12 (1970), p. 65.

[15] Lewis, p. 139.

[16] Lewis, pp. 124-5.

[17] Herbert Rowen, The King's State - Proprietary Dynasticism in

Early Modern France (Rutgers, New Jersey, 1980), pp. 16-18. Also see: Henry Myers, Medieval Kingship (Chicago, 1982) on the establishment of primogeniture with Louis IX's father, Louis VIII.

[18]Viard, "Introduction", vol. 7, pp. v-xix.

[19]Viard, "Introduction", vol. 7, p. xvii; Geoffroi de Beaulieu, Vita et sancta conversatio piae memoriae Ludovici quondam regis francorum, Recueil des historiens des Gaules et de la France (Paris, MCCCXL), vol. 20.

[20]Eric Kemp, Canonization and Authority in the Western Church (London, 1948), p. 104.

[21]Guillaume de Nangis, Vie de saint Louis, Les Grandes Chroniques de France, ed. J. Viard, vol. 7. See Henri Delaborde, Jean de Joinville et les seigneurs de Joinville, suivi d'un catalogue de leurs actes (Paris, 1894), pp. 140-141. For informed discussion of written and oral traditions in historiography see: A. Momigliano, "Historiography on Written Tradition and Historiography on Oral Tradition", Studies in Historiography (London, 1969), pp. 211-220. Also see: D. Hay, Annalists and Historians, Western Historiography from the VIII to the XVII Century (London, 1977).

[22]Natalis de Wailly, HSL, pp. 488-491.

[23]Nangis, Vie, 7.74, p. 188; "De celui qui jura vilain serement".

[24]Beaulieu, Vita, 33, p. 19 c.

[25]Nangis, Vie, 81, p. 203; "Comment le roy donnoit ses prouvendes".

[26]Beaulieu, Vita, 20, p. 12 d.

[27]Nangis, Vie, 72, p. 183; "Comment le roy amenda l'estat de son reaume".

[28]Nangis, Vie, 80, p. 198; "Comment le roy fist plusseurs religions".

[29]Beaulieu, Vita, 19, p. 11 b.

[30]Nangis, Vie, 115, p. 277; "Comment le roy endoctrina Phelippe son fils".

[31]Beaulieu, Vita, 52, p. 26 c.

[32]Nangis, Vie, 116, p. 280; "Comment le saint roy morut".

[33]Beaulieu, Vita, 44, p. 23.

[34]de Wailly, HSL, pp. 488-491.

[35] Nangis, Vie, 73, p. 186; "De la prevosté de Paris".
[36] Nangis, Vie, 80, p. 201.
[37] de Wailly, HSL, pp. 490-491.
[38] King Louis was accused by contemporaries of being king of the monks rather than of his kingdom. See: Guillaume de Saint-Pathus, Vie de saint Louis, éd. H.F. Delaborde (Paris, 1899), p. 118. See the same theme in Rutebeuf, Oeuvres complètes, pub. E. Faral (Paris, 1960), vol. 1, p. 429. In relating the historiography on pious traditions of the religious king to state traditions of a dynasty, Andrew Lewis has made an important contribution to our understanding of the period and its written traditions: Royal Succession, ch. 4. Current tendencies in hagiographical studies focus on the relationships between hagiography and social and political processes; the role of the miraculous in popular and elite cultures and their literary traditions; the role of hagiography in advancing proprietary claims. See Hagiographie, cultures et sociétés, IVe - XIIe siècles: Actes du colloque organisé à Nanterre et à Paris (2-5 mai, 1979) (Paris, 1981) for thirty-two essays in the field.

[39] Margaret Wade Labarge, Saint Louis - The Life of Louis IX of France (Toronto, 1968), p. 184. This thorough and well-balanced presentation of King Louis IX captures the monarch as a moral reformer rather than as an innovator providing a sound guide to the context of his financial and administrative developments. The literary traditions of the genealogical legitimacy of the Capetian monarchy have been treated in W. Ullmann, The Carolingian Renaissance and the Idea of Kingship (London, 1969); Reto Bezzola, Les origines et la formation de la littérature courtoise en occident (Paris, 1963), vol. 2, p. 366; Dominique Boutet, "Les chansons de geste et l'affermissement du pouvoir royal (110-1250)", Annales, jan.-fev. no. 1 (1982), pp. 3-15. For descriptions of Louis' realisation of his powers as suzerain and the growth of the idea of sovereignty during his reign: J.F. Lemarignier, La France médiévale (Paris, 1970), 26-3; B. Guenée, "Etat et nation en France au moyen âge", Revue Historique, CCXXXVII (1967), pp. 17-30, esp. 24-5; Elizabeth M. Hallam, Capetian France-987-1328 (London, 1980), pp. 207-272.

[40]The representation of King Louis as an official saint is not so incongruous a partner to his representation as official king. Both were advantageous to men of the cloth who saw in the royal person the elect of God and practically speaking, the defender of the Church and churchmen. These traditional and official forms of depicting sanctity served not only to further the monarch's canonization but further the prestige of the monarchy and its protection of the Abbey where Nangis collected the biographical material. For the beginnings of this 'quasi-hagiographic' tradition in the royal biographies by medieval monks see: Helgaud, *Epitoma Vita Regis Rotberti Pii*, éd, tr. et annoté par R-H Bautier & G. Labory (Paris, 1965); *Vita Aedwardi Regis, qui apud Westmonasterium requiescit: S. Bertini monacho ascripta*, ed. and tr. F. Barlow (London, 1962). See Joel T. Rosenthal, "Edward the Confessor and Robert the Pious: 11th Century Kingship and Biography", *Mediaeval Studies*, XXXIII (1971), pp. 7-20; M.J. Semmler, "La naissance des abbayes royales au haut moyen âge", *Revue du Nord*, 50 (1968), pp. 110-111.

[41]On the development and significance of medieval royal biography see H. Beumann, *Die Historiographie des Mittelalters als Quelle, fur Idungeschichte des Königstums, in Idungeschichtliche Studien zu Einhard und anderen Geschechtsschreibern des fruheren Mittelalters* (Darmstadt, 1969), pp. 40-79.

[42]Lewis, p. 120-1.
[43]Lewis, p. 122.
[44]Lewis, p. 113.
[45]Lewis, p. 125.
[46]Lewis, p. 126-7.
[47]Lewis, p. 123.
[48]Fawtier, pp. 3-5.
[49]Hallam, p. 127.
[50]Georges Duby, *Le dimanche de Bouvines* (Paris, 1973), p. 180.
[51]Lewis, p. 129.
[52]Lewis, p. 129.
[53]Lewis, pp. 122-133.
[54]Lewis, pp. 122-133.

[55] HSL 142. 720, p. 390.
[56] HSL 142. 722, p. 392.
[57] HSL 142. 723, p. 392.
[58] HSL 142. 726, p. 394.
[59] HSL 142. 727, p. 396.
[60] HSL 139. 692, pp. 380-382.
[61] HSL 139. 692, pp. 380-382.
[62] Labarge, p. 215.
[63] HSL 128. 685, p. 378.
[64] HSL 128. 685, p. 378.
[65] HSL 146. 755, pp. 404-406.
[66] HSL 146. 759, p. 406. Consult Robert Folz, "La sainteté de Louis IX d'après les textes liturgiques de sa fête", Revue d'histoire de l'Eglise de France, 57 (1971), pp. 31-45.
[67] J. F. Lemarignier, La France médiévale (Paris, 1970), pp. 260-3. The king's power was extended from his vassals, to the vassals of his vassals. Then it was extended to the burgesses and peasants. It gradually spread into the political, religious, financial and military spheres of what became known as 'Francia' or the French kingdom. Hallam, pp. 239-263. By the latter part of the thirteenth century, jurists referred to the French realm as "communis patria", the community of the fatherland with the king as its embodiment
[68] Hallam, p. 263; Elizabeth R. Brown, "Taxation and Morality in the Thirteenth and Fourteenth Centuries: Conscience and Political Power and the Kings of France", French Historical Studies 8 (1973), pp. 16-28.
[69] Hallam, p. 241; B. Guenée, "Les Généalogies entre l'histoire et la politique: la fierté d'être Capétien en France au moyen âge", Annales 33 (1978), 461 and passim. For further background on the conflict between the development of monarchical sovereignty and feudal suzerainty see: Marcel David, La souveraineté et les limites juridiques du pouvoir monarchique du IXe au XVe siècle (Paris, 1954), pp. 23-67; Walter Ullmann, "The Development of the Medieval Idea of Sovereignty", English Historical Review 64 (1949), pp. 1-34; Peter Riesenberg, Inalienability of Sovereignty in Medieval Political Thought (New York, 1956); and E. H. Kantorowicz, The King's Two Bodies, A Study in

Medieval Political Theology (Princeton, 1957). For Louis' own views on the nature of his office see the article by C.T. Wood, "The mise of Amiens and Saint Louis's theory of kingship", French Historical Studies vi (1970), pp. 300-310.

[70] HSL 140. 693, p. 382.

[71] HSL 140 . 704-706, pp. 384-386.

[72] HSL 140. 710, p. 386.

[73] HSL 140. 711, p. 386.

[74] HSL 141. 716, 717, pp. 388 & 390.

[75] For the lawyers' views on the kingship see J. J. Pegues, The Lawyers of the Last Capetians (Princeton, 1962). While the word 'souverain' was in use during the last half of the thirteenth century, sovereignty as 'auctoritas superlativa' did not come into use until the end of the century and common use in the late fourteenth century. Sovereignty was distinguished from 'public power' or 'potestas' , David, pp. 23-67. Classic works which treat the growth of the medieval monarchical institution and its written laws and traditions are: F. Lot & R. Fawtier, Histoire des institutions françaises au moyen âge 3 vols, (Paris, 1957), vol. 2 "Institutions royales"; Ch. Petit-Dutaillis, La monarchie féodale en France et en Angleterre (Xe - XIIIe siècle) (Paris, 1933), still an excellent guide for the period 987-1270.

[76] For the place of the king in the feudal system refer to L. Halphen, "La place de la royauté dans le système féodal", Annario de historia de derecho espanol, IX (1932), pp. 313-321.

[77] The incorporation of legal texts into Joinville's work responds to a different conception of the law and the king than that represented in his oral and visual sources which depicted the king as an integral part of the community and its traditional customs. As Carlyle explains... "at least as early as the thirteenth century there began to reappear the conception of laws as being made, not that the idea of custom as law disappears, but that there gradually grew up alongside of this the conception that laws could be made under certain conditions and by suitable authority... We have here arrived at the beginning of the modern conception of sovereignty, that is, of the conception that there is in every independent society the power of making and unmaking laws,

some final authority which knows no legal limits, and from which there is no legal appeal." See: R.W. Carlyle & A.J. Carlyle, A History of Mediaeval Political Theory in the West (London, MCMLXII), vol. 3, p. 45. Also see H. Wallon, Saint Louis et son temps, 2 vols. (Paris, 1876), vol. 2, p. 66.

[78] The bailliages under Louis IX included: Paris, Senlie, Vermandois, Amiens, Arras, Saint-Omer, Gisors, Nantes, Rouen, Caux, Verneuil, Caen, Bayeun, Cotentin, Sens, Mâcon, Etampes, Orléans, Tours, Bourges, Auvergne, Beaucaire, Carcassone, Périgord, la Rochelle and Quercy. These were administered through the power of the king as suzerain. However, all of France was divided into bailliages and it was in this more theoretical but implicating sense, that the bailliages came to represent a more unified royal power, still dependent upon its feudal base. See Wallon for a meticulous presentation of the baillis' powers, vol. 2, pp. 71-167. Beaumanoir, a bailli seems to have been influenced by the revived thirteenth century study of civil law in representation of the king as legislator through the bailliages: Les Coutumes de Beauvaisis, ed. Salmon (Paris, 1899), vol. 2, ch. XLV, p. 235.

[79] See Vincent de Beauvais, De Eruditione Filiorum Nobilium, edited by Arpad Steiner (Cambridge, Mass.: 1938) introduction, p. xiii. For a good introduction to Vincent's work, De Eruditione, see Dora M. Bell, L'Idéal éthique de la royauté en France au moyen âge (Genève, 1962) ch. III, "Vincent de Beauvais", pp. 41-49. Also see: Lester K. Born, "The Perfect Prince. A Study in Thirteenth and Fourteenth Century Ideals", Speculum, III (1928) pp. 470-504.

[80] HSL, CXLV, 740, p. 400. The text which Joinville borrowed on King Louis' instructions to his son is not as ample as that recorded in French by Guillaume de St. Pathus, which agrees with the Latin text of Duchesne. For further discussions see: Le Nain de Tillemont, Vie de Saint Louis (Paris, MDCCCXLIX), vol. 5, pp. 164-168. Also consult: H.F. Delaborde, Le texte primitif des enseignements de Saint Louis à son fils, BEC, vol. LXXIII (1912) pp. 73-99 & 237-262. Ch.-V. Langlois, "Les Enseignements de Saint Louis", La Vie en France (Paris, 1924), vol. IV, pp. 23-46.

[81] Lewis, pp. 130-131.

CHAPTER FIVE
CONCLUSION

INTRODUCTION

The historians of the medieval west inherited at least two major intellectual traditions: on the one hand, the Judeo-Christian tradition with Moses at its head down to Jerome and Eusebius of Caesarea; on the other hand, the western Latin tradition of such historians as Sallust, Tacitus and Valerius Maximus. Within these intellectual traditions, we may ask how did the medieval chroniclers conceive their history, what were their sources and what was their relationship to their audiences? There are many questions to ask of the complex array of medieval annalists, four out of five of whom were clerics, educated members of the ecclesiastical social order.

Through the work of such researchers as Taylor, Croce, Collingwood, Huizinga, Febvre, Momigliano, Stern, Lacroix, Smallwood, LeGoff and others, we have come to see these medieval chroniclers as a rich source for studying the mentalities of western Europe, not only through their literary traditions, but in their visual witness and oral sources, both of which were also influenced by oral traditions. Literary and oral traditions blended in medieval histories not only in their origins and sources but in their purposes and audiences. From the first grammarians of Rome to Jean Bodin in the sixteenth century, the role of the historian was to transform the events which occurred into narrative to be listened to as well as read.

As Lacroix has documented in his study of medieval historians, it was the great personnages of the day who made the pages of the chronicles: princes, saints, soldiers, judges, priests, heads of monasteries, heads of churches, heads of kingdoms. But among the great, it was the king who occupied the centre stage as protector of his people and their lands, as mediator between their God and their history. Even God was conceived as a king.

From Abbot Suger on Louis VI, to Joinville on Saint Louis, to Christine de Pizan on Charles V, to Commynes on the spider king, Louis

XI, the largest number of medieval chronicles were written on the kings. Most frequently, they were composed by their former counsellors, or, as in the case of Christine de Pizan, by a daughter and wife of former counsellors.

This research work has concentrated on a lay work of the French Capetian king and saint, Louis IX, by the Champenois seneschal, Jean de Joinville. Joinville came from within the charmed circle of nobility who alone could look upon the monarch as an equal. The seneschal's account of the good king's words and deeds is one of the first lay vernacular sources on a Capetian king.

Under the illusions of a printing press culture and even in the critical spirit of Natalis de Wailly's celebrated 1874 edition of the text, it has been taken for granted that Joinville's guide for his account of the king's life were written chronicles. However, a careful reading of the manuscripts and a return to the original title: a book of holy words and good deeds, led the author to conclude that the knight's oral and visual sources take priority over his written sources.

This study re-examines the traditional literary manner of reading Joinville's <u>Le Livre des saintes paroles et des bons faiz de notre roy saint Looys</u>. Sensitive to the most recent findings in the sister disciplines of sociology, psychology and anthropology, it analyzes the modes of perceiving the king in each of Joinville's source-types. This new methodology extracts greater cultural richness from a medieval text which designates its source-types utilized within a largely oral society. The results of this methodology illustrate a startling diversity in the respective cultural perceptions of the king in Joinville's oral, eye-witness and written sources.

This distinctive reading of the Crusader and saint brings Louis to us in a picturesque and vivid manner, close to the layers of tradition which surrounded him, close to the social mentality of his lay aristocratic milieu, close to the transitional perceptions of his own Crusading companion and historiographer, Jean de Joinville.

PORTRAIT SUMMARIES

a) The Portrait of the Oral Sources

As witness to the oral sources of his lay aristocratic milieu, Joinville recounts the sacred and feudal heredity of his hero as well as the Crusading values popular in his milieu. Here, Louis IX appears close to the collective rituals of symbol and myth. He is the accumulation of kings who have gone before him. He is talked about as a kind of hebraic David dubbed King of the Franks, the new Chosen People. Tales and anecdotes multiply around him. Oral tradition likes good deeds and wise words of epic proportions. Few occasions are missed to aggrandize the monarch traditionally loved or the sultan traditionally feared.

Through the rituals of the oral stories, the monarch appears present to the Crusaders' paternal needs, contained in ambivalent and sometimes contradictory archetypal functions of theocratic and feudal heritage. Louis emerges as a sacred myth unifying the Crusaders. He is both a warrior-God's lone leader in a dualistic battle for the world against the Devil's agents and a corporate caste Christ-figure who can redeem his people even in defeat. The king's name is a divine theatre for hermeneutic and didactic meanings. The king's function is one of central interpreter and interpretation. He is the moral judge of his peers and people. The king's acts are attached to aristocratic objects of power and abundance.

In Joinville's oral sources, we find many of the fundamental myths surrounding the French monarchy: myths which justified its legitimacy: the French king as a sacred personnage of God; myths which protected it from Rome: the French as a new Chosen People led by their Chosen monarch; myths which perpetuated feudalism: the French king as protector of the peasants; myths which eventually led to sovereignty: the French king as 'sword of the world'. The textual analysis of Joinville's oral sources brings out the ancient richness of the enduring myths surrounding the thirteenth century French monarchy.

b) The Portrait in the Visual Source

Then, there is Joinville, the most reliable first-hand eye-witness of the king, Louis' confidante. This time, the reader approaches the familial king of worthy exempla, the warrior king, the prud'homme among his peers, the judge and the foibled king in personal relationship with Joinville.

In this material, we find two levels of perception. On the one hand, Joinville relates a king who is similar to the perceptions of his oral sources. This is a public king of collective caste rituals. He is a stylized king of justice, holiness and aristocratic prud'homie. He is a cosmic figure who relates God's disposition to his people: 'sword of the world', the aristocrat of all aristocratic wealth and abundance, theatre of meaning, justice, holiness. It is reasonable to assume that being part of his milieu, the seneschal was influenced by the collective traditions present in his oral sources.

On the other hand, Joinville brings the king to eye-level in the latter half of his eye-witness Crusade account. In increasing personal exchanges with Louis, the king emerges from collective rituals into an individual of emotion, thought, beliefs and humour. Louis is presented with the first individualizing characteristics of thirteenth century portraiture.

It is significant that this portrayal of Louis, the individual, takes place through a demythologization of the central images of both Joinville's oral and early visual sources: king of justice, holiness and chivalry. Joinville was questioning the very myths of which he and the king were a part, perhaps illustrating his own disenchantment with the Crusade, perhaps illustrating the cultural conflict within himself during a transitional period.

As the seneschal comes to know Louis well in their four years in the Holy Land after the dismal Egyptian campaign, he develops a critical stance vis-à-vis the king. He questions the perfection of his justice, the universality of his holiness, the appropriateness of his chivalry. With a sense of familial irony and intimacy, he presents the great king's foibles as he curtly dismisses a Christian convert to Mohammed, throws his brother's gambling dice into the sea, argues over the liturgical sign of peace, fails to greet his wife and new-born child while fixed in prayer, ignores the injustice to a Champenois knight, refuses to give a spare horse to a poor knight.

Joinville's eye-witness account, analyzed in relation to his oral sources, makes a remarkable transition from the collective rites on a faithful knight's eulogy on his king to a critical biography approaching early modern standards of psychological insight on the limits of this ascetic and extraordinary monarch. Within the limits of this knight's Champenois culture, the reader is permitted a close three-dimensional look at the man behind the mythic tapestried king and translucent saint.

c) The Portrait in the Written Sources

Finally, Louis appears in formal selections from the official written sources borrowed from the reputed Benedictine Saint-Denys chronicles, official dynastic chroniclers of the French monarchs for centuries. Here, we find Louis in a withdrawn state of dynastic deeds and saintly words and paternal instructions. Within this documented tradition of long literary precedent, Louis is presented as a unifying feudal suzerain expanding Capetian power towards sovereignty with new <u>ordonnances</u> which regulate his whole kingdom. The king also appears as the saint worthy of canonization in pious acts of benevolence and charity to the poor, the suffering, the religious orders, the churches; absolute acts of moral judgment branding the mouth of a blasphemer with a hot iron. Lastly, Louis is seen as the virtuous dynastic father intent on instructing his son and heir in the religious and moral virtues of Capetian kingship.

This is a dynastic source which emphasizes the conventional, binding or written acts and words of the king. It is based in the literary traditions of secular biography and ecclesiastical hagiography. Louis is a king of institutions: his monarchy, his church, his family. He fulfills the legal requirements to function admirably in each institution. He promulgates <u>ordonnances</u> for his monarchy's growing <u>imperium</u> in the Roman legal sense. He fulfills the canonic requirements for sanctity as required by the Papal court. He formally instructs his son and dynastic heir in the "De regimene principum" for the virtuous continuity of the Capetian lineage.

Joinville is no longer a participant in this king of his written sources. This makes a difference to the kind of monarch presented. King Louis is represented in the written traditions of a monk's king rather than the oral traditions of a knight's king.

Although Joinville selected certain passages which either blended with or compensated for his own view of the king as a prud'homme, the over-all picture of the king in the written sources is more in keeping with a monk's ideals which were closely related not only to pious traditions of the religious life but to state traditions of dynasty. While Guillaume de Nangis in the Saint-Denys chronicles took the whole kingdom for his field, Joinville took the king and himself as a social and finally, as a personal concern.

All the subjects treated in Joinville's written sources are of a legally binding or legally demonstrable nature: ordinances, precepts, judicial proceedings, legally witnessed deeds. This is in contrast, on the one hand, with the royal-knightly tension of his visual images and, on the other, with the popular traditional trends of his oral images. In particular, there is a contrast between the spontaneous and traditional qualities of the orally imagined king and the rigid and conventional qualities of the king in the written sources.

Joinville's written king is further from the mouths of his people. There is no description of his relationships in any social or personal sense. Even as a father, he is a formal instructor. What is remarkably absent in the king of the written sources is emotion: either on the part of the chronicler or the king. As a result, there are no lived values presented within or around the monarch. King Louis is distant, serious, abstract, proper, universal.

In the written sources, Louis is above all, a king of state, an official saint of the church. He is the king of the kingdom and of his religious institutions, more than a king of his people. He is a king of orthodox entities. In his private life, he appears as a crowned monk, the king the church had traditionally sought. In his public life, he appears as a ruler representing the written traditions of his lineage and office.

THE SECONDARY SOURCE-MATERIAL

There is a contrast in the ways of perceiving Louis IX between Joinville's auxiliary sources: his oral and written material. This difference can best be approached by first treating the distinct character of each source-type's material before treating the content of that material. There are also some common themes which emerge and these will be treated.

a) General Character and Comparative Content

    1. Historical Epistemology

In the historical interpretations of the king in Joinville's written and oral sources, there is a different epistemology, a different interpretation of the place of the king and saint in events.

The Saint-Denys selections present Louis IX as an agent of reform and through that, of change in his kingdom. He is a moral and administrative reformer through rational principles of conduct and law to which he adheres. Christian action in accord with Biblical directives is seen as an initiating force in the society of the time.

The private acts of the saint, the public deeds and laws of the Christian monarch reform the kingdom and change the conditions of the poor, the suffering, the religious orders, as well as the baillis, the prevôts, the maieurs. Guillaume de Nangis' passages reflect the growing humanist concerns of the Church for "De regimene principum". King Louis' Enseignments to his son synthesize Christian principles of good personal and governmental disposition: spirituality, prayer, counsel, justice, truth, fairness, immunity from influence. The reasoned attitudes of the king to his faith in God and his religion are presented as the core of his sanctity and monarchy. The logical mode of thought employed in Nangis' selections are reminiscent of the scholastic method flowering in the universities of the period. His presentation of Louis is a Summa of his reforming accomplishments of change.

We could describe the epistemology employed by Nangis as Aristotelian. Empirical evidence is gathered like matter to build up the form of the argument.

Significantly, Joinville's oral sources reveal, if anything, a popular neo-Platonism at work in the noble mentality. The tales show the extent to which the king was the given meaning of an event before it occurred. The king was the central interpreter and interpretation of historical events. There seems to be little perception of historical change. Interpretation is concentrated on King Louis conforming himself to God's Will as revealed in oral custom, established ritual and ceremonious rites. The king-figure is a sign of conservation not of change. He conserves God's continuous actions in the society through his personal and public morality.

Birth, coronation and death; crossings of perilous waters, landings on enemy shores, openings of collective ventures and deeds, lone lunges from heights into battle, ritual confrontations with enemies' envoys, rich aristocratic gifts to allies , feudal councils, theatres of paternal justice and meaning - all provide the customary occasions to interpret the eternal illuminations of God's Words and Acts in history through the king. It is as if the world has few innate laws of reason: battles are lost or won through the king's observation of custom, Crusades are undertaken with God's sign in royal sickness;good shores are sighted with signs of royal splendour and dangerous shores are avoided with processions recommended through authoritative oral report. The new is experienced in terms of the old. The old is conveyed on the tongues of authoritative oral report: ancestors, parents, priests, travellers, kings.

In the seneschal's oral sources, the king conserves the past to assure God's favour on the present. History is the tale of how well or badly the king accomplishes this sacred duty. The meaning of the royalty is its mediation of the supernatural truth into the natural day-to-day world of the Crusading nobles.

2. Social Anthropology

Interdependent with historical epistemology is the question of social anthropology. While Joinville's oral sources speak of a charismatic king, his written sources document a bureaucratic monarch.

In the written selections, King Louis is a part of a permanent structure with a system of rational rules fashioned to meet calculable needs by means of a normal routine, normal categories of requirements. The purpose of the written material was to deliberately prove, according to defined thought-categories that Louis IX enhanced the religious, administrative and genealogical character of the dynasty. The perception of the king in these sources suggests a reordering of stresses in royalist chronicles of the monarchy. Lewis has demonstrated in his research on royal succession, the evolution in the conceptualization of the king in the Saint-Denys chronicles. Louis' biography illustrates the progressive development of expressions about Capetian dynasticism. Criteria for the legitimacy of his sanctity, monarchy and paternity are presented not only to exalt his name but to buttress the dynasty.

As a bureaucratic monarch, Louis rules a kingdom not a social hierarchy. His setting in space is dominant, uniform and territorial. His setting in time is retrospective. This is a review of his whole reign. This is a king of the long-term in which war and crises are minor. There is little military or social emphasis. The king's monarchy rests upon an ordered base of his household, his bureaucratic agents, his system of taxation, judicial inquiry and legislation.

He is a saint who has been analyzed into appropriate categories for the purposes of the bureaucratic canonization requirements. His deeds are systematized, regularized, quantified. Beaulieu's *exempla* follow the proto-*exempla* style. They are exemplary proofs of virtue suitable for the Papal court. As a Capetian who literally fulfills his title "most Christian of the Christian kings", Louis is the fitting representative of his lineage. His sanctity is a politically pertinent accomplishment not only for the church but for his kingdom and the continuity of his dynasty.

In Joinville's oral sources, the king is a popular religion. There is little differentiation between what is sacred in him by custom, blood-right, coronation, lineage or personal holiness. The sacred in the king is to be found rather than created. The seneschal's oral tales tell of the expectations for the sacred functions with which the Crusaders endowed their king. Magic and religion are blended in the royal religion. His sacredness is embodied in myths, rites, divine signs and superstitions.

The general character of the king in the tales is charismatic. Louis is the Crusaders' natural leader in a time of psychic, physical, economic, religious and military distress and extravagant hope. The royal leader of the Crusade is endowed with specific gifts of the body and the spirit, not accessible to everybody. These gifts are supernatural. This sets Louis alone, apart and above his knights. As a military leader, he is the arm of God, the sword of the world. As a judge, he endows his cases with a sense of mystic mission, knowing wisdom; he is also the judge of events, the theatre for veracity, import, meaning. As an aristocrat, he is the aristocrat of aristocrats: abundant, providing, generous.

By virtue of his Crusading mission, the king of the oral tales demands obedience and recognition as a duty of his Crusading men. His is a charismatic domination which is not based on reason. He and his followers stand outside the normal routines of their lives, the normal ties to the world and their country, as well as outside the routine obligations of family life. His space is the territorial call of the Crusading mission. This is a sacred journey to far-way shores: Egypt and the Holy Land. It is a journey to recover the centre of the world for God and His Christian people. His time is a time of crisis and sacred war. In this crisis, everything is replete with meaning; everything is a question of life and death. The royal time of the oral sources is a microcosmic time of collective struggle. The king's leadership rests upon constant proof of his divine mission. In the Crusade, this proof is victory. Conversion is a secondary proof.

In Joinville's oral material, we see a profound dualism at the heart of his circle's beliefs about the Crusade and the king. Their world is divided into the good Christians and the evil non-Christians. The king is the symbolic figure for the good society which externalizes evil. He ties their history to a cult which represents a theogonic drama. God is a deity who helps his Chosen People in their battles against the wicked. Conquest is granted through a hierarchical order issuing from the king. Louis fights on God's side to control the <u>plenitudo temporum</u>. His warrior lust, generosity and justice represent God's attributes.

The modes of thought present in these royal perceptions do not make conceptual distinctions around the king-figure. The major distinction present in these oral sources is the moral one. This has a specific social anthropology attached to it: one which absolutizes the good from the bad and which represents characteristics of a closed society which needs to externalize evil on its outsiders. Because these royal perceptions emerge from a Crusading time of war, it is possible that these perceptions may represent a mentality of crisis.

The royal perceptions in Joinville's oral tales correspond to anthropological categories of participation, analogy and symbolic laws. Together, they characterize the mental universe of archaic societies. The king is an hierophany in the anecdotes. He represents himself but he also represents something beyond himself: something sacred. By participation in this hierophany, his shield, his helmet, his ring, his lance also become sacred objects Secondly, the belief is strong that like produces like, and that by analogy, if three Saturday processions warded off a dangerous coast-line and mountain, three more Saturday processions will bring the king's brother to the shores of Damietta. If Louis had followed the oral custom of properly dividing up the provisions in Damietta between Crusaders and inhabitants, the Crusade might have been won as other Crusades had been won. Thirdly, there is an identification between symbols of the mind and laws of the universe. When Louis sends a magnificent red tent to the converted Mongol leader, it depicts on its walls many scenes of Christian doctrine. The oral tale suggests that there was a correspondence between this gift and the Mongol's subsequent power to reduce princes to his submission.

Joinville's oral informers speak of the king from within the lay mentality of the king's own aristocratic Crusading milieu. They are not external to his values, nor to his way of life. They represent the collective milieu within which both Joinville and the king lived for six years. In this sense, these oral sources are an index, not only to the king's images among the Crusading nobility, but they must be taken seriously as an index to the mentality of which the king was a part.

Spoken when the king was alive and events were fresh and close to the spokesmen and author, the oral sources are contemporary commentary on the Crusading king and the general mentality within which he crusaded.

Not spoken to formally prove, they nonetheless carry with them the weight of authoritative interpretation. These stories are laden with values and interpretations. They celebrate these beliefs within the events to which they are integrally attached. With vivid images, these tales relate how these beliefs effected and were affected by events themselves. While not explicitly shaped by clear-cut categories of thought, the structure of these anecdotes show implicit attitudes, and mythical structures of thought close to the profound emotional and religious needs of the Crusaders.

3. Political Beliefs

Joinville's collective oral sources introduce us to the early medieval character of the sacral king still alive in thirteenth century circles of Crusading nobility. The structures of meaning with which the king is endowed in Joinville's tales are quite ancient and reflect early theocratic images of the medieval kingship. The lone and saving warrior, the sick king rescued by God for the Crusading mission, the defeated leader punished by God who defends His oral customs - these are perceptions of a theocratic king which survive in these oral reports.

The corporate monarch of constant consultations, baronial council, the king of provisions for his men who hold from him, the king who must listen to the advice of his peer-group and council; this is the feudal suzerain of limited power and obligations to his men. This is a monarch of reciprocal ties, duties and services, held in check by his peer-knights.

The mixture of these sacral and suzerain perceptions in the seneschal's oral sources suggest that the sacral and suzerain stages of the French monarchy were not as clearly delineated as historians such as Ullmann and Lemarignier suggest through their extensive research on the written legal records of the dynasty. In the minds of the knights who fought with Louis IX and spoke with Joinville, the monarch was both theocratic and feudal at a time when the French monarchy was moving towards sovereignty.

While the seneschal's oral tales depict a sacral and feudal king, his written sources document the last stages of feudal suzerainty and emerging sovereignty. The king is the legislator of _ordonnances_ which seek to unify and regulate essential royal powers and services throughout his disparate feudal kingdom with universal application to every corner of that land.

The clerical author praises the progress of the dynasty to which his monastic house is bound and views Louis' expanding legislation with pride. In the noble oral accounts, the same king is divinely censured with a Crusade disaster for departing from oral custom which is found, not made.

The disparate political views of the monarchy contained in Joinville's oral and written sources deserve further investigation. The simultaneity of divergent political layers of belief illustrates the complex and fragmented nature of the evidence with which we are dealing, evidence which may, if augmented, reflect the culture itself.

Nobles who had much to lose in territorial and familial dynastic kin-structure with the growing centralizing of the French crown, did not share the enthusiasm of the good monk of Saint Denys. The Benedictine monks of Saint Denys buried the Capetians on their grounds and housed the memorabilia of their power. Their monastic interests were not those of the nobles.

Through an analysis of Joinville's oral sources, we see how the early patterns of the French monarchy clung to the new forms of the kingship. While historians have relied heavily on written sources as leading historical evidence on certain political aspects of the medieval French monarchy, Joinville's oral sources touch another vein of the kingship as it existed in the minds of thirteenth century noble élite.

b)   Joinville's Privileged Oral Witness

In the seneschal's collection of anecdotes, the nobles look to the king for the extraordinary. His function is still held sacred. The line between the magical expectations accorded the royal leader and the religious evaluation of his person is not distinguished. Magic and religion co-exist in this collective witness.

When Louis fails collective hopes for victory, breaks with oral custom and loses the Crusade according to the oral interpretation, there is silence in Joinville's collective oral reports. At this juncture, the seneschal records the king's own words concerning his captivity experience. Louis gives a mystical interpretation to the loss, living it as a Crucifixion related to Christ's Resurrection. His suffering is represented as that of a Head of a Mystical Body of Crusaders: together they fight, together they suffer, together they hope, as all need each other. Louis the king is prepared to suffer the torture of the bernicles before he will blaspheme to the Saracen captors with the promise they ask of him.

The holy man's privileged witness records a more sophisticated religious self-understanding, than appears in the collective oral tales. The principled endurance of loss, the immense sense of collective destiny expressed between the king and his Crusaders, the mystery of the defeat in God's hands and the Crucifixion-Resurrection, all manifest a more internalized Christianity than the other oral sources show. However, it is culturally instructive to note the extremities to which Louis connects oath-taking. Louis is prepared to suffer the torture of repeated bone-breaking and watch the effect his resistance has on the torture of an old Christian man, rather than swear to give away castles he does not own or stamp on God's Cross if he breaks the settlement. The king is prepared to suffer death for the sake of Christian principles.

The king's preference of death to blasphemy illustrates in literal religious terms an anthropological phenomenom. Just as the oral sources connect intentions with results, mental thoughts with actual facts, so did the medieval mind make a close connection between the use of certain words and their direct influence on results. As the king, Louis was surrounded with sacred expectations of a charismatic leader who must prove himself worthy of the divine mission. His sacredness was ambivalent. It was also dangerous. A blasphemous promise to the Saracens would not only be a sin, it would be the provocation of a collective evil. A sin of verbal intention to defame the God who led Him was also a cultural and anthropological taboo. In this example, we observe the relationship between Louis' personal religion and his collective magic.

There is indirect evidence that Louis' pristine interpretation of the Crusade defeat did have some impact within the Crusading circle. Joinville introduces two Saracen oral reports which laud the king for his Christian heroism in defeat, principles in prison. Whether these tales truly originated with Saracen sources is irrelevant for our purposes here. The fact which interests us is that these two tales were repeated among the Crusaders. There is a possibility that Louis' Suffering Servant interpretation of the disaster was received with some meaning among his disappointed warriors. Conversion of the Saracens to recognition of Christian superiority was some consolation to these sickened men. It is doubtful that many nobles fully embraced the level of the king's mysticism. Suffering as a form of rebirth was not a military theme.

Joinville's oral sources portray Louis in two different forms, one of which corresponds to noble aspirations, the other reflecting the monarch's religious vision and enemy recognition. First, the king appears as a divine exemplar, endowed with semi-magical attributes. He is graced with the imagery of an Old Testament King leading his Chosen People. He is a mythical religious figure not bound to fact but responding to simple, profound and customary aspirations of his nobility. These aspirations were evidently worldly and archaic.

Their anthropomorphic dream of God as their aristocratic conquest and power was specifically associated with their king as their political and military leader on Crusade. Strange and extravagant as these noble tendencies may seem to us, they were sincere expressions of these men's faith in their social destiny as Christians of the thirteenth century. When their collective phantasy of conquest fails, Joinville turns to the privileged information from the king and the complimentary witness of the Saracens. Noble report falls silent on the disaster.

In the second constellation of Joinville's oral images, King Louis shares his Crusaders' reconciliation with stunning defeat through a theological and mystical interpretation of the Christian message. The king is like a new Christ, braving temptation, threats, and even death for the sake of his will to redeem his men in God. Louis is stripped of magic and clothed in the crucified cloak of martyrdom.

c) Common Themes

The seneschal's oral and written sources on King Louis each present a partial presentation of the monarch related to a particular environment, heritage and social caste. The character and content of each source-type illustrate specific historical epistemologies, social anthropologies and political beliefs. In the overall work of Joinville on Louis, it is the oral sources which are the index to the Crusading monarch's social milieu and values. The manner in which the Champenois knight's oral anecdotes and written selections depict the king reflect the diversity of traditions, social, political and religious values attached to his person and function. But while the literary traditions of the written sources influenced Joinville's portrait, the oral traditions of his oral sources influenced the mentality of the king, Joinville's visual witness and the very core of his work.

The separate analysis of the seneschal's source-material permits us to emancipate ourselves from our cultural pre-suppositions and to appreciate a work which is both a product of oral and written traditions. Moreover, it allows us to better comprehend both official and popular aspects of King Louis himself.

After reading Joinville's oral stories of kings and King Louis, we can no longer dismiss as unhistorical the sacral king, the king of religious veneration and collective myth linked to the beliefs of his people and his knights. The mixture of sincere conviction and heroic phantasy in these tales exercised a real, and in this case, disastrous, influence on the French fate during the seventh Crusade. In these tales, we sense the passion for honor, for glory and for vengeance which acquired the splendour of virtue and duty in the Crusade mission led by the king. It is not possible to understand the king on Crusade nor the Crusade itself if one neglects these elements. For the thirteenth century noble, the Crusade was a combination of sacred vengeance and religious justice. The king was at once, its sacred and religious charisma.

The ideals of didactic justice and transcendent meaning attached to the king-figure in the oral tales finds a lofty place in the written sources. These ideals, popular and ambivalent in the oral stories, become the official virtues of the Church's model monarch and saint in the written selections. King of justice, king of holiness: these two themes find their reasoned counterpart in the literary and monastic traditions of the written material. While the social and military chivalry of the Crusade images is remarkably absent in the Saint Denys *exempla*, the values of justice and holiness are their major emphasis. Transposed onto a new plane of administrative reforms and sanctified deeds, interpreted within long-standing biographical and hagiographical traditions of literature and attached to the legitimacy of a dynasty, these themes serve to define King Louis.

If there is anything which in a word, sums up the most important contribution of Joinville's oral sources to King Louis' history, it is this: they bring contemporary values to contemporary facts. If you will, Joinville's oral sources are the popular aesthetics of Louis' official history.

THE PRIMARY SOURCE-MATERIAL

Joinville's eye-witness account of King Louis takes on new highlights in reference to the character and contents of his secondary source-material, particularily that of his oral anecdotes which were part of his milieu. We have noted how the holy king of the privileged oral witness emerged in relationship to the sacred and semi-magical myths of the seneschal's general oral reports. In Joinville's visual source, a foibled king develops from traditional views of a king of justice, holiness and chivalry.

The Champenois knight's introductory recital of Louis' holy words presents socially oriented <u>exempla</u> of the king who places religious <u>prud'homie</u> on a higher scale than feudal <u>prud'homie</u>. Louis espouses the religious values of chivalry over the social and traditionally feudal values of chivalry. Joinville plays the role of the feudal <u>prud'homme</u> who enjoys his wine in moderation, dislikes kissing the feet of the poor on Holy Thursday and prefers thirty mortal sins to leprosy He serves as the foil for Louis' holiness. The king teaches the knight that he must put social values of his caste beneath his faith in the <u>Credo</u>. In Louis' teachings to the seneschal: watered wine is more virtuous than wine which leads to either gout or intoxication; the example of Christ who washed the feet of his disciplines before his Crucifixion and Resurrection is superior to social qualms; and when a leper dies, he is cured of that illness, when a mortal sinner dies, he runs the risk of perpetual punishment.

In these social <u>exempla</u>, two decent ideals are illustrated: those of the king and those of Joinville. This is in contrast to the proto-<u>exempla</u> of Joinville's written selections in which only one exemplary ideal is exalted. In Joinville's introductory section, the king instructs him that the love of God is paramount to all other desires. He begs his knight that for love of the king, he should follow his example. Louis relates faith in the words of the <u>Credo</u> said in the liturgy from the words of the apostles, to Joinville's faith in the words of his mother that his father's name was indeed, Simon. Love of God is related to love of the king. Faith in the <u>Credo</u> is related to faith in a mother's words about the father's identity.

These _exempla_ illustrate a king of incomparable holiness. This is a monarch who manifests a love of God the Father above all else. He advocates love of himself as an authoritative guide for Joinville to God. This is a king who recommends faith as belief in oral words of familial authority. This is a king of perfect justice, chivalry, holiness.

This eye-witness portrayal serves as a bridge between the magico-religious king of Joinville's oral sources and the official saint of his written sources. In these court scenes, Joinville shows how Louis surpasses social chivalry and its values for the austere and almost monastic values of a saintly aristocrat. This is a king with the ascetic qualities of a monk and the social charms of an aristocrat.

In the middle of Joinville's visual memories, we accompany the king through the Egyptian Crusade campaigns. Joinville shows us the sea at Limassol filled with the expansive sails of Louis' fleet, the battle-field of Mansurah stilled to the strength of his German helmet shining in the sun, the protection of his shield, the courage of his sword. We watch the battle's progress through Louis' feudal consultations with his Council of war: movements forward, movements backward, no movement at all, and then a sortie to save his trapped brother, Robert of Artois. Joinville's images of sacred awe and feudal corporate groupings present the king in a stylized Gothic form. The perceptions of the monarch's military might and aristocratic expansiveness resemble the motifs of Joinville's collective oral sources.

The seneschal's images of the early Crusade years, 1248-1250, present Louis in two visual settings: alone, above and apart from his men; corporate and engaged with feudal groupings. Alone, the king is the sacred king of God. He descends from a chapel alone to settle a chivalrous dispute among his rivalling knights. He lunges waist-deep into the waters of Damietta, following the ensign of Saint Denys ahead of all his troops, to the landing beaches where the Saracens' horns blow terrible warnings. Corporate, Louis is the feudal king. He is related to a social and military hierarchy and a Council of war in which obedience is the key to honour and the common good. Joinville is the outsider to the Council, a distant spectator of the king among 15,000 men. He sees Louis as the visual focal point for the Council of war's decisions. We see Louis and Council forbidding Joinville to risk his life in a feat of bravery on the land-side of Damietta's walls. Louis and his Council become the centre of decision for crossing the canal of Bahr-as-Saghir to Mansurah. Cat-castle and causeway burned by Saracen Greek-fire, Louis and his Council reconvene to find another way around the obstacle of the canal surrounded by Saracen fire.

In these two visual settings: sacred and feudal; alone and corporate; ritual events, objects, deeds and people abound. Louis could be almost any king. He is represented in rituals and rites of collective perception. He is archetypal. The spatial pattern along with the themes resemble those of Joinville's oral source-material.

Whereas the early part of Joinville's visual witness depicts a perfect king of holiness, chivalry and justice through his _exempla_ of holy words, and the first half of his Crusade account describes in established sacred and feudal rituals, a king of heroic deeds, the last four years of the Crusade account, 1250-1254, break this collective mode of royal perception. There is a perceptual development of the king from a two-dimensional Gothic form into a three-dimensional sunlight painting with highlights and shadows, solidity and depth.

This metamorphosis occurs with the development of a personal relationship between the trusty knight and his admired monarch. The royal alliance is founded on the basis of moral conscience. Having proven himself to the king through a series of deeds of valour and feats of arms, Joinville becomes a member of the royal Council after the Egyptian captivity. At Acre, a number of crucial Council meetings debate whether the king should stay in the Holy Land until all the prisoners-of-war are freed or return to France, as his royal barons and mother advise. On the basis of his familial honour and Champagne pride in chivalry, Joinville opts to stay. He is ridiculed by the majority of the Council members. But he finds a vital ally. It is the king.

In the light of the contrast between the themes of Joinville's oral military motifs and his visual _exempla_ motifs, this Council alliance takes on serious moral meaning. The king's two remaining brothers and the majority of the barons elect to return to France. For them, the military defeat and the financial costs of staying take precedence over moral commitment to the remaining prisoners-of-war. But for Joinville, as he explains it, his chivalrous familial pride will not permit him to return until these prisoners are freed. It is a moral principle of chivalry for the seneschal. This is more important than military conquest or financial expenditure. Joinville's chivalry transcends its more shallow virtues. And while these moral principles do not reach the religious heights of his king, they are sufficiently exceptional for his caste to make him a moral confidante of King Louis.

In the absence of his established Council, in the new and untried circumstances of the Holy Land, an increasing dialogue develops between Joinville and Louis. For the first time in the Crusade account, Joinville's separate autobiographical theme interacts with his royal biography. In this exchange, inner emotions, private thoughts, personal humour come to the fore. Familial Champenois traditions, monarchical Crusading rituals recede into the background. For four years, they live in close quarters, dining together, debating together, attending the liturgy, consulting in Council.

Joinville becomes more than the royal confidante. He becomes the king's private keeper. He is the social conscience to the king's justice; the familial guard to the king's ascetic holiness; the feudal correction to the king's religious chivalry. It is not that the loyal seneschal questions his king's evident justice, sanctity or chivalry. It is that he calls it into a range of human limitation, a tension of human dialogue. It is that Joinville, as he tells the king, does not wish to kiss the holy king's bones before they are relics. How could he be an honest prud'homme of limits and do otherwise?

BIBLIOGRAPHY

EDITIONS OF THE TEXT

Wailly, Natalis de. Jean, sire de Joinville, Histoire de saint Louis, Credo et Lettre à Louix X. Texte original accompagné d'une traduction. Paris, Didot, 1874.
Joinville, Histoire de Saint Louis. Texte original, précédé de notions sur la langue et la grammaire de Joinville et suivi d'un glossaire. Paris, 1881; 20e éd 1931.

TRANSLATIONS
French Translations

Mary, André. Le Livre des saintes paroles et des bons faits de notre saint roi Louis, mis en français moderne. Paris, 1928.
Longnon, Henri. La Vie du saint roi Louis, dictée et faite écrire par Jean, seigneur de Joinville et mise en nouveau langage. Paris, 1928.
Pauphilet, Albert. Jean de Joinville, Histoire de Saint Louis. Historiens chroniqueurs du moyen âge. Paris, 1952.

English Translations

Evans, Joan. The History of Saint Louis, by Jean, sire de Joinville, seneschal of Champagne, translated from the French text, ed. by N. de Wailly. Oxford, Oxford University, 1938.
Hague, René. The Life of St. Louis, translated from the text edited by N. de Wailly. London, Sheed and Ward, 1955.
Shaw, M.R.B. Life of Saint Louis, in Chronicles of the Crusade. London, Penguin, 1963.
Wedgwood, Ethel. The Memoirs of the Lord of Joinville. A new English Version. London, 1906.

PRIMARY SOURCES

Beaumanoir, Philippe de. Coutumes de Beauvaisis, ed. A. Salmon. 2 vols. Paris, Picard, 1899-1900.

Bourbon, Etienne de. Anecdotes historiques, légendes et apologues, ed. A. Lecoy de la March. Paris, Librairie Renouard, 1877.

Gaufrido de Belloloco. Vita et sancta conversatio piae memoriae Ludovici regis, Historiens des Gaules et de la France, ed. Bouquet. Paris, l'Imprimerie royale, 1840, 20, 3-27.

Guillaume de Nangis. Vie de Saint Louis, Grandes Chroniques de France, ed. J. Viard. Paris, Société de l'Histoire de France, 1932, VII.

Guillaume de St. Pathus. Vie de Saint Louis, Historiens des Gaules et de la France, ed. Bouquet. Paris, de l'Imprimerie royale, 1840, 20, 58-121.

Guillelmi Tyrensis Archiepicopi. Historia rerum in partibus transmarinis gestarum, Patrologiae cursus completus, series latina, ed. J. P. Migne. Paris, 1884-1885, CCI, 209-891.

Guillelmo Carnotensi. De Vita et Actibus Regis Francorum Lucovici, Historiens des Gaules et de la France, ed. Bouquet. Paris, de l'Imprimerie royale, 1840, 20, 24-41.

Matthieu de Paris. Chronica Majora et Liber Addimentorum, ed. H. R. Luard. London, Rolls Series, 1876-1882, III-IV.

Primat. Chronique, tr. Jean de Vignay, Historiens des Gaules et de la France, ed. Bouquet. Paris, de l'Imprimerie royale, 1840, XXIII, 8-88.

Rutebeuf. Oeuvres Complètes, ed. E. Faral and J. Bastin. 2 vols. Paris, Picard, 1959-1960.

Salimbene. Cronica. 2 vols. Bari, Laterza et Figli, 1942.

Sarrasin, Jean. Lettre à Nicholas Arrode, ed. A. L. Foulet. Paris, Lettres françaises du XIIIe siècle, 1924.

Suger. Vita Ludovici Regis, éd. Molinier. Paris, Picard, 1887.

Tillemont, le Nain de. Vie de Saint Louis, roi de France, ed. J. de Gaulle. 6 vols. Paris, Jules Renouard, 1847-1851.

Wailly, N. de, ed. Récits d'un Ménestrel de Reims au XIIIe siècle. Paris, Société d'histoire de France, 1876.

Vincent de Beauvais. De Eruditione Filiorum Nobilium, ed. Arpad Steiner. Cambridge, Mass., Harvard University Press, 1938.

SECONDARY SOURCES

Aebischer, P., ed. Le Voyage de Charlemagne à Jerusalem et à Constantinople. Genève, Librairie Droz, 1965.

Ambroise. The Crusade of Richard Lion-heart, tr. M. G. Hubert. New York, Columbia University Press, 1941.

Barbazan, Ed., ed. Fabliaux et contes des poètes français. Paris, Warée, 1808.

Champagne, Thibaut de. Les Chansons de Thibaut de Champagne, ed. A. Wallenskold. Paris, Champion, 1875.

Clari, Robert de. De Chiaus qui conquistrenet Constantinople, ed. Philippe Lauer. Paris, Classiques français du moyen âge, 1924.

Dante, Alighieri. De Monarchia libri tres, ed. C. Witte. Vinobonae, 1884.

Freising, Otto of. Chronica sive Historia de duabus civitatibus, ed. Hofmeister. Leipzig, SRG, 1912.

Gesta Frederici I Imperatoris, ed. G. Waitz. Hanoverae Hahniani, 1912.

Friedman, Lionel J., ed. Text and Iconography for Joinville's Credo. Cambridge, Mass., The Mediaeval Academy of America, 1958.

Glaber, Raoul. Historiarum libri V, ed. M. Prou. Paris, 1886.

Gregorii Papae, Sancti. Dialogorum, Patrologiae cursus completus, series latina, ed. Migne. Paris, 1849' LXXVII, 49-430.

Halphen, L. and Poupardin René, eds. Historia Gaufredi ducis Normannorum et comitis Andegavorum. Paris, 1913.

Hippeau, C., ed. La Chanson du Chevalier au Cygne et de Godefroid de Bouillon, suivie des extraits de la Chanson de Chétifs. Genève, Slatkine Reprints, 1969.

La Conquête de Jérusalem. Genève, Slatkine Re-rints, 1969.

John of Salisbury. Policraticus sive de Nugis curialium, ed. C. C. I. Webb. 2 vols. Oxford, Clarendon Press, 1909.

Langlois, Ed., ed. Le Couronnement de Louis. Paris, Classiques de France au moyen âge, 1925.

Mas-Latrie, L. de, ed. Chronique d'Ernoul et de Bernard le Trésorier. Paris, Société de l'histoire de France, 1871.

Meredith-Jones, C., ed. Chronique du Pseudo-Turpin. Paris, Droz, 1936.
Map, Gautier. De Nugis Curialium, ed. M. R. James. Oxford, Clarendon Press, 1914.
McMillan, Duncan, pub. La Chanson de Guillaume. 2 vols. Paris, Société des anciens textes français, 1949-1950.
Meyer, Paul, ed. L'Histoire de Guillaume le Maréchal, comte de Striguil et de Pembroke. Paris, Société d'Histoire de France, 1891-1901.
Meyer, P., and Longnon, A., pub. Raoul de Cambrai. Paris, Société des anciens textes français, 1882.
Mousket, Philippe. Chronique Rimée. 2 vols. Bruxelles, 1836-1838.
Navarre, Philippe de. Les quatres âges de l'Homme, ed. Marcel de Freville. Paris, Société des anciens textes français, 1888.
The Wars of Frederick II against the Ibelins in Syria and Cyprus, tr. J. L. La Monte. New York, Columbia University Press, 1936.
Orr, J., ed. Les Oeuvres de Guiot de Provins, poète lyrique et satirique. Manchester, Manchester University Press, 1915.
Paris, P., pub. La Chanson d'Antioche. Genève, Slatkine Reprints, 1969.
Pseudo-Denis. De Divinis Nominibus, Patrologiae Graeca, ed. J. P. Migne. Paris, 1857, III, 586-984.
Ricardo, Canonico Sanctae Trinitatis Londoniensis. Itinerarium Peregrinorum et Gesta Regis Ricardi, ed. W. Stubbs. London, Longman, 1864.
Tarbé, P. Le roman de Girard de Viane, de Bertran de Bar-sur-Auble. Reims, 1850.
Valere Maxime. Actions et paroles memorables, tr. P. Constant. Paris, Garnier, 1935.
Van Moe, E. A. Saint Louis, Enseignements à son fils aîné. Paris, 1944.
Villehardouin. La conquête de Constantinople, ed., tr. E. Faral. 2 vols. Paris, Classiques de l'Histoire de France, 1938-1939.
Vitry, J. de. The Exempla or illustrative stories from the sermones vulgares, ed. T. F. Crane. Mendeln/Liechtenstein, Kraus Reprint Limited, 1967.

SELECTED WORKS

The following Bibliography includes those works which we consider most pertinent to our work. For further study, consult the <u>Manuel bibliographique de la littérature française au moyen âge</u> of Robert Bossuat, as well as his two supplements for the years 1949-1961. For the years following 1961 - 1984, we have utilized the bibliographical notices of the review <u>Romania</u>, well known to specialists in the field of medieval historical research. Another helpful source is in R. C. van Caenegem and F. L. Ganshof, <u>Guide to the Sources of Medieval History</u> (Amsterdam/New York/Oxford, 1978).

Aigrain, R. <u>L'Hagiographie, ses sources, ses méthodes, son histoire</u>. Paris, Bloud et Gay, 1953.

Alphandery, P. and Dupront, A. <u>La Chrétienté et l'idée de croisade</u>. 2 vols. Paris, Editions Albin Michel, 1954-1959.

Aries, Philippe. <u>L'Homme devant la Mort</u>. Paris, Seuil, 1977.

Atiya, A. S. <u>The Crusade: Historiography & Bibliography</u>. Bloomington, Indiana University Press, 1962.

Auerbach, E. <u>Mimesis. Dargestellte Wirklichkeit in der Abendlandischen Literatur</u>. Bern, Francke, 1964.

Bachelard, G. <u>La psychanalyse du Feu.</u> Paris, Gallimard, 1949.

Bahn, E. & Bahn, M. <u>A History of Oral Interpretation</u>. Minneapolis, Minn., Burgess, 1970.

Barber, R. <u>The Knight and Chivalry</u>. London, Longman, 1970.

Bartok, B. & Lord, A. B. <u>Serbo-Croatian Folk Songs.</u> New York, Columbia University Press, 1951.

Bedier, J. "Jean de Joinville", <u>Histoire de la littérature française illustrée</u>. Paris, Larousse, 1923, I, 82-85.

Bedier, J. & Aubry, P., ed. <u>Les Chansons de Croisade.</u> Paris, 1909.

Bekker-Nielsen, Hans, et al. <u>Oral Tradition - Literary Tradition - A Symposium.</u> Denmark, Odense University Press, 1979.

Beer, J. M. A. "Villehardouin and the oral narrative", <u>Studies in Philology</u> LXVII (1970), 267-277.
<u>Villehardouin, epic historian.</u> Genève, Droz, 1968.
<u>Narrative Conventions of Truth in the Middle Ages.</u> Genève, Droz, 1981.

Bell, Dora M. L'Idéal ethique de la royauté en France au moyen âge. Genève, Librairie Droz, 1962.

Bement, Newton, S. "Latin remnants in Joinville's French", Philological Quarterly, XXVI (1947), 289-301.

Benton, M. J. F. "The Court of Champagne as a Literary Centre", Speculum, XXXVI (1961), 551-591.

Berger, Samuel. La Bible française au moyen âge. Paris, Imprimerie nationale, 1884.

Bessinger, J. B. "Beowulf and the Harp at Sutton Hoo", University of Toronto Quarterly, XXVII (1957-1958), 148-168.

Bezzola, R. R. Les Origines et la formation de la littérature courtoise en occident. Paris, Champion, 1944-1963.

Bloch, Marc. Feudal Society, tr. L. A. Manyon. Chicago, University of Chicago Press, 1964. 2 vols.
La France sous les derniers Capétiens, 1223-1328. Paris, Librairie Armand Colin, 1958.
Les rois thaumaturges. Paris, Istra, 1924.

Bonjour, A. "Beowulf and the Beasts of Battle", Publications of the Modern Language Association, LXXII (1957), 563-573.
The Digressions in Beowulf. Oxford, Basil Blackwell, 1950.

Bossuat, Robert. "Jean de Joinville", Dictionnaire des lettres françaises: le moyen âge, ed. R. Bossuat, Mgr. L. Pichard et G. Raynaud de Lage. Paris, Fayard, MCMLXIV.

Bouthoul, Gaston. Les Mentalités. Paris, P. U. F., 1966.

Brecy, René. Portraits de rois et reines de France. Monaco, les documents d'art, n.d.

Boissonade, P. Du nouveau sur la Chanson de Roland. La genèse historique le cadre géographique, le milieu, les personnages, la date et l'auteur du poème. Paris, Champion, 1923.

Brehier, Louis. Les sculptures de la façade de la cathédrale de Reims et les prières liturgiques du sacre. Paris, Belles Lettres, 1915.

Brooke, Rosalind. "The Lives of St. Francis", Latin Biography, ed. T. A. Dorey. London, Routledge and Kegan Paul, 1967.

Brown, E. R. "Taxation & Morality in the Thirteenth and Fourteenth Centuries: Conscience and Political Power and the Kings of France",

French Historical Studies 8 (1973), 16-28.

Bruyne, Edgar de. Etudes d'Esthétique médiévale. 3 vols. Brugge, Templehof, 1946.

Buisson, L. Konig Ludwig IX, der Heilige und das Recht. Verlag Herder Freiburg, 1954.

Burgière, A. "The Fate of the History of Mentalités in the Annales", Comparative Studies in Society and History 24 (1982), 424-427.

Calin, W.C. The Epic Quest, Studies in four old French Chansons de Geste. Baltimore, John Hopkins Press, 1966.

Campbell, G. J. "The Attitude of the Monarchy towards the use of ecclesiastical censures in the reign of Saint Louis", Speculum XXXV (1960), 535-555.

"The Protest of Saint Louis", Traditio XV (1959), 405-418.

Carlyle, R. W. & A. J. A History of Mediaeval Political Theory in the West. 6 vols. London, Blackwood, MCMLXII.

Cassirer, E. Language and Myth, tr. S. Langer. New York, Dover, 1946.

Catel, M., Maillet, G., et al. Visages de la Champagne. Paris, Editions des Horizons de France, 1947.

Chaytor, H. J. From Script to Print. Cambridge, Heffer & Sons, 1945.

Cheyney, E. P. The Dawn of a New Era, 1250-1453. New York, Harper, 1962.

Clapham, J. H. "Commerce and Industry in the Middle Ages", The Cambridge Mediaeval History. Cambridge, University Press, 1936, VI, 413-453.

Cohen, Gustave. Histoire de la chevalerie en France au moyen âge. Paris, P. U. F., 1954.

Corbett, Noel Lynn. Joinville's Vie de Saint Louis, A Study of the Vocabulary, Syntax and Style. Ottawa National Library, Public Archives Microfilms, no. 12937, 1968.

(Collectif) "Saint Louis et son temps", Archeologia, XXXVII (1970), 6-41.

Coulton, G. G. Five Centuries of Religion. 4 vols. Cambridge, University Press, 1923-1950.

Coupez, A. & Kamanzi, Th. Récits historiques du Rwanda. Tervuren, Annales du musée royal d'Afrique centrale, 1962é
Littérature de cour au Rwanda. Oxford, Clarendon Press, 1970.

Coutau-Begarie, H. Le Phenomène "Nouvelle Histoire" - Stratégie et Idéologie des Nouveaux Historiens. Paris, Economica, 1983.

Crosby, Ruth. "Oral Delivery in the Middle Ages", Speculum, XI (1936), 88-110.

Creed, R. "The Making of an Anglo-Saxon Poem", English Literary History, XXVI (1959), 445-454.

Crosland, J. The Old French Epic. Oxford, Oxford University Press, 1951.

Culley, R. C. Oral Formulaic Language in the Biblical Psalms. Toronto, University of Toronto Press, 1967.

Dahmus, J. Seven Medieval Kings. New York, Doubleday & Co., 1967.

David, M. La souveraineté et les limites juridiques du pouvoir monarchique du IXe au XVe siècle. Paris, Dalloz, 1954.
Le serment du sacre du IXe au XVe siècle, contribution à l'étude des limites juridiques de la souveraineté. Strasbourg, Palais de l'université, 1951.

Delaborde, H. F. "Jean de Joinville, l'homme et l'écrivain", Revue des Deux Mondes, LXXII (1892), 602-636.
Jean de Joinville et les seigneurs de Joinville, suivi d'un catalogue de leurs actes. Paris, Imprimerie nationale, 1894.
"Le texte primitif des Enseignements de saint Louis à son fils", Bibliothèque d'école des chartes, LXXIII (1912), 237-262.
"Notes sur Guillaume de Nangis", Bibliothèque d'école des chartes XLIV (1883), 198-199.

Delaruelle, Etienne. ""L'Idée de croisade chez Saint Louis", Bulletin de littérature ecclésiastique (1960), pp. 242 et suivant.

Delehaye, H. Cinq leçons sur la méthode hagiographique. Bruxelles, Bollandistes, 1934.
Les Légendes hagiographiques. Bruxelles, Bollandistes, 1905.
Les Passions des Martyrs et les genres littéraires. Bruxelles, Bollandistes, 1921.

Delisle, L. "Chartes du sire de Joinville pour le prieuré de Remonvaux", Bibliothèque de l'école des chartes XVIII (1856).

Delooz, Pierre. Sociologie et Canonisation. Liège, Faculté de droit, 1969.

Denholm-Young, N. "Feudal society in the thirteenth century: the knights" History XXIX (1944), 107-119.

Dewick, E. S. The Coronation Book of Charles V of France. London, H. Bradshaw Society, Harrison & Son, 1899.

Diamond, R. "Theme as Ornamentation in Anglo-Saxon Poetry", Modern Languages Association of America LXXVI (1961), 461-468.

Diringer, D. The Illuminated Book. London, Faber & Faber, 1967.

Dornseiff, F. "Literarische Verwendung des Beispiels", Vortrage der Bibliothek Warburg, IV (1924-1925).

Doutrepont, G. Les Mises en prose des épopées des romans chevaleresques. Bruxelles, Palais des Académies, 1939.

Dragonetti, R. La Technique poétique des trouvères dans la chanson courtoise. Contribution à l'étude de la rhétorique médiévale. Bruges, de Tempel, 1960.

Dronke, P. Medieval Latin and the Rise of the European Love-Lyric. Oxford, Clarendon Press, 1965.

Droun, Maurice. "Saint Louis et la notion de justice", Revue des deux-mondes   Déc.(1970), 524-532.

Duby, G. Adolescence de la Chrétienté occidentale, 980-1140. Genève, Skira, 1967.

"Histoire des mentalités", L'Histoire et ses méthodes. Paris, NRF, 1961, 937-965.

"Une enquête à poursuivre: La noblesse dans la France médiévale", Revue historique, CCXXVI (1961), 1-22.

Duby, G. & Mandrou, R. Histoire de la civilisation française. Paris, Colin, 1968.

Dunbar, H. F. Symbolism in Medieval Thought and its Consummation in the Divine Comedy. New York, Russell & Russell, 1961.

Dupin, Henri. La Courtoisie au moyen âge. D'après les textes du XIIe et du XIIIe siècle. Paris, Picard, 1931.

Eliade, M. The Sacred and the Profane, tr. W. R. Trask. New York, Harcourt, Brace & World, Inc., 1959.

Myth and Symbol, ed. F. W. Dillistone. London, SPCK, 1966.

Evans, Joan. "The End of the Middle Ages", The Flowering of the Middle Ages, ed. J. Evans. London, McGraw Hill, 1966.

Faral, E. La Vie quotidienne au temps de Saint Louis. Paris, Hachette, 1942.

Faral, E. Les Jongleurs en France au moyen âge. Paris, Bibliothèque de l'Ecole des Hautes Etudes, 1910.

Fawtier, R. "L'Europe occidentale de 1270 à 1380", Histoire du moyen âge, pub. G. Glotz. Paris, P.U.F., 1940, VI.

The Capetian Kings of France. London, MacMillan and Co. Ltd., 1964.

Febvre, L. "La Psychologie et l'histoire", Encyclopedie française. Paris, Larousse, 1938, VIII.

"La Sensibilité dans l'histoire", Annales d'histoire sociale. Paris, 1941.

"Man or Productivity", Rural Society in France, Selections from the Annales, ed. R. Forster and O. Ranum. London, John Hopkins, 1977.

A New Kind of History and other essays, ed. P. Burke, tr. K. Folca. New York, Harper, 1973.

Febvre, L. & Martin, H.-J. L'Apparition du Livre. Paris, Editions Albin Michel, 1958.

Figgis, J.N. The Divine Right of the Kings. 2nd ed. Cambridge, 1914.

Finnegan, R. "Note on Oral Tradition and Historical Evidence", History and Theory, IX (1970), 195-201.

Flach, G. Les origines de l'ancienne France. 4 vols. Paris, Larose et Forcel, 1886-1917.

Flandrin, Jean-Louis. Le Sexe et l'occident - évolution des attitudes et des comportements. Paris, Seuil, 1981.

Flick, A. C. The Decline of the Medieval Church. 2 vols. London, Burt Franklin, 1930.

Focillon, H. Art d'occident: le moyen âge roman et gothique. Paris, Colin, 1947.

Fontaine, Jacques. "La Composition: dessein et structure de la Vita Martini": Introduction to Sulpice Sevère, Vie de Saint Martin. Paris, Cerf, 1967.

Foulet, Aflred. "Joinville et le Conseil tenu à Acre en 1250", Modern Language Notes, XLIX (1934), 464-468.

"Notes sur la Vie de Saint Louis de Joinville", Romania, 58 (1932), 551-565.

"The Archetype of Joinville's Vie de saint Louis", Modern Language Quarterly, LX (1945), 404 and following.

Foulet, Alfred. "When did Joinville write his Vie de Saint Louis?",
    Romanic Review, XXXII (1941), 233-243.
Frankfurt, H. La Royauté et les Dieux. Paris, Payot, 1951.
Frappier, Jean. Les Chansons de Geste du Cycle de Guillaume d'Orange.
    Paris, Société d'edition d'enseignement supérieur, 1955.
Frazer, J. G. The Golden Bough. London, MacMillan, 1922.
Frazer, J. C. Lectures on the early history of kingship. London, 1905.
Friedman, L. J. "A Mode of Medieval Thought in Joinville's Credo",
    Modern Language Notes, LXVIII(1953), 447-452.
    "On the Structure of Joinville's Credo", Modern Philology, LI (1953),
    1-8.
Gaiffier, Baudoin de. "Mentalité de l'hagiographe médiéval d'après
    quelques travaux récents", Analecta Bollandiana, LXXXVI (1968),
    391-399.
Ganshof, F. "Qu'est-ce que la chevalerie", Revue générale belge,
    CXVIII (1947), 77-86.
    Qu'est-ce que la féodalité? Bruxelles, Lebeque, 1944.
Gautier, L. La chevalerie. Paris, Quantin, 1891.
    Les epopées françaises. 6 vols. Paris, Victor Palmé, 1882.
Genicot, L. "La noblesse dans la société médiévale", Le moyen âge,
    LXXI (1965), 539-560.
    La Spiritualité médiévale. Paris, Fayard, 1958.
Gevirtz, S. Patterns in the Early Poetry of Israel. Chicago, Chicago
    University Press, 1963.
Gierke, Otto. Political Theories of the Middle Ages, tr. F.W. Maitland.
    Boston, Beacon Press, 1959.
Gilson, E. Discours de Reception à l'Académie française. Paris,
    Flammarion, 1947.
Godefroy, T. & D. Le céremonial françois. 2 vols. Folio, 1649.
Goodich, Michael. Vita Perfecta: The Ideal of Sainthood in the
    Thirteenth Century. Stuttgart, Anton Hiersemann, 1982.
    "A Profile of Thirteenth - Century Sainthood", Comparative Studies
    in Society and History, 18 (1976), 429-437.
    "The Politics of Canonization in the Thirteenth Century: Lay and
    Mendicant Saints", Church History, 44(1975), 294-307.

Grolier, Eric de. *Histoire du Livre.* Paris, P.U.F., 1954.

Grousset, R. *Histoire des Croisades.* 3 vols. Paris, Plon, 1936.

Guenée, B. "Les Généalogies entre l'histoire de la politique: la fierté d'être Capétien, en France au moyen âge", *Annales: Economies, Sociétés, Civilisations,* 33(1978), 461.

Guenée, B. & Lehoux, F. *Les entrées royales françaises de 1328 à 1515.* Paris, C.N.R.S., 1968.

Guiette, R. "Chanson de geste, Chronique et mise en prose", *Cahiers de Civilisation médiévale*, VI (1963), 423-440.

Gunter, H. *Psychologie de la légende. Introduction à une hagiographie scientifique.* Paris, Payot, 1954.

Hatzfeld, H. "A sketch of Joinville's prose style", *Medieval Studies in honor of J.D.M. Ford.* Cambridge, Mass., Harvard University Press, 1948.

Heer, F. *The Medieval World: Europe, 1100-1350*. Cleveland, World Publishing Co., 1962.

Heers, J. *Fêtes, jeux, et joutes dans les sociétés d'occident à la fin du moyen âge.* Paris, Vrin, 1971.

Henry, A. "Joinville, Histoire de Saint Louis", *Romania*, LXXIV (1953), 223-224.

Herlihy, D., ed. *Mediaeval Culture and Society*. New York, Harper, 1968.

Hilka, Alfons von, ed. *Chanson de Roland.* Halle, Auflage besorgt von Gerhard Rohlfs, 1948.

Hoekstra, A. "Hésiode et la tradition orale", *Mnemosyne*, X (1957), 193-225.

Holmes, U. T. *A History of Old French Literature.* New York, Crofts, 1938.

Holzknecht, K.J. *Literary Patronage in the Middle Ages*. New York, Octagon 1966.

Hooke, S.H., ed. *Myth, Ritual & Kingship.* Oxford, Clarendon, 1960.

Huizinga, J. *Homo Ludens*. Boston, Beacon, 1955.

Jackson, W.T.H. *The Hero and the King: an Epic Theme.* New York, Columbia University Press, 1982.

Hutton, Patrick. "The History of Mentalities: The New Map of Cultural History", *History and Theory*, 20 (1981), 237-259.

Johnson, A.R. Sacral Kingship in Ancient Israel. Cardiff, University of Wales Press, 1955.

Jonin, P. "Le climat de croisade des chansons de geste", Cahiers de civilisation médiévale, VII (1964), 279-288.

Jordan, W.C. Louis IX and the Challenge of the Crusade - A Study in Rulership. Princeton, Princeton University Press, 1979.

Jubainville, M. d'Arbois de. Histoire des ducs et des comtes de Champagne. Paris, 1865.

Jung, C.G. Symbols of Transformation. New York, Harper, 1964. 2 vols.

Kagame, A. Introduction aux Grands Genres lyriques de l'Ancien Rwanda. Butard, Editions Universitaires du Rwanda, 1969.

Kantorowicz, E.H. Laudes Regiae, A Study in Liturgical Acclamations and Mediaeval Ruler Worship. Berkeley & Los Angeles, University of California Press, 1958.
The King's Two Bodies, A Study in Mediaeval Political Theology. Princeton, Princeton University Press, 1957.

Ker, W.P. Epic and Romance. Essays on Medieval Literature. London, Oxford University Press, 1908.

Kern, F. Kingship and Law in the Middle Ages, tr. S.B. Chrimes. Oxford, Oxford University Press, 1957.

Kienast, Walther. Untertaneneid und Treuvorbehalt in England und Frankreich. Weimar, H. Bohlaus Nachf, 1952.

Kiley, J. F. Einstein and Aquinas: A Rapprochement. The Hague, Martinus Nijhoff, 1969.

Kissane, E. The Book of Pslams. Dublin, Richview Press, 1953-1954.

Kraus, H.J. Psalmen. Biblischer Kommentar. Neukirchen, Neukirchener Verlag, 1960.

Labande, E. R. "Saint Louis pèlerin", Revue d'histoire de l'église en France, LVII (1971), 5-19.

Labarge, Margaret Wade. Saint Louis, the Life of Louis IX of France. London, Eyre & Spottiswoode, 1968.

Lacroix, Benoît. L'Historien au moyen âge. Paris, Vrin, 1971.

Lagarde, G. De. La Naissance de l'esprit laique, au declin du moyen âge. 6 vols. Paris, Nauwelaerts, 1934-1946.

Langlois, Ch. V. "Le Credo de Joinville et Les Enseignements de Saint Louis", La Vie en France au moyen âge. Paris, Hachette, 1928, IV, 1-46.

"Observations sur un missel de Saint-Nicaise de Reims, conservé à la Bibliothèque de Leningrad", Comtes-rendus de l'Académie des Inscriptions et Belles-Lettres, oct. - déc. (1928), 362-368.

Lawrence, W.W. Beowulf and Epic Tradition. London, Hafner, 1967.

Leclercq, Dom Jean. L'Idée de la royauté du Christ au moyen âge. Paris, Cerf, 1959.

"Monastic Historiography from Leo IX to Callistus II", Studia Monastica, XII (1970' 65.

Lecoy de la Marche, A. La Chaire française au moyen âge. Paris, Renouard, 1886.

Saint Louis. Tours, Alfred Mame et fils, 1898.

Leeuw, Gerardus Van Der. Fenomenologia della religione. Torino, Editore Boringiere Societa per Axione, 1960.

Lefebvre, Georges, La Naissance de l'historiographie moderne. Paris, Flammarion, 1971.

Legg, L.G.W. Three Coronation Orders. London, Harrison & Sons, 1900.

Le Goff, J. La Civilisation de l'occident médiéval. Paris, Arthaud, 1964.

Lemarignier, J.-F. "Autour de la royauté française du IXe au XIIIe siècle" Bibliothèque de l'Ecole des chartes, CXIII (1955), 5-36.

"Hiérarchie monastique et hiérarchie féodale", Revue historique de droit française et étranger, XXXI (1953), 171-174.

La France médiévale. Paris, 1970.

Levis - Mirepoix, A. de. Saint Louis, roi de France. Paris, Michel, 1970.

Levy-Bruhl, L. Le Surnaturel et la nature dans la mentalité primitive. Paris, Alcan, 1931.

Levi-Strauss, C. The Savage Mind. Chicago, University of Chicago Press, 1969.

Levron, J. Saint Louis. Paris, Amoit-Dumont, 1957.

Lewis, Andrew W. Royal Succession in Capetian France: Studies in Familial Order and the State. Cambridge, Mass., Harvard University Press, 1981.

Loew, C. Myth, Sacred History and Philosophy. New York, Harcourt, 1967.

Lohr, C.H. "Oral Techniques in the Gospel of Matthew", Catholic Biblical Quarterly, XXIII (1961), 403-435.

Loomis, R.S. "Morgain la Fée in the Oral Tradition", Romania LXXX (1959), 337-362.

Lord, A.B. "Composition by Theme in Homer and South Slavic Epos", Transactions and Proceedings of the American Philological Association, LXXXIII (1951), 71-80.

"Homer and Other Epic Poetry", A Companion to Homer, ed. A.J.B. Wace and F.H. Stubbings. London, Macmillan, 1962.

"Homer, Parry and Huso", American Journal of Archaeology, LII (1948), 34-44.

"Homer's Originality: Oral Dictated Texts", Transactions and Proceedings of the American Philological Association, LXXXIV (1953), 724-734.

"The Poetics of Oral Creation", Comparative Literature, ed. W.P. Friederich. Chapel Hill, University of North Carolina Press, 1959.

The Singer of Tales, Harvard Studies in Comparative Literature. Cambridge, Harvard University Press, 1960.

Lot, F. Etudes sur les légendes epiques françaises. Paris, Champion,

Lot, F. & Fawtier, R. Histoire des Institutions françaises au moyen âge, vol. II: Institutions royales. Paris, P.U.F., 1958.

Lottin, O. Psychologie et morale aux XIIe et XIIIe siècles. 3 vols. Louvain, Abbaye de Mont César, 1942-1960.

Lozinski, G. "Recherches sur les sources du Credo de Joinville", Neuphilologische Mitteilungen, XXXI (1930), 170-231.

Lubac, H. de. Exégèse médiévale. Les quatre sens de l'ecriture. 3 vols. Paris, Aubier, 1959-1964.

Lutz, J. & Perdrizet, P. Les sources et l'influence iconographique principalement sur l'art alsacien du XIVe siècle. Mulhouse, 1907.

Lyons, Faith. Les Eléments descriptifs dans le roman d'aventure au XIIIe siècle. Genève, Droz, 1968.

MacKinney, L.C. "The People and Public Opinion in the eleventh century Peace Movement", Speculum, V (1930), 181-206.

Magoun, F.P., Jr. "Bede's story of Caedmon: The Case History of an Anglo-Saxon Oral Singer", Speculum, XXX (1955), 49-63.

Magoun, F.P., Jr. "Oral-Formulaic Character of Anglo-Saxon Narrative Poetry", Speculum, XXVIII (1953), 446-467.

Maillet, Germaine. La vie réligieuse au temps de saint Louis. Paris, Bibliothèque chrétienne d'histoire, 1950.

Male, E. L'art réligieux de XIIIe siècle en France. Paris, Colin, 1948.

Malraux, A. Metamorphosis of the Gods. New York, Doubleday, 1960.

Marichal, R. "Manuscrit", Dictionnaire des lettres français. Le moyen âge, ed. R. Bossuat, L. Pichard, G. De Lage. Paris, Fayard, 1964.

Marrou, H.-I. La connaissance historique. Paris, Seuil, 1954.

Martene, Dom Edmond. De antiquis Ecclesiae ritibus. 2 vols. 1736-1737.

Matthews, W. Medieval Secular Literature. Los Angeles, University of California Press, 1965.

Matuszak, Juliane. Das Speculum exemplorum als quelle volkstunilicher Glaubensvorstellungen des Spatmittelalters. Siegburg, Verlag F. Schmitt, 1967.

Maumené, Ch., Harcourt, L. d'. Iconographie des rois de France. Paris, Colin, 1927-1928.

McIlwain, Ch. H. The Growth of political thought in the West. New York, MacMillan, 1932.

McLugan, M. The Gutenberg Galaxy. Toronto, University of Toronto Press, 1962.

Meredith-Jones, E.G.C., ed. Chronique du Pseudo-Turpin. Paris, Droz, 1936.

Miller, E. "The State and Landed Interests in Thirteenth Century France and England", Change in Medieval Society, ed. S. Thrupp. New York, Appleton-Century Crofts, 1964.

Miller, S.J. "The Position of the King in Bracton & Beaumanoir", Speculum, XXXI (1956), 263-296.

Misch, Georg. Geschichte der Autobiographie im mittelalter. Frankfurt, Verlag G. Schulte-Bulmke, 1962.

Sachsenspiegel und Bible. Notre Dame, Indiana, University of Notre Dame, 1941.

Misrahi, J. "Girard de Vienne et la Geste de Guillaume", Medium aevum, IV (1935), 1-15.

Molinier, A. "Les Capétiens", Les Sources de l'histoire de France. Paris, Picard, 1903, III.

Mollat, M. Genèse médiévale de la France moderne, XIVe-XVe siècles. Paris, Arthaud, 1970.

Maranvillé, H. "Note sur le MS. français 13568 de la Bibliothèque Nationale: Histoire de Saint Louis par le sire de Joinville", Bibliothèque d'Ecole des chartes, LXX (1909), 303-312.

Mosher, J.A. The Exemplum in the Early Religious and Didactic Literature of England. New York, Ams Press, 1966.

Mura, E. Le Corps mystique du Christ. Paris, Blot, 1937.

Murphy, T.P. The Holy War. Columbus, Ohio, Ohio University Press, 1976.

Nichols, S.G., Jr. Formulaic Diction and Thematic Composition in the Chanson de Roland. Chapel Hill, University of North Carolina Press, 1961.

Nielsen, E. Oral Tradition. London, SCM Press, 1961.

Notopoulos, J.A. "Homer, Hesiod and the Achaean Heritage of Oral Poetry" Hesperia, XXIX (1960), 177-197.

"The Homeric Hymns as Oral Poetry: A Study of Post Homeric Oral Tradition", American Journal of Philology, LXXXIII (1962), 337-368.

Pacaut, M. La Théocratie. L'Eglise et la pouvoir laique au moyen âge. Paris, Aubier, 1957.

Painter, S. French Chivalry. Baltimore, The John Hopkins Press, 1940.

The Rise of the Feudal Monarchies. New York, Cornell University Press, 1962.

William Marshal, Knight Errant, Baron and Regent of England. Baltimore, John Hopkins Press, 1933.

Pange, J. de. Le Roi très chrétien. Paris, Fayard, 1949.

Paris, Gaston. "Jean, sire de Joinville", Histoire littéraire de la France. Paris, 1898, XXXII, 291-459.

"La Chanson composée à Acre", Romania, XXII (1893), 541-547.

"La Composition du livre de Joinville sur Saint Louis", Romania, XXIII (1894), 508-524.

Paris, J. L'Espace et le regard. Paris, Seuil, 1965.

Paris, Paulin. Etudes sur la vie et les travaux de Jean, sire de Joinville. Paris, Didot, 1870.

Rost. H. Die Bible im Mittelalter. Augsburg, 1939.

Rowen, H. The King's State - Proprietary Dynasticism in Early Modern France. Rutgers, New Jersey, 1980.

Runciman, S. A History of the Crusades. 3 vols. Cambridge, The University Press, 1955.

Rychner, Jean. "La Chanson de geste, épopée vivante", La Table Ronde, CXXXII (1958), 152-167.

La Chanson de geste, essai sur l'art épique du jongleur. Genève, Droz, 1955.

Contribution à l'Etude des fabliaux, variantes, remaniements, dégradations. Genève, Droz, 1960.

Saxer, V. "Légende épique et légende hagiographique", Revue des sciences religieuses, XXXIII (1959), 372-395.

Schnurer. L'Eglise et la civilisation au moyen âge. Paris, Payot, 1933.

Schramm, P.E. "Coronation Ritual and Festivities", A History of the English Coronation, tr. L.G.W. Legg. Oxford, Clarendon, 1937.

Der Konig von Frankreich: Das Wesen der Monarchie. vom 9. zum 16. 2 vols. Weimar, Jahrhundert, 1939.

Setton, K.M, ed., A History of the Crusades. Oxford, Clarendon, 1962.

Simonnet, J. Essai sur l'histoire de la genéologie des sires de Joinville. Langres, 1876.

Smalley, Beryl. The Study of the Bible in the Middle Ages. Notre Dame, Indiana, University of Notre Dame Press, 1964.

Southern, R.W. Saint Anselm and his Biographer. A Study of Monastic Life and Thought. 1059-1130. Cambridge, Cambridge University Press, 1963.

Western Views of Islam in the Middle Ages. Cambridge, Mass., Harvard University Press, 1971.

Stoianovich, I. French Historical Method: The Annales Paradigm. Ithaca, New York, Cornell University Press, 1976.

Strayer, Joseph R. Medieval Statecraft and the Perspectives of History. Princeton, Princeton University Press, 1971.

Teneze, M. "Introduction à L'Etude de la littérature orale: le conte", Annales, Economies, Sociétés, Civilisations, XXV (1969), 1116.

Tervarent, Guy de. Les Enigmes de l'art du moyen âge. Paris,
    Les Editions d'Art de D'histoires, MCMXLI.
Thomas, A. Francesco da Barbarino et la littérature provençale en
    Italie au moyen âge. Paris, Bibl. Ed. Franc. Athènes-Rome, 1883.
Thompson, J.W. The Literacy of the laity in the Middle Ages. New York,
    B. Franklin, 1963.
Thurston, P. The Coronation Ceremonial. 2nd ed. London, 1911.
Townsend, G.B. "Suetonius and his Influence", Latin Biography,
    ed. T.A. Dorey. London, Routledge and Kegan Paul, 1967.
Trachtenburg, J. The Devil and the Jews. The Medieval Conception
    of the Jew and its Relations to Modern Antisemitism. Yale, Yale
    University Press, 1943.
Tubach, F.C. "Exemplum in decline", Traditio, XVIII (1962), 407-417.
Tupper, F. Types of Society in Mediaeval Literature. New York, Biblo and
    Tannen, 1968.
Ullmann, W. Principles of Government and Politics in the Middle Ages.
    London, Methuen & Co. Ltd., 1961.
    The Carolingian Renaissance and the Idea of Kingship. London,
    Methuen, 1969.
    The Individual and Society in the Middle Ages. Baltimore, The John
    Hopkins Press, 1966.
Vallat, Xavier. "Louis IX, Saint Patron de la Maison de France", Ecrits
    de Paris, avril (1970), 64-75.
Van Gennep, A. "La Valeur historique du folklore", Religion, moeurs,
    légendes, 33, 11 (1909), 173-185.
Van Lier, Henri. Les Arts et l'espace. Tournai, Casterman, 1963.
Vansina, Jan. De la tradition orale, essai de méthode historique.
    Tervuren, Musée royale de l'Afrique centrale, 1961.
Varagnac, André. Civilisation traditionnelle et genres de vie. 2 vols.
    Paris, Editions Albins Michel, 1948.
Vauchez, André. La Sainteté en occident aux derniers siècles du moyen âge
    Les procès de canonisation et les documents hagiographiques.
    Rome, Ecole française de Rome, 1981.

Viard, Jules, ed. Les Grandes Chroniques de France. 10 vols. Paris, Champion, MDCCCCXXXII.

Viollet, P. "Les Enseignements de saint Louis à son fils", Bibliothèque d'Ecole des chartes, XXXV (1874), 1-56.

"Note sur le véritable texte de instructions de Saint Louis à sa fille Isabelle et à son fils, Philippe le Hardi", Bibliothèque d'Ecole des chartes, XXX (1869), 129-148.

Vollmer, H. "Bibel und deutsche Kultur Ver offentlichungen des deutschen Bibel-Archivs en Hamburg", Materialen zur bebelgeschichte und religiosen Volkskunde des Mittelalters. Neue Folge V, Potsdam, 1931.

Vries, Jan de. Heroic Song and Heroic Legend, tr. B.J. Timmer. London, Oxford University Press, 1963.

Wailly, Natalis de. "Joinville et les Enseignements de saint Louis à son fils", Bibliothèque d'Ecole des chartes, XXXIII (1872), 386 et suivant.

"Mémoire sur la langue de Joinville", Bibliothèque d'Ecole des Chartes, XXIX (1868), 329-478.

"Mémoire sur le romant ou chronique en langue vulgaire dont Joinville a reproduit quelques passages", Bibliothèque d'Ecole des chartes, XXXV (1874), 217-248.

"Recueil de chartes originales de Joinville, en langue vulgaire", Bibliothèque d'Ecole des chartes, XXVIII (1867), 557-608.

Wallon, H. Saint Louis et son temps. 2 vols. Paris, Hachette, 1876.

Weinstein, D. & Bell, R.M. Saints and Society: The Two Worlds of Western Christendom, 1000-1700.. Chicago, University of Chicago Press, 1982.

Welter, J.T. La Tabula Exemplorum. Paris, Guitard, 1926.

Weston, J.L. "Legendary Cycles of the Middle Ages", The Cambridge Mediaeval History. Cambridge, Cambridge University Press, 1936, VI, 815-841.

White, L.T. Medieval Technology and Social Change. Oxford, Oxford University Press, 1965.

Whitelock, D. "William of Malmesbury on the Works of King Alfred", Medieval Literature and Civilization, ed. D.A. Pearsall and R.A. Waldron. London, Athlone Press, 1969, 82-86.

Whitman, C.H. *Homer and the Heroic Tradition.* Cambridge, Mass., Harvard University Press, 1958.

Wood, C.T. *The French Apanages and the Capetian Monarchy.* Cambridge, Mass., Harvard University Press, 1966.

Yates, F.A. *The Art of Memory.* London, Routledge and Kegan Paul, 1966.

Yver, C. *Saint Louis.* Paris, Soes, 1947.

Marie-José Fassiotto

MADAME DE LAMBERT (1647–1733) OU LE FÉMINISME MORAL

American University Studies:
Series II, Romance Languages and Literature. Vol. 7
ISBN 0-8204-0131-5   approx. 154 pp.   hardcover/lam., approx. US $ 20.50

Connue pour son célèbre salon de l'hôtel de Nevers où elle reçut pendant plus de vingt ans (1710–1733) des écrivains, des savants et des artistes – tels Montesquieu, Fontenelle et Marivaux – la marquise de Lambert jouit aussi en son temps d'une solide réputation littéraire. Représentant un aspect essentiel de la pensée française au début du XVIIIe siècle, elle fut, en outre, une féministe convaincue. Sa pensée féministe, cependant, a été diversement et bien souvent faussement interprétée, certains trouvant la marquise trop tiède dans son féminisme, d'autres allant jusqu'à l'accuser d'antiféminisme même! L'étude détaillée de son essai, *Réflexions nouvelles sur les femmes,* le plus original et le plus personnel de tous ses écrits, montre, bien au contraire, que la marquise, mettant directement le monde masculin en accusation, sut passer et s'élever de constatations hardies, de réprimandes et d'accusations vives et manifestes, à de fortes et franches revendications. Et que, ce faisant, elle a bel et bien posé de nouveaux jalons pour la condition féminine.

PETER LANG PUBLISHING, INC.
34 East 39th Street, USA – New York, NY 10016

Wesley D. Camp / Agnes G. Raymond

JACK THE FATALIST AND HIS MASTER
A New Translation from the French of Denis Diderot

American University Studies:
Series II, Romance Languages and Literature. Vol. 8
ISBN 0-8204-0076-9   218 pp.   pb./lam., US $ 21.60

A valet and his master are journeying on horseback, whiling away the weary hours with many a strange anecdote, droll story and tale of love and vengeance that never fails to astonish or surprise. The author employs his talents of eigtheenth century French philosopher, dramatist, critic and storyteller to weave into this tapestry of fictions his reflections on Jack's fatalism – everything that happens here below was written Up-there on the great scroll of Destiny; on the human need for love and friendship, dominance and pets – dogs in particular; and on the relation of art to reality – all weighty subjects treated in a comic vein with profound human understanding.

Contents: Wesley Camp's new and lively translation of *Jack the Fatalist* is intended for the general reader and the student, but its racy dialogue cries out for adaptation to the theater or the screen.
Agnes Raymond's brief preface whets the reader's appetite while reserving for the postface a more detailed analysis of the novel and Diderot's debt to Laurence Sterne.
Eighteenth century French social satire – French literature – Denis Diderot – Novel – Comedy.

PETER LANG PUBLISHING, INC.
34 East 39th Street, USA – New York, NY 10016

Lloyd Bishop

THE ROMANTIC HERO AND HIS HEIRS IN FRENCH LITERATURE

American University Studies:
Series II, Romance Languages and Literature. Vol. 10
ISBN 0-8204-0096-3   approx. 295 pp.   hardcover/lam.,
                                            US $ 32.50

Our contemporary view of the romantic hero is blurred by infrequently examined assumptions. The purpose of Professor Bishop's book on *The Romantic Hero and his Heirs* is two-fold: to draw a precise and updated portrait of the original romantic hero in French literature and then to trace his legitimate heirs from the romantic period to the middle of the twentieth century – and beyond. By bringing together his own findings and those of other scholars he establishes the important fact of literary history that *the romantic hero is the central hero of modern French literature.* The book offers not only a detailed description and genealogy of a significant literary hero, it also provides a description of the modern sensibility. This is an ambitious and convincing work of vast and precise erudition.

Contents: A precise and updated portrait of the romantic hero in French Literature and of his legitimate heirs from the romantic period to the middle of the twentieth century – and beyond.

PETER LANG PUBLISHING, INC.
34 East 39th Street, USA – New York, NY 10016